HOW PORCUPINES MAKE LOVE III

HOW PORCUPINES MAKE LOVE III

Readers, Texts, Cultures in the Response–Based Literature Classroom

Alan C. Purves
State University of New York, Albany

Theresa Rogers
Ohio State University

Anna O. Soter
Ohio State University

Longman *Publishers USA*

How Porcupines Make Love III: Readers, Texts, Cultures in the Response-Based Literature Classroom

Copyright © 1995, 1990 by Longman Publishers USA.
All rights reserved.
No part of this publication may be reproduced,
stored in a retrieval system, or transmitted
in any form or by any means, electronic, mechanical,
photocopying, recording, or otherwise,
without the prior permission of the publisher.

Longman, 10 Bank Street, White Plains, N.Y. 10606

Associated companies:
Longman Group Ltd., London
Longman Cheshire Pty., Melbourne
Longman Paul Pty., Auckland
Copp Clark Longman Ltd., Toronto

Credits are listed on p. iv

Senior acquisitions editor: Laura McKenna
Production editor: Linda W. Witzling
Cover design: Susan J. Moore
Production supervisor: Richard Bretan

Library of Congress Cataloging-in-Publication Data

Purves, Alan C., Date
    How porcupines make love III : readers, text, cultures in the
response-based literature classroom / Alan C. Purves, Theresa
Rogers, Anna O. Soter.
        p.   cm.
    Includes bibliographical references (p.) and index.
    ISBN 0-8013-1260-4
    1. Literature—Study and teaching.   I. Rogers, Theresa.
II. Soter, Anna O., Date   III. Title.
PN59.P79   1995
807—dc20   94-6629
                                                     CIP

4 5 6 7 8 9 10-CRS-9897

Credits

This book is dedicated to
our students and friends

Contents

CHAPTER 9   BUT WHAT ABOUT WRITING AND ALL THAT?   151

CHAPTER 10   READING IN HYPERSPACE   175

Preface

Why Another Edition of an Old Chestnut? In 1988, fifteen years after the first edition of *How Porcupines Make Love* appeared, the three authors, who had worked together on other projects over the years since all were at the University of Illinois, came up with a prospectus for a new volume, which was published in 1990.

The first edition came out at a time when the idea of reader-response was barely beginning to take hold in schools and before it had made much headway in the world of literary criticism. When the team wrote the first edition, they saw a need to bring the reader, and particularly the student reader, into the consciousness of teachers who had been trained in close reading and the idea that there could be a verifiable reading of literary work. It was a time when many were beginning to see the importance of drama and talk in the classroom and that one way to enhance these ideas was to be irreverent.

The second edition tried to capture the same spirit as the earlier one, tempered by our realization of the nature of schools, students, teachers, principals, and parents. Although many more people knew about reader-response approach and several books and many articles had been written about it, we did not see that the approach was that common in practice. We have been teaching in every grade from Kindergarten through twelve and have been working with teachers in training and in-service teachers for a long time, and we know how daunting the reality of long days and weeks in unpainted classrooms can be. We know it is all too easy to slip back into a nice easy pattern of teachers doing the talking and students slouching around, not even trying to stay awake. Yet we know it is possible to keep one's spirits up and one's intellectual wits collected; a spirit of irreverence can only help.

In 1992 the editors at Longman asked us to consider a revision. We were aware of some changes we wanted to make. For one thing, there is a need for irreverence still; but this time the sacred cow is reader-response itself. Everybody says they do it, but we still don't see that much real engagement in talk and active response in classrooms.

We also see that the ideology of reader-response in the 1990s needs some correctives. Some advocates of a reader-response pedagogy hold that naive readers are "better" readers. They use this adaptation of the idea of the noble savage to attack such aspects of school literature programs as the teaching of literary terminology, generic study, and literary history, lumping these under such labels as "cultural literacy," or "product focus," or "traditional teaching," or "new criticism." In their place they would have readers engage in a form of group soul-searching. But from years of research on real readers in school, we know that readers are not naive; they have something in their heads put there by past experiences, particularly with literature and schooling in literature.

In addition, we have come to realize that a simplistic view of reader-response simply will not stand up in the face of a new realization of the multicultural nature of society, of the new media and technologies that we think are profoundly affecting the very nature of reading and are already influencing approaches to literature instruction. If we consider the culture of the writer, we must expect our students to come to know something of that culture. If we consider the impact of technology, we must face the fact that our students live in a world different from that in which many of us grew up and learned our trade.

Although we value the ideas about readers and reading literature that we held before, we see this change in our approach as a deepening of it and not a turning away. The reader whose response we value is willing to be informed, is willing to explore and learn, and is not satisfied with being naive and solipsistic. Literature is too serious an enterprise for us not to take it seriously. And if we take it seriously, we take the reader seriously as a curious, exploring, imaginative being. That is the focus of this book, and we hope its pages suggest ways to help foster that kind of reader.

We recognize that all of what we are concerned with in literature teaching and learning begins with the act of reading, with an individual coming into contact with a text and then having whole worlds open up. We call this a "reader-based" rather than a "response-centered" approach; it is not *centered* on the reader but *based* on a reader's reading. It is not a curriculum, but an approach to texts, curricula, and teaching. And it occurs in a postmodern frame, a world in which certainty and positivism are replaced by multiplicity and change.

There are, then, some subtle and not so subtle changes of emphasis in the book. There is more on multiculturalism. There is a new section on portfolio assessment, a buzzword that we think should be more than a slogan; it should be an integral part of any literature program. More attention is given to computers and particularly to hypertext (those multilinear collocations of text or text, picture, and sound which readers can access, connect, and revise as they will) and hypermedia (a hypertext-based media-retrieval system). We think the application of hypertext and hypermedia to literature and its teaching will truly bring the ideas of a reader-based approach into the lives of students whether teachers want it or not. There is also additional emphasis on drama, an act of engagement with text that we think is absolutely central to the curriculum. Drama can range from oral reading of the text to simulation and gaming to process drama and readers' theater.

But we decided to keep some things the same. We want the book's tone to remain informal. We use many examples and illustrations. (We call them vignettes.) We want to suggest, not prescribe. The reader-based teacher must be able to improvise, to move where the students are and not be bound to a rigid lesson plan. We want to be sure that the world of classroom literature and the world of student reading and viewing are connected, even though they are distinct. We want to encourage a spirit of joy and engagement in reading and responding to literature in schools, in addition to a set of clear curricular goals.

Writing this book required the collaboration of a number of people. We would like to thank the coauthors of the first edition of *Porcupines*, who generously turned over their rights and wished us well. Several are still teaching in the spirit of the original; we hope we have not violated their trust. We are also grateful to the many consultant readers for Longman who fed us their ideas, including:

Philip M. Anderson, Queens College, City University of New York

Jean Brown, Saginaw Valley State University

Jean Casey, University of New Mexico

Mark Andrew Faust, University of Georgia

David Laubach, Kutztown University of Pennsylvania

William Martin, George Mason University

Gary Negin, California State University, San Bernadino

Thomas Philion, University of Illinois, Chicago

Kyoko Sato, California State University, Northridge

Sheila Schwartz, State University of New York, New Paltz

Wayne H. Slater, University of Maryland

Betty Tutt, William Woods College

Jane Zaharias, Cleveland State University

We are grateful to a number of colleagues whose work we admire. Among these always are James Moffett, James Britton, Gunnar Hansson, Cecily O'Neill, Rob Eagleson, Don Murray, and, of course, Louise Rosenblatt. We are grateful, too, to all the teachers who invited us into their classrooms so we could try our approaches before we sold them. These include Chris Gibson, Merrlyn Cahill, Joe Quattrini, Marian Galbraith-Jones, Susan Zimmerman, Sarah Edelman, and Janet Lanka. Our thanks also to Mary Armentrout, who helped prepare the manuscript.

We are particularly grateful to our spouses (Anne, Rob, and Dan) and our children and grandchildren, all of whom let us work relatively uninterrupted, except for hugs.

HOW PORCUPINES MAKE LOVE III

chapter 1

By Way of an Introduction: Readers, Writers, and Literature

When we (Alan, Anna, and Terry) studied literature in college in the 1950s, 1960s, and 1970s, we mostly took courses organized by the country of origin (England, Australia, or America), by genre (poetry or drama or the novel), by period (the Victorians), or maybe by author (Shakespeare or Melville). Occasionally we studied literature on a theme (such as the individual and society). When we studied literature we were supposed to take it seriously. Pieces like the one on the opposite page were not supposed to be part of the course.

But all around us people were writing. Some were the sort of people who took the literature we were studying and put it into new contexts—like a comic.

At the same time that we read things like comic books or mysteries or Gothics (in our off time, of course), we were expected to be versed in molecular biology and Hindu mythology. We were barely aware that some poets took the comic book heroes and put them into poems like this parody of A. A. Milne:

GOODBAT NIGHTMAN

God bless all policemen
and fighters of crime,
May thieves go to jail
for a very long time.

They've had a hard day
helping clean up the town,

Now they hang from the mantelpiece
both upside down.

A glass of warm blood
and then straight up the stairs
Batman and Robin
are saying their prayers.

They've locked all the doors
and they've put out the bat,
Put on their batjamas.
(They like doing that!)

They've filled their batwater-bottles,
made their batbeds,
With two springy battresses
for sleepy batheads.

They're closing red eyes
and they're counting black sheep,
Batman and Robin
are falling asleep.

Roger McGough

While we were studying literature, writers took various parts of their world that interested or amused them and turned them into poetry or fiction or drama. We suspect that you went through a similar experience studying literature, although maybe you didn't do it in periods and genres. You have probably had a course or two in the literature of an ethnic group or in women's literature. You may even have had a course in adolescent or young-adult literature, or even "kiddylit." You may have taken a course in science fiction and a few more thematic courses than we did. Perhaps you have had a film course. Maybe you studied literary theory, that important stuff that fills the pages of many of our journals.

In any event, we suspect that, like us, you were supposed to take what you read seriously. The not-so-hidden message of your course was: This is important stuff that you are reading, and you are going to be tested on it, so you'd better know it cold.

Believe it or not, while you were doing that, writers all around you kept on writing about the world they live in and the ideas and feelings they have about that world and all its current events. They were not writing to be studied in courses.

Writers have always done that. The writers we studied, people like Jane Austen, Christina Rossetti, and Charles Dickens, were very much a part of their world. They lived and breathed and wrote about what they saw around them and how they thought and felt about it.

They were not writing "litchachure" to be studied in courses, but stories, novels, and poems to be read by whoever picked them up—pieces like the following:

WAITING ON ELVIS, 1956

This place up in Charlotte called Chuck's where I
used to waitress and who came in one night
but Elvis and some of his friends before his concert
at the Arena, I was twenty-six married but still
waiting tables and we got to joking around like you
do, and he was fingering the lace edge of my slip
where it showed below my hemline and I hadn't even
seen it and I slapped at him a little saying, You
sure are the one aren't you feeling my face burn but
he was the kind of boy even meanness turned sweet in
his mouth.

Smiled at me and said, Yeah honey I guess I sure am.

Joyce Carol Oates

Is that a poem? It's not like what we studied. It barely looks like a poem. There are no capital letters at the beginnings of the lines. Also, it talks about Elvis, and real poets don't write about such things.

It is a poem written by an American writer living in the last half of the twentieth century, a woman, a Caucasian woman who grew up as part of the culture of the 1950s and 1960s when Elvis was KING, and who is still living in a world where Elvis is spotted weekly and where the U.S. Postal Service has put him on a stamp. (They hadn't put him on a stamp when she wrote the poem in the 1970s, but Graceland was open to the public, and those headlines about Elvis sightings were just as popular as they are today.)

Is it literature?

We think so.

But is it the kind of literature we study in a college course or want our high school students to study?

Depends on what you mean by literature. We will take that up in Chapter 3 in some detail. But if you mean should it be put into an anthology or included in a literature course, why not? It is no more or less a comment on the popular culture of its time than is Jonathan Swift's *Gulliver's Travels*, which is filled with references to popular politicians and stage people, or George Eliot's *Middlemarch*, which refers to events and characters of the day. If you mean should it be put on a pedestal and seen as some great monument to be treated with fear, or as a word puzzle with a key known only to the teacher, our answer is no.

Literature is what people write. First of all, people write out of their experience, their daily lives, and the culture into which they were born and grew up. This is true of writers throughout the world, past, present, and future. It is certainly true of those writers we call American, a very small number of whom we studied in school.

Some American writers came from the peoples who were here before the European "discoveries" of the islands and continent we call North America—the people who call themselves the First Nations. Others came as immigrants, not as conquerors: some as slaves, some to make up the labor force that built the railroads or toiled in the factories. They came from Europe and its surrounding islands, from central Asia and the Indian subcontinent, from China and Japan and other parts of the Pacific rim, from the Caribbean and Central America. They came under cramped conditions, and many of them came because they were forced out of their homeland. Once they got here, they worked long hours in conditions that we would think unbearable; many who worked twelve-hour days were young children.

The immigrants came from parts of the world that had produced and are still producing serious and important poets, storytellers, and dramatists. They came with a literary and cultural heritage, for there is no society that doesn't have one. In some societies a good bit of the heritage is oral and communal; in others there is a long tradition of scribes and writers.

These writers and their descendants who are living in the United States and Canada today produced the literature and art that define the cultures of our multicultural societies and, more specifically, the ways in which the members of the culture deal with one another.

Much literature treats the major human and social rituals of a culture: birth, child rearing, maturation, marriage, old age, and death. Much literature describes a culture's religious practices. Much literature deals with the barriers that members of a culture establish to keep others out, and such barriers become the defining events of a culture's history. For African Americans of the United States, that defining event may be slavery and emancipation. For many Europeans that defining event may be the fact of revolution or the brutality of a civil war. For Jews it may be the pogroms or the Holocaust. For Arabs it may be the loss of Palestine and the imperialism of T. E. Lawrence. For the Irish it may be the famine of 1848. For many Latinos it may be Catholicism's supplanting of the Aztec or Mayan religions or the tyranny of dictators like Trujillo or the Somozas. For many in the United States, it may be symbolized by Ellis Island. For the Lakota it may be the Battle of Wounded Knee. For Japanese Americans it may be the internment camps during World War II. For Chinese Americans it may be the railroads and the whorehouses of San Francisco.

IMMIGRATION BLUES

At home I was in poverty,
    constantly worried about firewood and rice.
I borrowed money

to come to the Gold Mountain.
Immigration officers cross-examined me;
no way I could get through.
Deported to this island,
like a convicted criminal.
Here—
Mournful sighs fill the gloomy room.
A nation weak; her people often humiliated
Like animals, tortured and destroyed at others' whim.

Anonymous Nineteenth-Century Chinese American

Nearly all of these defining events are times of tribulation and survival, and it is from these, as well as from rituals and ceremonies, that the values of a culture emerge.

We have listed some of the defining events of the cultures that are mingled on this continent. Each culture in the world is defined by such events as well as by ceremonies and rituals that bring people together in times of celebration and times of trial.

Literature is a writer's expression of and an artist's lens into her or his culture and its celebrations and trials. Whenever we read a book or poem or see a play or film we realize this and honor it instead of treating it as a monument not to be touched or explored.

The literature of a culture turns these various expressions, beliefs, values, and ceremonies into verbal art that complements the plastic arts, music, and dance. The writers are habituated to their culture; they are also habituated to the world of art. It is the world of art (in our specific case, of literature) that serves to connect cultures and bring them into relationships with one another.

Regardless of a poet's culture, that poet uses rhythm, imagery, metaphor, typography, grammar, and syntax as the medium of the poem. Regardless of the race or religion of a playwright, that playwright uses the devices of stagecraft to make a play. August Wilson is a major African-American playwright; he is a major playwright. Related in his craft to Shakespeare, Oscar Wilde, and Federico García Lorca, he is shaped by and has shaped the dramatic tradition. Our students deserve to find out something both about the culture that drives Wilson's writing and about that shared craftsmanship.

They also deserve to read and explore the craftsmanship in this poem by a Latino poet:

INSTRUCTIONS FOR JOINING A NEW SOCIETY

One: Be optimistic
Two: Be well turned out, courteous, obedient.
(Must have made the grade in sports.)
And finally, walk

As every member does:
one step forward
and two or three back;
but always applauding, applauding.

Herberto Padilla

When we explore authors and their culture we must not forget the craft, for it is the craft that gives the reader a sense of the beauty or wryness of what has been written. The texts are not to be treated as sermons but as artifacts, objects shaped by an author to give power and beauty to a vision of the world. They are written to make us feel and see. They are written to make us respond, and in our responding we need to explore not only ourselves, the content of the work, and the culture of the writer, but the ways in which the writer has shaped and refined language to make us respond. Writers want us to feel and hear and imagine the experience, and they expect us to revel in the language and the images and the style. They also want us to be outraged or to cry or to bend over in laughter at what they are writing about. They want us to get the message and enjoy the getting of it and admire their craft. That's what being an artist is all about.

Those Literature Courses Missed Out on "Real" People Writing, but Now. . . . Everything Has Gotten Mixed Up Even More Than It Had Been When We Were at School and Ain't It Great? Let's Celebrate

We now have a collection of poems, plays, stories, and essays from all corners of the globe, and all demand to be treated equally.

We now have such a cross-fertilization between "high" and "low" culture in our writing that to use such a distinction to put down a writer doesn't make much sense. (Good and bad, yes; high and low, no.)

We now have a mingling of writing and the graphic arts (and the aural arts) into a media mélange. What these writers have created refuses to rest securely in 10-point type on the page. Literature from around the world includes both scripted and improvised theater, film, television drama, videotext, performance art, and ancient ritual.

Much of it demands to be looked at, to be heard, to be read all at once. It demands to be taken as fun—fun that has its serious moments, but fun nevertheless.

It demands that we enjoy it and feel its power.

It demands that we honor the writers and the cultures of the world from which they come.

It demands that we respond to it creatively. Ruth Krauss wanted us to read the following play but also to think of how it might be staged and who might be the actors. She wanted us to perform it.

PINEAPPLE PLAY

Narrator
In a poem you make your point with pineapples.
(Pineapples fly onto stage from all directions.)
Spy
And it would be nice to have a spy going in and out.
End
Ruth Krauss

Literature demands to be taken naturally; after all, it is organically grown in the hearts and heads of writers, who are people just like you and us. Writes the Czech biologist-poet Miroslav Holub:

> Most of all I like writing for people untouched by poetry for instance, for those who do not even know that it should be at all for them. I would like them to read poems as naturally as they read the papers, or go up to a football game. Not to consider it as anything more difficult, or effeminate, or praiseworthy.

Literature demands more strongly than ever before that the traditional barriers among genres be seen as inconsequential, that such classification fails because it does not provide useful distinctions. Is the following a story? A poem? An essay? How are we to think of the author, and how are we to think of ourselves as readers?

Borges and I
The other one, the one called Borges, is the one things happen to. I walk through the streets of Buenos Aires and stop for a moment, perhaps mechanically now, to look at the arch of an entrance hall and the grillwork on the gate; I know of Borges from the mail and see his name on a list of professors or in a biographical dictionary. I like hourglasses, maps, eighteenth-century typography, the taste of coffee and the prose of Stevenson; he shares these preferences, but in a vain way that turns them into the attributes of an actor. It would be an exaggeration to say that ours is a hostile relationship; I live, let myself go on living, so that Borges may contrive his literature, and this literature justifies me. It is no effort for me to confess that he has achieved some valid pages, but those pages cannot save me, perhaps because what is good belongs to no one, not even to him, but rather to the language and to tradition. Besides, I am destined to perish, definitively, and only some instant of myself can

survive in him. Little by little, I am giving over everything to him, though I am quite aware of his perverse customs of falsifying and magnifying things. Spinoza knew that all things long to persist in their being; the stone eternally wants to be a stone and the tiger a tiger. I shall remain in Borges, not in myself (if it is true that I am someone), but I recognize myself less in his books than in many others or in the laborious strumming of a guitar. Years ago I tried to free myself from him and went from the mythologies of the suburbs to the games with time and infinity, but those games belong to Borges now and I shall have to imagine other things. Thus my life is a flight and I lose everything and everything belongs to oblivion, or to him.

I do not know which of us has written this page.

Jorge Luis Borges
Translated by J. E. I.

The questions Borges asks here are questions that currently inform the world of hypertext and technology and literature, which we discuss in Chapter 10. Borges is playing with ideas and language, and literature is language at play . . .

Yet literature, like all art, demands to be taken seriously: When you make a poem you merely speak or write the language of every day, capturing as many bonuses as possible and economizing on losses; that is, you come awake to what always goes on in language, and you use it to the limit of your ability and your power of attention at the moment. You always fail, to some extent, since the opportunities are infinite—but think of the extent of your failure in ordinary conversation! Poetry bears the brunt, though; for in trying for the best it calls attention to its vivid failures. (Stafford, 1978, p. 3)

Literature even demands that the traditional language barriers be broken. Good translations of poets abound. Fiction and drama have become virtually international: Witness the awarding of a National Book Award to a Brazilian novel; witness the many national touring companies of major plays from around the globe; witness the polyglot (or monoglot, depending on how you look at it) cinema, with actors and directors from all over the world converging on a film.

It has long demanded not to be censored and has taken everything as its province: Hamlet, homosexuality, sadism, smog, masturbation, the flag, AIDS, Black Masses, computers, race. Revolution has been the topic of poems printed in the more staid journals.

Literature is bursting the bounds of the printed page to be read from beginning to end and is becoming a hypertext, a Nintendo game of words that everyone can play. And it wants to get into school that way, not condemned to an outer darkness by those who want to restrict literature to an elite group.

Literature courses once sought to create a private preserve of the cultivated few who worshipped monuments. Now primary and secondary schools and colleges are reveling in the anarchic, joyful, angry, strident, sentimental, and vital qualities of stories, poems, plays, novels, and essays—and not only of contemporary works but of works of the past. Teachers are beginning to recognize that the literature they teach is the creation of people. Of course it always has been, but schools have tended to make it much too serious and to take it away from the living, breathing struggle and celebration of the peoples of the earth.

Let's try to bring the struggle and celebration into our reading and teaching.

And help our students explore that world.

In fact, the term *literature*, once applied to what was in print, hardly applies to this conglomeration of writing, graphics, sound, music, film, and tape.

Forms have broken down. The regularity of print has been challenged. Subject matter taboos have shifted. But anarchy has not been loosed on the world. Literature is undergoing one of its periodic shifts whereby conventions are being tested and used as springboards for trying out new modes of expression. Many even want to do away with the word *literature* as being too elitist. We, the authors of this book, would like to keep it, however, because we think that it has its usefulness. We thing it is a term of value that helps inform what we are doing in school.

What Do You Mean by "Literature as a Term of Value"?

There are many ways of looking at literature as a term of value. If it is the "value" of a classic being a classic just because someone thought it was a classic and that everyone had to worship it as a classic, that value has come under increasing attack. We don't accept that use of "literature as a term of value." Nor do we accept that to be literature a text must be a complex structure of words, images, and ideas that form a puzzle to tantalize and dismay the uninitiated.

We do accept and argue that by using the word *literature* we place a premium of value on what students are reading. Using the term means that students are not simply developing a skill like typing when they read in school. It means that as teachers we consider what students read an important part of the curriculum. It also means we want students to read in a particular way; we want them to do more than mouth the words or jot down the main idea. We want them to make many connections, which we explore throughout this book. And we want them to learn something.

In selecting the texts that students will read in our courses, we must confront the issue of value. Why do we choose this novel instead of that one? Why do we think it is important to include more women or minority writers? Value remains important, but the criteria for judging pieces of writing have been challenged. One challenge that we have referred to is that of multiculturalism and the realization that literature in schools must reflect the pluralism of our society and the global village we inhabit.

There is another value we think important: the value of art. That, too, had been closely circumscribed to exclude what many call "subliterature." Who says a literary work must end with a period, have a single, static form, adhere to the "rules" of a genre, deal with the niceties, be written by one person, or be written by a person at all? Who says great literature must always be about humankind's deepest thoughts or must be taken seriously? Who says a work must have a single meaning? Who says a work must use words alone? That wasn't true for the Chinese and Japanese poets. That wasn't true for William Blake 200 years ago, when he created the picture poem "The Tyger." These matters are matters of taste, and taste is subject to change.

Values remain, but they are continually tested and challenged by new creations. One enduring value is the value of pleasure. Literature seeks to please the person who made it and the person who attends to it. Pleasure is not the same as laughter, but comes from a sense that what is written is as it should be. It is a satisfaction with the ways in which content, structure, and language converge. It can be highly complex or amazingly transparent. Pleasure is as important as the value of the writer's race, gender, or culture.

Has the Bursting of the Bonds of Convention, Genre, Standards Never Happened Before?

Of course it has. In England and the United States it happened when the Elizabethans played hob with dramatic form and with the Italian sonnet. It happened when opera introduced the mixing of media. It happened with the novel in the eighteenth century and again in the nineteenth century as writers returned from their travels around the world bringing back pieces of the cultures of the Orient and Africa. It happened when women began to gain a voice and a reputation as artists.

Magpielike, Chaucer borrowed plots, themes, lines from contemporary writers, and popular jokes and folktales, as well as borrowing from the "classics." He also had fun poking holes in literary conventions. So did Shakespeare:

> My mistress' eyes are nothing like the sun.
> Coral is far more red than her lips' red.
> If snow be white, why then her breasts are dun,
> If hairs be wires, black wires grow on her head.

The Tyger.

Tyger Tyger, burning bright.
In the forests of the night;
What immortal hand or eye,
Could frame thy fearful symmetry?

In what distant deeps or skies.
Burnt the fire of thine eyes!
On what wings dare he aspire?
What the hand dare sieze the fire?

And what shoulder & what art.
Could twist the sinews of thy heart?
And when thy heart began to beat,
What dread hand? & what dread foot?

What the hammer! what the chain,
In what furnace was thy brain?
What the anvil? what dread grasp.
Dare its deadly terrors clasp!

When the stars threw down their spears
And water'd heaven with their tears:
Did he smile his work to see?
Did he who made the Lamb make thee?

Tyger Tyger burning bright.
In the forests of the night:
What immortal hand or eye,
Dare frame thy fearful symmetry!

I have seen roses damasked, red and white,
But no such roses see I in her cheeks.
And in some perfumes is there more delight
Than in the breath that from my mistress reeks.
I love to hear her speak, yet well I know
That music hath a far more pleasing sound.
I grant I never saw a goddess go,
My mistress, when she walk, treads on the ground.
    And yet, by Heaven, I think my love as rare
    As any she belied with false compare.

Sonnet 130

Shakespeare is making poetry comic, just as Dave Morice did with Emily Dickinson's poem. Both did it to get us to see what might seem stale with new eyes.

In most societies writers have continually sought to "make it new," to modify the conventions set by their predecessors and forge their own forms, themes, and combinations of words, media, and ideas. Often they have failed; often they have succeeded.

Today's writers are no different, save that they have more traditions to play against, more gadgets to play with, more areas of information to assimilate into their writing, and—most important—a larger literate audience. They are no longer dependent on a small number of publishers, because with a computer and a laser printer they can produce their own books.

What makes the plethora of writings, forms, themes, and mixtures seem confusing to many in school is that the nice, neat, segregated world of literature courses has become reconnected with writers and what they do. A couple of hundred years ago, educators thought the only literature was Latin and Greek. English and American writers were not part of the curriculum (save for a few excerpts that were used to teach people how to read).

But around the world writers wrote.

When education became the province of all, Latin and Greek literature were replaced by English literature, but it was the English literature of the sixteenth, seventeenth, and eighteenth centuries. Even American literature was frowned on. In the universities literature was studied historically, in the context of the development of the language and the moral and political life of the times in which it was written. In the high schools works were read for their beauty of expression and their purity of thought—read, that is, as models of ethics and style. Only a few works by the "right sorts of people" made the reading list.

Writers went on writing.

Thomas Carlyle was so dissatisfied with the form of the philosophical thesis that he invented a German writer and an editor to present his ideas. The result was *Sartor Resartus*. Karl Marx imitated him and started a revolution.

Susan Glaspell was invited to write a play to open a new summer theater in the 1920s. What she produced was *Trifles*, a play that has become a feminist landmark.

Ambrose Bierce found that one of the most congenial forms for him was the dictionary. In his "Devil's Dictionary," he defines a critic:

CRITIC, n. A person who boasts himself hard to please because nobody tries to please him.

There is a land of pure delight,
Beyond the Jordan's flood,
Where saints, appareled all in white,
Fling back the critic's mud.

And as he legs it through the skies,
His pelt a sable hue,
He sorrows sore to recognize
The missiles that he threw.

Orrin Goof

Langston Hughes not only wrote "straight" poems and short stories, but worked with the photographer Roy de Cafava to make his classic "The Sweet Flypaper of Life," a mixed picture poem like Blake's.

Art Spiegelman wrote a searing satire on the Holocaust; it's a comic book, *Maus*.

But while writers were having fun writing, taking their experience of their culture and the world around them and making it into art, in colleges and secondary schools people were making the study of literature a big business. Pieces of writing acquired barnacles of articles, books, and dissertations, with definitive editions, annotated editions, scholarly editions, variorum editions; with examinations of structure, imagery, and metaphor; with interpretations political, social, psychological, aesthetic, and moral; with computerized concordances and bibliographies of bibliographies. Shakespeare, needless to say, has become one of the most encrusted. Students who want to know all that has been said about *Hamlet* would have to spend their lifetimes reading that body of scholarship alone.

Scholarship became such a growth industry it produced a spinoff: theory. And theory doesn't even seem to need writers and artists.

Today, theory is a bigger business than scholarship. In the schools this industry is evident in the many curriculum guides and teaching aids that accompany each text, and in drugstores' revolving book racks, which are often filled, not with novels, poems, plays, and nonfiction, but with master outlines and study guides to the great works. The accumulation of knowledge and secondhand opinions about what writers have written has superseded the reading and enjoyment of their work. Literary study, even at the junior high school level, is a serious business. The thousand or so students we have interviewed say literature study in school is reading to take tests and give the right answer.

And writers go on writing.

Annie Dillard writes meditations on the little things in nature; Jamaica Kincaid writes stories about her life and articles about her garden; Ursula LeGuin probes further and further into her world of fantasy and explores femininity at the same time.

Writers don't seem to pay too much attention to what goes on in school. Have they forgotten what they were taught? Or is it that they, like so many of their predecessors, realize that literature routinized becomes a literature that stagnates?

We aren't saying that theory and literary scholarship are valueless. On the contrary, critical commentary, historical study, textual editing, bibliographical enterprise, and theory are all valuable, particularly to teachers, not because of the truth they purport to give us, but because they allow us to see how people have responded to pieces of writing. They help to locate the various pieces of literature in the world of the past and in the broad scope of human intellectual history. Theory and literary scholarship have become a testimony to the power of the mind to read and to construct and test hypotheses about what is read. They testify to the ability of people to organize and build structures out of a collocation of objects that might otherwise be considered unique. They demonstrate another use of the imagination, but it is not the same as the artist's imaginative vision.

Like scientists' elaborate organization of natural phenomena, like historians' network of human events and actions, like psychologists' theories of human behavior, the literary scholars' web of biographical, historical, generic, structural, archetypal, and rhetorical connections between poem and poem, play and play, novel and essay is a triumph. But literary scholarship is not the same thing as works of literature themselves, just as science is not nature and history is not human events.

Northrop Frye, one of the great teachers, described how literature defies our attempts to tame it by scholarship or theory this way:

> . . . the organizing principles are myth, that is, story or narrative, and metaphor, that is, figured language. Here we are in a completely liberal world, the world of the free movement of the spirit. If we read a story there is no pressure to believe in it or act upon it; if we encounter metaphors in poetry, we need not worry about their factual absurdity. Literature incorporates our ideological concerns, but it devotes itself mainly to the primary ones, in both physical and spiritual forms: its fictions show human beings in the primary throes of surviving, loving, prospering, and fighting with the frustrations

that block those things. It is at once a world of relaxation, where even the most terrible tragedies are still called plays, and a world of far greater intensity than ordinary life affords. In short it does everything that can be done for people except transform them. It creates a world that the spirit can live in, but it does not make us spiritual beings. (Frye, 1991, p. 16)

Sing, goddess, the anger of Peleus' son Achilleus and its devastation, which put pains thousandfold upon the Achaians, hurled in their multitudes to the house of Hades strong souls . . . of heroes, but gave their bodies to be the delicate feasting of dogs.

What happens to a dream deferred?

We real cool

When shall we three meet again in thunder, lightning, or in rain?

The curfew tolls the knell of parting day, The lowing herd wind slowly o'er the lea, The plowman homeward plods his weary way, And leaves the world to darkness and to me.

For if he like a madman lived At least like a wise one he died.

I am an invisible man.

They told me, Heraclitus, they told me you were dead.

"you, Tom!"

He who has a thousand friends has not a friend to spare And he who has one enemy will meet him everywhere.

We shall never understand one another until we reduce the language to seven words.

It is a truth universally acknowledged, that a single man in possession of a good fortune must be in want of a wife.

Let us go then, you and I, When the evening is spread out against the sky . . .

By and by God caught his eye . . .

I will fight no more forever.

I, too, dislike it.

I'm lighting out for the territory.

Hope is a thing with feathers

As far as many readers are concerned there are poems, and plays, and stories, and the Bible, and myths, and cartoons, and jokes, but literature? Literature is an abstraction, a network that binds the various pieces together. For different people, literature is different networks. For some it is all the information about authors and publishers and audiences, just as, for some, the Beatles were everything about Paul, Ringo, George, and John but their music. For some it is an elaborate code set to trap the unwary reader, who must continually read between the lines. For some it is an infinite series of variations on a few themes. For some it is a verbal manifestation of the totality of the human psyche—a model of the human.

We have taken the broadest definition in this chapter and tried to illustrate it in Figure 1.1. It is one that states: Literature is a vast assortment of imaginative verbal (usually) utterances; each utterance comes from some writer(s), who has a voice and is a voice for his or her culture; and each

FIGURE 1.1 Defining the World of Literature

Writers	Texts	Foci	Responses
Gender	Poems	People	Horror
Nationality	Plays	Images	Laughter
Ethnicity	Essays	Moods	Boredom
Date of Birth	Novellas	Metaphors	Longings
Religion	Comics	Plots	Imaginings
Education	Films	Settings	Hope
Culture	Stories	Words	Fear
Sexual Preference	Novels	Punctuation Marks	Tension
Interests	Epics	Rhythms	Despair
Family	Performances	Rhymes	Affirmation
etceteras	etceteras	etceteras	etceteras

utterance in itself is defined by style and order, which give pleasure above and beyond the experience conveyed. It includes the comic strip *Calvin and Hobbes* and the *Divine Comedy*. Pieces of literature arouse in us a response— a sense of knowing, of feeling, of moving, of pattern and insight. When these senses coalesce for one of us, we have a kind of pleasure, a sense of the fitness of things. Out of having read what we've read, we construct a theory— a theory building on the nature of language and the nature of the mind and the meeting of language and mind in what we would call response.

But If What You Have Said Is True, Then Your Definition of Literature Doesn't Matter. Does It?

Of course not. But yours does.

Well, Then, What about Literature Courses?

At the center of the curriculum are not the authors, those living people who made the literature; not the works of literature, those collections of words in print or in sound wave; not the various parts of the works that readers and writers fasten onto at certain times; not the individual reader's psyche, with its neurological movements and its constantly changing psychological states and constantly modifying sets of beliefs, images, and concepts . . .

but

all those imaginary quill-like lines connecting the cells in the four columns in Figure 1.1: the mind as it meets the book and, through the book, the author; the response; the small bit of the book that captures the writer's or the reader's fancy; the meeting of writer and reader on the barrier reef of the text or the image.

The Response of the Reader to the World of the Writer through the Text

That is the center of a curriculum in literature. Treat a lot those quills carefully, touch them lightly, or the book will become dead and the mind will retreat into itself. But don't avoid them; you must touch those quills, and you will have a response-based curriculum.

References

Frye, Northrop. *The Double Vision: Language and Meaning in Literature and Religion*. Toronto: University of Toronto Press, 1991, p. 16.
Stafford, William. *Writing the Australian Crawl: Views on the Writer's Vocation*. Ann Arbor: University of Michigan Press, 1978.

Resources

What follows is a number of pieces that we have used and found useful. Some are old, some are new. We've probably missed a lot as well. Let us begin with Perennial Sources:

> *New York Times Book Review*
>
> *Paperback Books in Print*
>
> *The Drama Review*
>
> *English Journal*
>
> *Language Arts*
>
> *College English*
>
> *Hornbook*
>
> *The New York Review of Books*
>
> *The Journal of Reading*
>
> *Poetry*
>
> *Reader*
>
> *The American Poetry Archives*

Abrahamson, Richard F., and Betty Carter, eds. *Books for You: A Booklist for Senior High School Students*. Urbana, IL: National Council of Teachers of English, 1988.

Atwan, Robert, and Harvey Wiener, eds. *Enjoying Stories*. New York: Longman, 1987.

Barrier, Michael, and Martin Williams, eds. *A Smithsonian Book of Comic-Book Comics*. Washington, D.C: Smithsonian Institution Press, 1981.

Fader, Daniel N., and Elton MacNeill. *Hooked on Books: Program and Proof*. Los Angeles: Berkeley Publishing, 1969.

Guriand, Felix. *Larousse Encyclopaedia of Mythology*. London: Paul Hamlyn, 1959.

Hall, Stuart, and Paddy Whannel. *The Popular Arts*. New York: Pantheon, 1964.

Hill, Karen, and Michael Winfield, eds. *Tapestry: A Multicultural Anthology*. Englewood Cliffs, NJ: Globe Book Co., 1993.

Smith, Ron. *Mythologies of the World: A Guide to Sources*. Urbana, IL: National Council of Teachers of English, 1975.

Stanford, Barbara Dodds, and Karima Amin. *Black Literature for High School Students*. Urbana, IL: National Council of Teachers of English, 1978.

Townsend, John Rowe. *Written for Children: An Outline of English Language Children's Literature*. 2nd ed. Philadelphia: Lippincott, 1983.

White, David M., and Robert H. Abel, eds. *The Funnies: An American Idiom*. New York: Free Press, 1963.

chapter 2

Those Kids: Readers, Rappers, Writers, Talkers, Listeners

Michael Jordan
Mystically he soars
In his own
Created world
He jams
and slams with
Ease

By Chuck
(in Lanka, 1990, p. 3)

They come in all shapes, hair colors and styles, peachy skin and fuzz, short and tall. They come from all kinds of cultures . . . and subcultures. At thirteen they are at the threshold of (for them) an unmapped terrain even though millions of us before them have passed the same way. They know nothing and yet everything. Filled with exuberance in the morning and dashed to the floor by the afternoon, they are puzzling, frustrating, challenging, and, in their own way, refreshingly wonderful.

Some still have the innocence of childhood with them but it's fast becoming tempered by "knowledge." Some didn't have that innocence in the first place—life had already begun its lessons at birth. But although we talk about this group of people as one, adolescents are not one amorphous group; they are not totally molded yet by the social system and its instrument—school.

Furthermore, we are increasingly reminded that they come from an extremely wide diversity of backgrounds. (Didn't they always?) This diversity in the adolescent school population must be faced, if only because, as we discuss later in this chapter, we also have to reconsider the kinds of selections we make on behalf of this diverse population. Recent debates on the validity of a literary canon that consists primarily of male, white authors have direct relevance here. Such a canon assumes a culturally homogeneous society and a society in which no one questions the dominance of one group over others.

These assumptions are no longer unchallenged. In traditional literature courses and anthologies, features such as ethnic stereotyping, gender bias, and a narrow selection of authors representing other cultures are now found to be extremely problematic. Perhaps, if research on student attitudes toward school literature anthologies is to be taken seriously, students always knew such features were problematic!

Why should we bother to write a chapter about adolescents? After all, despite the differences we'll discuss in this chapter, they're a recognizable age group about whom we've heard a great deal. Why bother to bring up the characteristics of adolescence in the context of discussing literature? There are three compelling reasons for doing so:

> First, there is the question of what literary selections to present to them, if we want to keep their interests in mind.
>
> Second, there is the question of how best to engage them in literary discussion and succeed in bringing about that often elusive goal of having them develop a love and appreciation of literature (one of the most frequently stated aims of literature curricula though often the least achieved).
>
> Third, they know a great deal more than we allow them to tell us. The *way* we teach literature, therefore, is at least as important as what we teach.

Selection and relevance are important components of the literature curriculum. However, if we close off what adolescents can say and write in response to literature through too much "telling" and too little "doing" on their part, and through too much narrow questioning not so much about the literature itself but about how we analyze it, we rarely, if ever, discover the richness and perceptiveness of their literary understanding. We simply make them inarticulate and dependent on others to read for them.

Curricular Goals and the Readers, Rappers, Writers, Talkers, and Listeners

Ask aspiring English teachers their aims in teaching literature and most say, "I want my students to *love* literature." Then follows a litany of other objectives related to understanding literature, appreciating it, comprehending it, being able to identify literary elements.

But the primary aim is related to getting them to love literature (presumably just as we English teachers love it). Yet we approach that objective from an adult's perspective.

Proof, you say?

Let's ask another question: "How do you intend to teach your literature classes?" A survey of 230 aspiring English teachers in a secondary English certification program revealed a less than unanimous response to this question.

Surprisingly few suggested that the literature chosen for study should be relevant to the adolescent student.

Surprisingly few suggested allowing extensive choice by the student.

Prodding them still further, we found an assumption that reflects our own experiences rather than that of the contemporary adolescent student: "I" love literature and "I" managed to "get hooked on it," and somehow, so will they; "I" will help them get there. The teacher is still the director and the student is still "the student"—a generic breed that lacks individual identities.

Perhaps such assumptions worked (up to a point) some twenty years ago, and perhaps they worked even ten years ago. The current generation of aspiring teachers still has one foot set in a more book-oriented time, but there seem to be fewer and fewer of these hardy survivors.

Yet current teenagers come to us loaded with stiffer competition—a media world far more accessible than any book, far more immediately engaging than reading, despite our protests. It is a world that began for many of them with escapes into Nintendoland, Segaland, and Gameboyland in restaurants, airplanes, and cars—the engrossing modern distracters and sedatives. Although these teenagers have far more to amuse and entertain them than did preceding generations, their world also demands a higher level of literacy for successful performance in many fields. And it is a world that does not consider essential the moral and ethical avenues traditionally available through organized religion.

In such a world, literature, from the classics to young adult selections, can offer many opportunities for exploring important questions ranging from issues of ethics and morality to purposes for living, as this extract from Walter Dean Myer's *Motown and Didi* aptly illustrates:

> "Mostly I just think about what I'm going to be doing from one day to the next," Motown said. "Sometimes I think about what the people around here are doing. This guy I know, I call him the Professor—I get books from him—sometimes we talk about how you see people doing things and they look like they're doing one thing and they're really doing something else."
>
> "Like what?" Didi asked.
>
> "Like they using dope and they saying it makes them feel good, only what they really doing is killing themselves." (pp. 101–102)

Finally, it is a world where many adolescents come from families in which both parents work, where divorces often result in divided loyalties, and where adults no longer provide the images of stability and security that we once fondly believed they did. In such a world, literature can provide many opportunities for helping adolescents find answers to the enduring questions common to their age group: "Who am I?" "Where Will I Be Going?" "How Will I Get There?" "What Kind of Person Will I Become?" (Winegard and Gruber, 1988, p. 2). Yes, their need to do well, to get those grades up still helps us in our task of promoting good literature, but we believe the arguments for making literature "live" in the classrooms are more urgent than ever.

VIGNETTE I: TEACHERS AS READERS

In a recent project, one of our teacher colleagues conducted a study in which she explored both her own and a volunteer seventh grader's response to several literary selections. Although her collaborating student has always been an avid reader and is a member of a challenge class, Susan Zimmerman observed that

> . . . once again, I was reminded that even though she is an above average reader, she still has not the adult experiences that I have had and therefore her responses will be different from my responses. . . . The project forced me to realize that even talented seventh grade readers are *not* adult readers.
>
> I learned the most about myself as a reader and teacher and about Tina as a person when I received her journal response about *Anastasia, Ask Your Analyst*. To Tina this book was the best one she had read all summer and to me it was a simple book with few qualities that I would consider exemplary in the field of young adult literature. I did not want to express this to Tina so I never wrote her my journal response. I wanted to be honest with her when writing all my journal entries but I did not want to tell her that her favorite book was my least favorite. Somehow I did not want to do anything that would discourage her love of reading or keep her from responding freely to liter-ature, which she obviously valued. . . . When I stepped away from the literary baggage I carry, I could understand why she loved this book. Firstly it is a light-hearted and humorous book. It therefore provides escape, which Tina needs in her hectic adolescent life. She has made it clear to me that escape from the everyday world is the main reason why she likes to read so much. In light of her recent family difficulties, I can see why this book provides a safe and loving place to which this young lady can run when reading. . . . I found I need to view the book

> from Tina's perspective to see its real value to her. Perhaps
> what she gets from the book and the series of which it is one
> part is far more valuable than what I get from some of the more
> complicated books we both read in the course of this project.
> (Zimmerman, 1993, p. 5)

Generally, we have regarded adolescents as a group to be controlled and classrooms as battlefields on which students' cooperation must be won. We suspect this perception is generally right—many students, including English majors, have seen their English classes in high school as dull and confusing. English was a riddle they never really solved.

They survived by finding out what the teacher wanted and delivering it as best they could. Sitting in classrooms where the teacher does most of the doing (i.e., talking, reading, sometimes even writing, if we include blackboard work) generates isolation and apathy. Adolescents are not without energy. Physically, emotionally, intellectually, they hum outside the classroom. Although much of the energy may be misdirected, according to adult eyes, creative and insightful teachers can draw on it and thereby find themselves in more dynamic classrooms than even they may have envisioned.

Another teacher we recently observed in an eighth-grade classroom had tapped the hum. It wasn't a literature class but a spin-off writing workshop where the students were working on a newspaper to be produced for some weeks to come. They talked with each other; some were busy writing drafts of their contributions; others were reviewing pieces already written and discussing them with the relevant writers. Perhaps there were kids in there who chatted about things other than the newspaper, but we'd be living in fantasy if we thought that sort of thing didn't go on in regular classrooms. Remember all those notes we used to write to each other while keeping track of the teacher's questioning and talking?

The enormous energy of adolescence can be drawn on to engage students in active participation in the literature classroom. Many current high school classrooms are mini-versions of college classrooms. Students sit and make notes while teachers lecture. As we've stated already, this may work for adult students but many high school classroom observations indicate it is hardly productive nor is it a way of "hooking" students on good literature.

Kids and Books

What is it that hooks kids on books? Why is it that some of us become avid readers and some don't? These questions still perplex educational researchers who are more interested in skill-based reading instruction. Increasingly such researchers are finding evidence that those who become literate do so for a number of reasons that go beyond skills levels and even "effective teaching."

Among such reasons is the role of background knowledge—that is, the kind of knowledge books assume we have in order to make sense of them. Another reason lies in the literacy-rich environments that produce children who read before they come to school and provide continuous support for reading throughout school.

So far, however, we really haven't tackled the delicate question of the relevance of materials in the school context, partly, we suspect, because we would then consider the unthinkable—that the literature we think all students should be able to read and should love to read (i.e., "the classics") is not of any particular relevance to them. If we find this as an answer, what do we do?

Thinking about this dilemma leads us to one of the interesting facts about literature that is sometimes overlooked in the "relevancy" argument and that young children, at least, have inadvertently provided powerful argument for: The world of imaginative discourse (that is, literature) can help us leap across domains we find unthinkable in the skills-based world.

If this were not so, how can young children love fantasy? If this were not so, how is it that science fiction can command a sizable readership? If this were not so, how can young adolescent readers (and even older ones) continue to become engrossed with the challenges faced, for example, by characters such as Cassie Logan in Mildred Taylor's *Let the Circle Be Unbroken* as she struggles to find herself a person of worth in a society that denies that worth because she is African-American?

It seems that when we pick up a literary book, we already accept that the unreal is possible. We suspend our disbelief, just as Samuel Coleridge said we do. We engage in flights of fancy and become totally involved in ways that may elude some of us with nonfictional reading. The same students who have trouble with a geography text don't quail from exploring the fantastic world of J. R. R. Tolkien. We won't discuss why in this chapter because the issue is covered elsewhere in this book, but at least one answer lies in the nature of literature as a distinct genre different from fact-based genres and, therefore, drawing forth different responses from readers.

Despite what we have just said, however, the relevance issue is not easily dismissed. At least one of us has tried to introduce the wonders of *Wind in the Willows* to an eighth grade class and largely been defeated, only to turn to a reader-based choice—a little novel entitled *Thursday*, aimed at the adolescent reader aged about fourteen, with a fourteen-year-old antihero and a heroine who brings him to his senses. They loved that! Yet we have also taught ninth graders who were spellbound by hearing and reading Shakespeare's *King Lear*. They were so still during the last act that we could, literally, hear a pin drop, and they intuitively understood the enormity of the pain Lear experienced as he carried Cordelia from the dungeon.

Selection, nevertheless, is a significant factor in engaging many adolescents (and any reader) in what they read. And, as teachers have reported, students from different cultural backgrounds engage more readily and powerfully with literature about their own cultures than they do with literature in which they never see themselves represented through heroes and heroines of their own cultures.

To help us determine on what basis selections might be made, we suggest considering the nature of adolescents and their social and cultural backgrounds, not in terms of the limits this implies but in terms of the scope it offers.

Who Is "the Adolescent"?

What is the identity of the high school student? Can we even really generalize about the adolescent? Any seasoned secondary teacher will talk about seventh graders as still being fresh and enthusiastic and pliable and eighth graders as unpredictable, yet still delightfully spontaneous and, yes, still interested in learning. Then there are those ninth graders—ugh! Increasingly incomprehensible, intractable, bored, moody, dominated by hormones. Somehow, the rigors of test-taking and meeting college-entry requirements take care of the tenth through twelfth graders, for we tend not to hear about their characters, their development, their inability to sit still quite so frequently. They are swallowed up in the need to do well and to get on in the grade grind. They have learned to be passive students, not active readers.

Phases of adolescent development are reasonably well covered in educational psychology, so we don't intend to cover the same ground in this chapter. We can, however, bring to the literature classroom some of the findings of that research and integrate them with such factors as literary selection, the question of relevance, and what we can expect in literary understanding and appreciation.

Personal/Social Development

> None the less, now that the time had come, there was a kind of ache in her at having to say good-bye; for it was in her nature to let go unwillingly of things, places, people once known. Besides, glad as she felt to have done with learning, she was unclear what was to come next. . . . Hence, her parting was effected with very mixed feelings; she did not know in the least where she really belonged, or under what conditions she would be happy; she was conscious only of a mild sorrow at having to take leave of the shelter of years.
>
> *Henry Handel Richardson*

Laura's intimations of "the cold, hard world" of reality as revealed in the passage from Richardson's *The Getting of Wisdom* illustrate part of the adolescent's ability to see patterns and significance in what were once just isolated events. Contemporary writers of adolescent literature also depict this movement from the relatively untroubled world of childhood into adulthood, as can be seen in the following extracts:

> "Meg, don't you think you'd make a better adjustment to life if you faced facts?"
>
> "I do face facts," Meg said. "They're lots easier to face than people, I can tell you."
>
> *Madeleine L'Engle*, A Wrinkle in Time

or

> She was in a different line and a few feet behind, and as she looked at the back of his head she was overwhelmed by the fact that at that very moment she was creating her own past. To let Dennis go his way and for her to go her own without even saying a word would be a memory she'd have to have for the rest of her life. It seemed as if it was something Liz should have known, and Sean. They should have known what they were risking. The present becomes the past, and it continues inside you.
>
> *Paul Zindel*, My Darling, My Hamburger

And there are many examples from Charles Dickens and other classical writers of heroes, sometimes even younger than adolescents, undergoing the same development. As social beings, adolescents often question adult authority while wishing to figure out adult reality:

> I began to realize that my coffee trips were futile—they only brought temporary relief whereas these people needed something more permanent with more individual care and attention. But the needs of these outcasts were insufficiently met or even understood by the public. To give them practical help needed money, time and professional skills. Of which I had none. My own inadequacy to assist them haunted me, so I went in search of others who felt the same. I found people kind and sympathetic, but not prepared to stick their necks out and become involved. What is so frustrating was that most of the objections were reasonable.
>
> *Sally Trench*, Bury Me in My Boots

Adolescents' developing ability to see shades of gray amid the black and white world of childhood makes adult reality confusing at times. An adolescent has already had time and experience to discover, for example, that when something is promised it doesn't necessarily happen immediately, or sometimes, ever. Another reality to be faced is that ethics and morality may, in fact, be relative, not absolute. People in adult life do get away with things. Adults are inconsistent and imperfect even though they expect children not to be so, and their kids know it:

> There was a rule at Lark Creek, more important than anything Mr. Turner made up and fussed about. That was the rule that you never mixed up troubles at home with life at school.
> When parents were poor or ignorant or mean, or even just didn't believe in having a TV set, it was up to their kids to protect them.
> *Katherine Paterson,* Bridge to Terabithia

In both the classics and contemporary adolescent literature we can find examples of the realities adolescents begin to reflect on as being part of adult life—for example, "the unfair," the "hard to explain." They may not like these realities, but when confronted with them in literature they take them seriously, as the following vignette illustrates.

VIGNETTE II: CONNECTING WITH LITERARY TEXT

About 1,000 eighth- and ninth-grade students were watching the dramatization of several stories by Poe and other writers, among them Shirley Jackson's "The Lottery." Between performances there had been a good deal of wriggling and talking. But once the performances began, total silence prevailed. The students were particularly riveted by the dramatization of Jackson's story. "The Lottery" is not a story written for or about adolescents. It tells of the brutality of ritualized control over this small rural community, the fate of individuals in it from infancy to old age controlled by a mindless casting of lots. Its drama and potential relevance did not escape this audience of fourteen- and fifteen-year-olds.

Prior to the performance, the students in one eighth grade class had read the story. After the performance, the teacher asked them to write their responses to the story as read and another response to the dramatization of it.

The dramatized version acted as a catalyst for reflection about what they had felt when they originally read the story. Their initial responses included anger, dismay, feelings of powerlessness, shock, and sadness. Significantly, the dramatized version brought out more forcibly connections between what they saw and similar situations seen and heard of in their daily lives; fraternity induction rituals, teen club membership rituals, gang behaviors.

Those parallels had not emerged in their initial readings of the story. With discussion, led by the teacher, and sharing of their written responses, the students moved away from seeing the witnessed events as perpetrated by a "bunch of uncivilized weirdos" to seeing them as incidents that they were uncomfortably aware could occur only too easily in their own lives.

One of the harder lessons an emerging adult faces is isolation from peers. The isolation may be a consequence of being different (interpreted as "oddness" by the peers) or a consequence of making a moral or ethical choice at a significant price. A number of classical novels and contemporary adolescent novels deal with this issue (without happy endings), offering an opportunity for students to explore how they would face such situations themselves.

In Dickens' *Great Expectations*, for example, we can see three situations in which characters are isolated: Pip, the orphan; Magwitch, the convict; and Miss Havisham, the embittered, jilted old woman. The novel focuses on Pip's personal and moral/ethical development against the backdrop of his illusions about wealth and what it represents. His great moments come when he can genuinely love the social outcast, Magwitch, and accept that it was this man who was responsible for Pip's having had "great expectations." Pip's struggles to accept the truth of the origin of his temporary fortune and his ability to see real worth in contrast to the glitter that formerly blinded him is representative of the growth we must all experience:

> But I must say more. Dear Joe, I hope you will have children to love, and that some little fellow will sit in this chimney corner of a winter night, who may remind you of another little fellow gone out of it forever. Don't tell him, Joe, that I was thankless; don't tell him, Biddy, that I was ungenerous and unjust; only tell him that I honored you both, because you were both so good and true, and that, as your child, I said it would be natural to him and grow up a better man than I did.
>
> *Charles Dickens,* Great Expectations

Another example that generates empathy among adolescent readers is found in Myer's *Motown and Didi*. Motown has just faced the choice of killing the youth who was responsible for selling drugs to Didi's younger brother or holding back the urge for revenge so that something better and more hopeful might emerge:

> He had thought, for some reason, that he had pulled himself together. Thought that the steel that he had forged in the streets and in the darkness of the buildings and in the solitude of his own soul had again hardened. . . . Gently he took her hand and held it against his cheek, gently turned it in his own hands, hands that would have

killed for her, but now would work for her and protect her, and gently, he brought her hand to his lips and kissed it.

Adolescents we have known and taught empathize with these heroes and heroines whose isolation and exclusion, trials and challenges are still essentially those of the contemporary teenager. Another compelling contemporary example is Robert Cormier's *The Chocolate War*, in which the young hero, Jerry, faces death largely because he doesn't go along with the crowd:

> Jerry raised himself toward the voice, needing to answer it. He had to answer. But he kept his eyes shut, as if he could keep a lid on the pain that way. But it was more than pain that caused an urgency in him. The pain had become the nature of his existence but this other thing weighed on him, a terrible burden. What other thing? The knowledge, the knowledge: what he had discovered. Funny, how his mind was clear suddenly, apart from his body, floating above his body, floating above the pain.
>
> *Robert Cormier,* The Chocolate War

Although Jerry's pain is a consequence of what other boys his age have done, the knowledge is that first sign of understanding of the significance of events. Similarly, in John Neufeld's *Lisa, Bright and Dark*, the students who attempt to help a fellow sixteen-year-old cope with her developing mania come to realize that they cannot expect cooperation and help from the adults closest to her—her parents and school authorities—all of whom turn a blind eye on the situation. The disbelief eventually becomes the foundation for not only disillusionment with the adults but an understanding of what makes them tick.

Other issues or problems related to adolescence include the preoccupation with peers, wide swings of mood and intense passions, feelings of isolation, and questioning the purpose in life. But it needn't all be grim. Heroes and heroines may also be admired for achieving greatness.

We've already mentioned Shakespeare's *King Lear* and can find similarly powerful experiences of coming of age, of facing who one really is, or of facing choices one has to make, in Jane Austen's *Emma*, Richard Hughes's *A High Wind in Jamaica*, Mark Twain's *The Adventures of Huckleberry Finn*, and Emily Brontë's *Wuthering Heights*.

Many writers suggest organizing a literature curriculum around the interests of adolescents but point out that this need not be a limiting factor. Rather, it can be a starting point in creating a program that is a developmental exploration leading students to confront more sophisticated and intellectually challenging questions at each grade level (Carlsen, 1981).

As one teacher has observed, in hoping for greater sophistication in literary tastes and responses to literature among adolescents, we forget the obvious differences in age and experiences between ourselves as teachers and our adolescent students. The teacher at one point notes adolescents' strong resistance to being "critical" about what they read as, possibly, being developmentally appropriate. Of her avid reader but reluctant critic she writes, "I respect her literary naiveté and find a small part of me longing for her innocence." (Zimmerman, 1993, p. 4)

Perhaps we should capitalize on these interests and differences as a way of hooking adolescents to literature. They can, for example, explore their passions through books that present adolescent perceptions of the range and kinds of love. *Romeo and Juliet* does a pretty good job of exploring the consequences of loving someone one's parents don't approve of. In contrast to the sometimes superficial representation of adolescent "passions" in popular magazines, the play presents the potential strength, beauty, and steadfastness of adolescent love. Remember Juliet's impassioned dismissal of sweet-nothings when Romeo swears his everlasting love with the romantic moon as his witness?

> **R:** Lady, by yonder blessed moon I swear, that tips with silver all these fruit-tree tops—
>
> **J:** O, swear not by the moon, th' inconstant moon, that monthly changes in her circled orb, lest that thy love prove likewise variable.
>
> **R:** What shall I swear by?
>
> **J:** Do not swear at all. Or, if thou wilt, swear by thy gracious self. . . .
>
> Romeo and Juliet, *2.2.107–14*

From contemporary young adult literature we can draw an example of another kind of passion, jealousy, in Katherine Paterson's *Jacob Have I Loved*, a brilliant exploration of a twin's struggle to discover herself while in the shadow of her more sparkling, musically gifted sister.

> There was no place to run to, no tip of the marsh where I could sit alone on a stump of driftwood and watch the water. I wanted to cry and scream and throw things. Instead, under almost perfect control, I got a broom and began savagely to attack the sand that was stuck like cement in the corner of the living room.
>
> *Katherine Paterson,* Jacob Have I Loved

The intensity of love/hate, guilt/remorse pulls us back to adolescence and its incredible swings of mood, unreasonableness, "black holes," and soaring wonder in a very compelling way. We adults find it quite simple to forget the intensity of these feelings, having long ago worked reason into the matrix of our emotions.

However, that we survived those topsy-turvy years without the aid of literature that presented us with realistic images of ourselves and our experiences (i.e., without adolescent fiction) is not an argument for expecting current students to do so.

As we have already noted, the current teenager is not identical to the teenager of the 1970s and 1980s. We read everywhere of high school students who do not "buy" the authority of schooling today. If nothing else, television and suggested alternatives to the status quo have eroded much of our traditional authority.

In many classrooms we can see the impact of irrelevant curricula and teaching styles: students slouching over desks, paying the minimum amount of attention to what is happening to get by, and, interestingly enough, still managing to get by. At the same time, to exclude the classics on the grounds of irrelevance denies adolescents the opportunity to explore themselves and their concerns from other perspectives. Our dress, manners, and even language may change, but the issues of life that face all of us are timeless.

Intellectual/Cognitive Development

Various people have commented on the depth of intellectual development that adolescents exhibit. Linguistically, this is often manifested in their attraction to metaphor, to irony, and, hence, to levels of meaning. In humor, we see it in their love of punning, double entendres, non sequiturs, parodies, and caricature.

According to developmental psychologists, adolescents are capable of thinking about abstract problems, applying logical rules to ideas that violate reality; thinking in increasingly flexible and abstract ways, solving problems through logical processes after having considered all possibilities, and making hypothetical judgments.

Social psychologists have found that adolescents are capable of notions of relativity regarding behaviors that may vary depending on internal states, external situations, or other transitory factors. They are also capable of seeing networks or systems of perspectives (e.g., society's perspectives versus their own points of view relating to group identity) and are capable of grasping the full complexity of human thoughts, feelings, and intentions.

More recently, we have begun to realize that many of these capabilities are also related to intellectual experiences adolescents have in their own lives, both in and out of school. We may find that the more literate adolescent will exhibit these capabilities to a greater extent—an argument, perhaps, for promoting extensive reading for this and younger age groups.

How might we capitalize on this potential in the literature classroom? As we see with the tenth-grade essay on *Animal Farm* (Chapter 9), asking students to consider a hypothetical argument such as whether George Orwell's novel is simply an animal story written for children or a symbolic representation of power is not beyond their capabilities. However, when we focus exclusively on the abstract, we run the risk of developing the switch-off atti-tude to literature we have observed in many high school classrooms.

Although the stated preoccupations of adolescents are usually related to their own emerging adulthood, their need for peer acceptance, and their increased sense of their own inadequacies (concerning figure, hair color, clothes, gamesmanship, height, and so on), we don't believe teachers must focus exclusively on these preoccupations to hook them on literature. But we can, through young adult literature, connect them with issues that *are* contemporary, such as gender bias or orientation. Cynthia Voigt's novels enable us to explore life from the perspective of a strong, independent girl who not only must care for her abandoned family but must face her own growth as a woman. Voigt's *Tillerman Cycle* offers many opportunities for exploring literature from a feminist perspective. Indeed, many young adult novels are being written by an impressive group of women writers, who are published in numbers unheard of in mainstream classical literature.

Library surveys show that among the most popular types of adolescent fiction are mystery, suspense, and fantasy (particularly science fiction and sci-ence fantasy).

A study of the topics and issues that most concern high school students reveals that nuclear holocaust and the deteriorating environment are two central concerns among the adolescent readers surveyed. Postholocaust dystopias from Wells to LeGuin are popular choices on public library shelves. These books also deal with "growing up," "coming of age," the agony of young love, and the like. Among the classics, both J. R. R. Tolkien and Edgar Allan Poe are popular, as are e. e. cummings, George Bernard Shaw, and the Bröntes. Furthermore, many classics with adult heroes and heroines deal with themes that intrigue adolescents if only because these characters face situations adolescents know they will someday face.

However, we need not fear that adolescents restrict themselves to books dealing only with the heavier issues of life, often focused on in contemporary realistic fiction. Library surveys also indicate adolescents like lighter fare tending toward the humorous, mysterious, and wonderful. We have heard both teachers and students in secondary schools groan that the literary diet is far too heavy, serious, and concerned with pain and sadness. Students will also connect with the "marvelous, extraordinary . . . metamorphoses, crystal palaces, gold and silver . . . (and) all that enchants me" (Hazard, 1944, p. 22).

Equally important, adolescent readers need not and should not be lim-ited to books that deal primarily with Anglo-American mainstream authors. Powerful, excellent literature representing a wide diversity of cultures is available, and, as we have already argued, there are compelling reasons for its inclusion in literature curricula. We have cited some of this literature elsewhere in this book, but some titles with relevance to the discussion here include Sonia Levitin's *The Return*, Suzanne Fisher Staples' *Shabanu*,

Daughter of the Wind, Jill Kerr Conway's memoir *The Road From Coorain*, Kunikida Doppos' *River Mist and Other Stories*, and the Arlene Hirschfelder and Beverley Singer collection, *Rising Voices: Writings of Young Native Americans*.

Connecting Adolescents and Literature in the Classroom

Let's draw the various threads of the chapter together so that we might explore literature with adolescents, now that we know who we are dealing with. The primary fact is that adolescents know more than we have expected and allowed them to reveal in the traditional literature classroom, where we emphasize "the" theme, "the plot," and "the meaning." We thought we'd start with the first two-thirds of Pooh's dream song, his response to hearing that his animal friends were going to give him a party but fearing that no one knows what he did to deserve it:

3 Cheers for Pooh!
(For Who?)
For Pooh—
(Why, what did he do?)
I thought you knew;
He saved his friend from a wetting!
3 Cheers for Bear!
(For Bear—
He couldn't swim,
But he rescued him!
(He rescued who?)
Oh listen, do!
I am talking of Pooh—
(Of who?)
Of Pooh!
(I'm sorry I keep forgetting.)
Well, Pooh was a Bear of Enormous Brain
(Just say it again!)
Of enormous brain—
(Of enormous what?)
Well, he ate a lot,
And I don't know if he could swim or not,
But he managed to float
On a sort of boat
(On a sort of what?)
Well, a sort of pot—

So now let's give him three hearty cheers
(So now let's give him three hearty whiches?)
And hope he'll be with us for years and years,
And grow in health and wisdom and riches!

A. A. Milne, Winnie-the-Pooh

We can celebrate adolescents' qualities or we can make fun of them and see them as irritating obstacles we have to bypass to get on with the task we have set for them. We may not want to go as far as *student-centered* curriculum but we can have a *student-sensitive* classroom. Such a classroom would give these students the opportunity to voice what they know and permit them to open our own eyes to new perspectives on what we read together. Such a classroom would not insist that every student share the same understanding or perspective of the same literary work. Let's have a look at some random comments adolescents have made about literature they have read.

> I like poetry like this; it's sensitive.

> I thought [of *Brave New World*] that it was pretty fascinating that in 1940 he's seen all those trends in our societies.

> If this guy had really loved youth . . . he wouldn't have turned the boy in but also you could see it like he loved him enough to turn him back to his father . . . but it seemed . . . he would have more taken the side of the boy.

> You could take it literally . . . or it could have sort of more deep meaning like . . . you can't trust adults.

> It's weird in the end because you can't really say that he's a traitor because he says . . . "you ought to make him happy."

> They're searching for themselves . . . and eventually, that finally happens . . . they're really beautiful books.

> The Indian boy was kind of a small and skinny thing . . . he is a stubborn boy and is also curious and thinks about things a lot. . . . And he just didn't like grown-ups because he had to go to school and didn't have much freedom.

> It tells a story about people's outlook on life. The guy that wrote it must have been a real philosopher.

We strongly advocate throughout this book providing frequent opportunities for small- and large-group discussions of literature. However, given that we have also said adolescents are very peer-oriented and dislike, more than other age groups, to stand out, we suggest that the more idiosyncratic response—that which reflects the reader's own experiences more closely—is more likely to occur when we allow for open response situations. We've seen that outside the classroom, given the opportunity, adolescents can have a great deal to say about literature, without needing "guidance" or prompting.

So, what's good about letting them tread unknown paths some of the time?

To answer this question, we need to go back to what we've argued elsewhere about becoming a reader. Developing expertise as a reader is obviously a cumulative experience. Even very competent and experienced readers may flounder when first encountering a text that presents information in an unfamiliar form and language. The information itself may be unfamiliar, in which case our early attempts at discerning meaning in the text are, at best, exploratory. But that solo exploration is also a part of becoming a competent reader.

We have heard teachers say that when students don't respond to questions such as "What does the story mean," they feel obliged to give them the answers.

Perhaps we are asking the wrong questions.

We could try asking what the words say to the students.

Similarly, having large or small group discussions does not ensure that all of the readers in the group will have negotiated the meaning of the text for themselves.

Yet however "off the wall" or "wide of the mark" an individual interpretation may be, we believe it is necessary to allow students to experience some solo interpretive activity at some point as a means of developing the confidence required to offer a perspective at another time (for example, sitting for the Scholastic Aptitude Test). And, of course, it's necessary to allow choice. As another teacher we know observed:

> While reflecting on my own reading and learning behaviors, likes and dislikes, I came to realize that I had much in common with my students. Many of them like to read in their beds at night. So do I. . . . Very little of my current reading is mandatory—required by someone else—and so I find I am again like my students who prefer to read about subjects they choose as well as when and where they choose. (Lawton, 1993, p. 3)

We also believe that confidence in one's own negotiation of meaning in a text is a precursor to the development of individual appreciation of literature. If we are continually dependent on others for defining meaning in text we will not experience the levels of enjoyment and aesthetic appreciation that are possible when we have a well-developed sense of content and context ourselves.

The *variability* of response, rather than being something to frown on or sigh over, may in fact represent just the elusive, individualized engagement with text that we, paradoxically, also hope for, as the following vignette illustrates.

VIGNETTE III: RANGES OF RESPONSE

Judith Lawton's eleventh-grade American literature and composition class completed a unit on election year literature from actual speeches written by present and past presidents to student-selected literature on issues that developed throughout the campaign and concluding with a study of Gore Vidal's *The Best Man*.

In the course of the unit, students studied campaign literature of each election candidate, responding to these in writing by offering their own positions and defending them. They also read speeches by former presidents and delivered short speeches themselves as a part of a mock election. They read poetry about presidents and about politics and wrote their own poems in response to the election year.

The unit provided them with many opportunities to reveal a great range of responses, perhaps more than would have occurred had they been limited to more traditional literary texts and more traditional ways of responding to texts.

Ms. Lawton's evaluation of the unit and course reflects many of the comments we have made about issues of relevance and interest with regard to adolescent reading. She noted:

> The students responded well to this unit of study, as evidenced by their high degree of participation in class as well as by their comments during a student evaluation of the unit. They liked the connection between literature we studied and the world outside their classroom.
>
> Many students wrote that they found the unit "more interesting than normal classroom topics" and that the unit "made me think harder." Several liked expressing their opinions in poems. I was gratified with the positive reinforcement from the students and wondered again, how can I offer my students a stimulating learning environment, one in which there is more relevance as well as more options, more connections to the world in which they live, more opportunities for intellectual and literary travel? I am more aware than ever that my own favored learning modes are not modes I can or do make readily available to my students. (Lawton, 1993, p. 3)

References

Carlsen, G. Robert. *Books and the Teenage Reader: A Guide for Teachers, Librarians and Parents*, 2nd rev. ed. New York: Harper & Row, 1981.

Hazard, Paul. *Books, Children and Men*. Translated by Marguerite Mitchell. Boston: The Horn Book Co., 1944.

Lanka, Janet. "Instead of Faking It . . . I Told My Students How I Felt." *Literacy Matters* 3, no. 2. Columbus, OH: Ohio State University, Martha King Literacy Center, 1990, 3.

Lawton, Judith. "On Side-Trips and Journeys Theatrical and Literary." *Literacy Matters* 5, no. 1. Columbus, OH: Ohio State University, Martha King Literacy Center, 1993, 3.

Winegard, William, and Gary R. Gruber. *Understanding and Enjoying Adolescence*. New York: Longman, 1988.

Zimmerman, Susan. "Rediscovering the Obvious." Unpublished manuscript. Columbus, OH: Ohio State University, College of Education, 1993.

Resources

Applebee, Arthur N. *The Child's Concept of Story: Ages Two to Seventeen*. Chicago: University of Chicago Press, 1978.

Atwell, Nancie. *In the Middle: Writing, Reading and Learning with Adolescents*. Upper Montclair, NJ: Boynton/Cook, 1987.

Barr, Mary, Pat D'Arcy, and Mary K. Healy. *What's Going On: Language/Learning Episodes in British and American Classrooms, Grades 4-13*. Portsmouth, NH: Heinemann, 1988.

Brannon, Lil, and C. H. Knoblauch. "On Students' Rights to Their Own Texts: A Model of Teacher Response." *College Composition and Communication* 33 (1982): 157-166.

Britton, James, Tony Burgess, Nancy Martin, Alex McLeod, and Harold Rosen. *The Development of Writing Abilities*. London: Macmillan, 1975, 11-18.

Hunt, Kellog J. *Grammatical Structures Written at Three Grade Levels*. Urbana, IL: National Council of Teachers of English, 1965.

Hynds, Susan. "International Cognitive Complexity and the Literary Response Processes of Adolescent Readers." *Research in the Teaching of English* 19 (1985): 386-404.

Judy, Stephen. "The Experiential Approach: Inner Worlds to Outer Worlds." In *Eight Approaches to Teaching Composition*. Edited by Timothy R. Donovan and Ben W. McClelland. Urbana, IL: National Council of Teachers of English, 1980.

Kohlberg, Lawrence, and Carol Gilligan. "The Adolescent as Philosopher: The Discovery of the Self in a Post-Conventional World." *Daedalus* 100 (1971): 1057.

Loevinger, Jane. *Ego Development: Conceptions and Theories*. San Francisco, Jossey-Bass, 1976.

Moffett, James. *Teaching the Universe of Discourse*. Boston: Houghton Mifflin, 1968.

Probst, Robert. *Response and Analysis: Teaching Literature in Junior and Senior High School*. Upper Montclair, NJ: Boynton/Cook, 1988.

Romano, Tom. *Clearing the Way: Working with Teenage Writers*. Portsmouth, NH: Heinemann, 1987.

Stevenson, Chris. *Teaching Ten To Fourteen Year Olds*. New York: Longman, 1992.

Vygotsky, Lev S. *Mind in Society: The Development of Higher Psychological Processes*. Edited by M. Cole, V. John Steiner, S. Scribner, and E. Souberman. Cambridge, MA: Harvard University Press, 1978.

chapter 3

Being a Chapter That Deals in Literary Theory and Its Relation to the Curriculum

Before we go into any detail about the response-based approach to literature we recommend and its various ramifications, we think it might be useful to discuss some of the major issues and controversies surrounding the teaching of literature at the end of the twentieth century. These issues include what literature and literature study are, what culture and cultural literacy mean, and what the implications of current critical theories are for the classroom.

First of All, We Must Remember That School Changes the Reading of Literature

When most children and adults talk about reading they are often talking about the reading of a poem or a story in a magazine or a book, or perhaps a novel. These are the literary texts that we pick up voluntarily. They are surrounded by a cover, a dust jacket with some information about the author, and perhaps a brief introduction or even a footnote or two. Consider that for the most part, 75 percent of the text we are reading appears to be produced by an author, the rest by the publisher. We use the word *appears* because we know in many instances there may have been others involved. Keats's poems went through several hands before they were published; his original manuscript is not what we read and study. Thomas Wolfe relied on editors; so do Gary Paulson, Alice Walker, and most writers.

When you look at a literary text placed in a school literature anthology, you will find that the text has new surroundings. There is a unit or chapter introduction and a text introduction with biographical and other contextual information. Around the text are notes and vocabulary. Following the text are vocabulary drills, questions for literal comprehension, questions for inferential comprehension (as if there is any difference at all between the two), activities to do in class, and several writing assignments. There may also be an illustration or two. Note that perhaps 50 percent of the text material is produced by the author (less if it is a lyric poem). The rest is produced by unknown hordes.

Put very boldly, the physical text in a literature classroom frequently becomes a different object from what it is in the broader world of literature about which critics write so much. Even the class sets of a paperback novel may have various school insignia on them (not to mention the graffiti of other students), to signal that the readers are part of a different culture. This difference reflects a difference between the reading of the text in a classroom and the reading of a text in a living room.

Second, We Must Remember That Literature Is a School Subject with All That Implies

Many of the students described in Chapter 2 report that they perceive school literature as reading literary texts in order to take tests on them. When we mention this, many teachers of English gasp in horror. But aren't the students right? School is where you are supposed to learn something, and other people determine whether you have learned that something by giving tests. The problem is that the something and the form of testing are often trivializing. We will get to that at the end of the book. The point is that students realize that school literature is not reading at home. Literature courses have a content, something people are going to have to know and probably be held accountable for.

The content of literature instruction is usually limited to five basic groups: literary works, background information, literary terminology and theory, cultural information, and the responses of the students themselves. In terms of what students are to do with all this content, the foci of the curriculum range from recognition and recall through interpretation and evaluation to the categories of preference and value. We will set up our particular model later in the chapter. We can think of these five as being layered like the food pyramid (Figure 3.1).

Is it better to be the large chunk at the bottom or the small triangle at the top?

Depends on your point of view. The shifts of emphasis among these five and which gets to be the biggest layer depend on the purposes of the curriculum makers and pressure groups and their particular approaches to schooling, which may be nationalistic, scientific, pragmatic, moralistic, or artistic, to name a few. Teachers have to negotiate their objectives with those

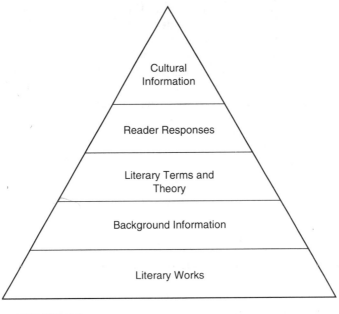

FIGURE 3.1

of principals, curriculum specialists, school boards, state mandates, parents, testing companies, and the students.

Through all these shifts of perspective, literature as a school subject is refracted through one of three main sets of lenses. One set of lenses reflects it primarily as a body of knowledge to be acquired, with literary works and background information becoming the two bottom layers. Proponents of this perspective suggest that a curriculum planner must attend to the selection of texts, either focusing on the "approved" author or on the supposed moral and social content of the text. They can be either conservatives or liberals, as witness the debate over cultural literacy, which we'll take up next.

The second set reflects school literature as the vehicle for training in the skills of literary analysis and interpretation, and literary works and literary terms (or critical methodology and discourse training) become the two bottom layers. The ideas of the literary skills approach can be seen in the "new critical," "deconstructive," "Marxist," "reader-response," and other labeled approaches to literature; the purpose is to train the mind to use particular sets of tools for analysis or interpretation. Some people also want the literature curriculum to serve something called "generic critical thinking skills." They argue that it doesn't matter what text the students read as long as they learn a procedure. We think literature texts do matter. If they didn't, we wouldn't have written this book.

The third set of lenses reflects school literature as the vehicle for social and moral development—what we call the development of habits—and reader responses and literary works become the two bottom layers, thus giving them the bulk of attention. Proponents of this perspective share some concerns with the knowledge group but are primarily concerned with supporting a society of readers—people committed to reading and literature. They see taste as important, not only taste in writing styles, but taste in the behavior and moral life of the students. Again, they can be both liberal and conservative.

Where do we stand? We see virtue in each set of lenses and want to try for a balanced, three-dimensional view.

One facet of the debate about ends is a debate about the importance of commonalty and what has been called cultural literacy.

Third, We Must Remember That School Literature Intends to Make People Culturally Literate

This may seem a radically conservative statement, but we want to observe that the debate over cultural literacy is not about whether schools should teach some form of cultural literacy but what form cultural literacy teaching should take. Although cultural literacy has come into the news over the past ten years, the idea is far from new. The notion of a "culture" goes back at least 3,000 years. As Edward Said has put it, culture is "all that which an individual possesses and which possesses an individual" (1983). Said wrote in *The World, the Text and the Critic*:

> . . . culture is used to designate not merely something to which one belongs but something that one possesses, and along with that proprietary process, culture also designates a boundary by which the concepts of what is extrinsic or intrinsic to the culture come into forceful play. (Said, 1983, pp. 8-9)

But Said also wrote in his book *Culture and Imperialism:*

> A confused and limiting notion of priority allows that only the original proponents of an idea can understand and use it. But the history of all cultures is the history of cultural borrowings. Cultures are not impermeable; just as Western science borrowed from the Arabs, they had borrowed from India and Greece. Culture is never just a matter of ownership, of borrowing and lending with absolute debtors and creditors, but rather of appropriations, common experiences, and interdependencies of all kinds among different cultures. (Said, 1993, p. 217)

Some people like to think of a single Western male culture, but that never really existed. Like the English language with its borrowing from dozens of other languages, the literary heritage of any country is permeated with the writings of many other cultures, masculine and feminine.

Anthropoligists tend to see culture somewhat differently from the way literary people do, but Said's notion about possession and being possessed applies both to family groups and to groups people join when they leave the family—a community, a school, a profession or trade, a regional or national group. Current "American" culture is one of affiliation, whether it be the culture of Nathaniel Hawthorne and Harriet Beecher Stowe, the culture of African-American studies, the culture of feminism, or the culture of punk. Current American or Canadian culture is also a collection of interpenetrating subcultures. A Navajo may live in a hogan, drive a Ford Ranger, listen to Ice T, and eat at Pizza Hut. Any culture usually tries to isolate its members from other cultures and is elitist and exclusionary by definition. People who have a culture see others as outside or beneath them. We are all snobs with respect to one "them" or another. Although few people transcend cultures or are full members of more than one culture, many do switch from one subculture to another as they go through life. They may be members of such subcultures as that of mycologists, joggers, film freaks, sailors, Poles, or English teachers, as well as members of the broader culture of literate Americans or Canadians.

Joining the Canon Club

To be a member of a culture, one must possess a fair amount of knowledge, some of it tacit, concerning the culture: its rules, rituals, little customs, heroes, gods, and demigods. This knowledge lies at the heart of cultural literacy, and the knowledge is brought into play when people read and respond to a piece of literature that comes from the same culture. It is such knowledge that, in fact, enables them to read that literature. By knowledge one must include semantic knowledge, knowledge of text structures and models, and pragmatic knowledge or knowledge as to how to act before, during, and after reading a particular text in a given situation. These kinds of knowledge are brought into play when we read and write as social beings. The lack of such knowledge keeps us outside, as witness the problems of visitors to our culture, who often suffer trifling embarrassments or serious misunderstandings.

How the Curriculum Helps

Given the idea of culture, one function of a literature curriculum in a school language program is to bring students into a broader culture than that of their home. We want them to read and come to know stories, poems, plays, and essays that they will have in common with other people.

The question is which ones.

A second function is to promote loyalty, acceptance, and valuing of those works and literature generally. We'd like culturally literate Americans to praise Mark Twain as a great writer and be offended when someone calls for the banning of *Huckleberry Finn*.

The question is which works should be valued most highly.

A third function of literature education is to develop individuality. Once a student has learned to share the culture and developed a loyalty to it, then a student should strike out to read new things, and write them, too.

The question is just how independent do we want them to be.

Some cultural literacy advocates want to restrict literacy to a particular culture, such as the "great tradition" or "the humanities" or "the American classics." They refer to a definite body of knowledge and suggest that specific titles are necessary. According to their view, it is this common knowledge that enables readers to read certain kinds of texts—notably texts that are shared by a group that one might define as "highly literate Americans." These would be people, for example, who can read *The New York Times* with understanding and might also read *The Atlantic Monthly* or Katherine Paterson's *Jacob Have I Loved*.

One argument for this sort of cultural literacy was that such literacy brought together a disparate immigrant population and helped the melting pot do its job. Such proposals bore with them the arguments of people like Matthew Arnold, Ralph Waldo Emerson, and T. S. Eliot, not to mention the major universities and educational reformers, that a common culture, or the Judeo-Christian American heritage, forged society into unity through affiliation. It did so not without cost.

> When our students are taught such things as "the humanities" they are almost always taught that these classic texts embody, express, represent what is best in our, that is, the only, tradition. Moreover, they are taught that such fields as the humanities and such subfields as "literature" exist in a relatively neutral political element, that they are to be appreciated and venerated, that they define the limits of what is acceptable, appropriate, and legitimate as far as culture is concerned. (Said, 1983, p. 21)

The political issue has raised a number of political questions, particularly who is to select the unifying texts. The second political question—how in the history of our educational system the idea of the cultural heritage came to disappear and why there is the lack of a cultural center—should become a political issue.

The Attack on the Canon Club

About twenty years ago a number of groups began to coalesce to push liter-ature and the notion of cultural literacy out of the forefront of the English curriculum. The first was a group that advocated making the secondary school more comprehensive rather than simply academic; the second group was made up of linguists, the third, of so-called functionalists, and the fourth were literature teachers. Their arguments (often the arguments and groups overlapped) against a single canon and a focus on literature can be enumer-ated as follows:

1. We have a comprehensive secondary school system, and more diverse groups are now passing through it. We must attend to the intellectual and cultural needs of those groups. The canon does not address these minority groups and it certainly does not address the concerns of women. In addition, the world is multicultural, and students need to learn a smattering about all cultures. Perhaps it is unnecessary to learn a smattering about all cultures. Perhaps it is unnecessary to learn about any one culture in depth.

2. English education should be dominated by language study and the appropriate teaching of the uses of language, whether one adopts a skills approach or an approach that looks at the personal growth of the individual student. There is no time for literature as such.

3. English education should meet the functional needs of the students and the workplace. There is little room in life for any attention to a cultural heritage, whosoever might claim the culture.

4. Many of the "cultural classics" are simply too difficult for the new students and beyond their range of experience or they deal with subjects that should not be in the classroom; they are no longer relevant. They were appropriate for people of greater and broader and different experience of life—the elite. Rather than bowdlerize them or present them in film, we should turn to the kinds of works that students can read, particularly adolescent and popular fiction.

Those who push for cultural literacy using the argument of the unifica-tion of a diverse nation through cultural literacy have not addressed these arguments. The argument is not *whether* cultural literacy, for all literature cur-ricula imply a body of works that constitute a canon and thus serve to accul-turate youth, as do television and other non-school phenomena; the argument is *what* should serve to define the culture or cultures of our society.

Our response to the four arguments is to wholeheartedly accept the first one and reject the other three. Language and literacy do not make any sense without literature, because it is literature that helps bind us as a nation made up of interesting and quirky subgroups. As a nation we are what we read, watch, listen to, and do. Literature is functional in our lives; it supports and sustains us as individuals and groups. Young people have a remarkably broad range of experience. People do other things besides work, and even in their work there is a place for the comfort and relief as well as the intellectual stimulation of reading, viewing, listening, and feeling satisfied by the experience of a text or other art form. As to the fourth charge, we haven't yet met a work of literature that is too difficult for any group of students, given a good teacher and the appropriate context; the only difficult works are those the culture people set up on a pedestal and say are too hard for the masses, thereby intimidating students and teachers.

That literature is an expression of and a lens into the cultures of the world and of North America is one of the main rationales through which literature is given value in the eyes of the people of this country. This cultural approach can be broadened to a global sweep. At this moment in the history of the world the cultural view of literature is what will sustain it in the schools, more so than the moral view or the universalistic view or the aesthetic view. It may not be the view that will prevail a generation hence, but we think it will. Any other view will only serve to perpetuate implicitly what the Western canon perpetuates explicitly. When one considers only the text or the reader, as many contemporary pedagogies would, one is tacitly assuming a monocultural view, a view that denies the roots of a literary work and the intellectual and cultural struggle that may have produced it. To assume a "universalism" is basically a form of imperialism. The cultural view of literature and literature teaching is the only moral basis on which to build a set of experiences for young people.

So we are for multicultural literacy. We do not want to remain within the confines of "dead white males," nor within the boundaries of this country. We see the world as our curricular oyster. We want to broaden the earlier definition and include Shakespeare and Chinua Achebe; Jane Austen and Amiri Baraka; Gary Soto and Lawrence Yep; Paula Gunn Allen and Ursula LeGuin and J. R. R. Tolkien; Amy Clampitt and Amy Tan. Some of these and other writers have written books that simply won't go away, won't get out of our heads and, we suspect, won't get out of your heads, either. We also think that when our students read them they won't go out of their heads. Students should join the Canon Club but be free to build their own canon.

Fourth, School Literature Is Guided by an Implicit Theory of Literature and Criticism

Let's try some definitions. Literary texts are artifacts produced by a type of person that one calls writer or author. Literary texts possess in common the broad features of having a content (that subject matter or referential world with which they deal), a structure, and a set of distinctive linguistic features, which are often referred to as style and tone. These three divisions are ones that readers and writers often make even though they realize that the sum of the text is greater than the parts and that the text may be perceived as an organic whole.

A Functional Definition of Literature

Writers may have in mind a variety of functions for the text they are writing when they write. Readers may also see a given text as having one of a number of functions as they read it: to say something about language itself, to say something about the writer, to say something about the reader, to say something about the world outside the text, to keep open the channel of communication, or to invite everyone to participate in the text itself. (This last is called the poetic function by many.) No writer or reader perceives any one text as being a pure representative of a single function. The functions mix and the labels are only partial descriptors. Nonetheless, they may prove useful.

Different communities of readers tend to focus on one or more of these functions as they deal with a text or a body of texts. These communities are the same as classrooms or schools but they may also be religious, business, social, or ethnic groups. One of these groups may say that a certain set of texts is poetic, that it is literature. Literature doesn't exist as a separate category of text that can be defined in terms of certain internal characteristics. Rather, literary texts tend to be those that communities of readers perceive as such, which is to say, they are texts that a significant number of readers read for the experience of reading them rather than to get information or moral guidance from them. They will say they read these texts *aesthetically* and claim others should so read them.

Literature from a Reader's Perspective.

Literature is often defined as the verbal expression of the human imagination, a definition broad enough to encompass a vast array of genres and forms of discourse. Recent literary theory has come to view literature less in terms of the writer and more in terms of the reader, for it appears to be the reader, particularly the informed and trained reader, who defines a text as literary. Such a definition allows for all sorts of works that once had been excluded or marginal (essays, letters, biographies, and the like) to be part of the literary canon. There is some sense in which the traditional literary genres of drama, poetry, and fiction have a more dominant role in most critics' thinking and thus a more prominent place in the curriculum than the other sorts of works. It is clear, however, that any definition must allow for new genres and new media.

Such a definition is closely related to the line of reasoning that readers help form the meaning of the text. The summary of the position is best expressed by Louise Rosenblatt, who says in *The Reader, the Text, The Poem*

(1978) that literary texts are grounded in the real world of writers, who may or may not intend them to be seen poetically. Once written, texts become alive only when they are read, and they become "literary" when a sufficient body of readers (a community) chooses to read them as aesthetic objects rather than as documents. These readers bring to bear a great deal of background knowledge concerning the substance, structure, and style of the texts to ascertain the meaning and significance of the text. The meaning is that which can be verified by other readers of the text and by recourse to the historical grounding of the text, if such is available. The significance is personal or perhaps communal.

How Theory Defines What Literature Is.   The theoretical position thus argues that any text has the potential of being literary should a significant group of knowledgeable and experienced readers determine the value of reading it as an aesthetic object. In this way such works as the speeches of Abraham Lincoln, Chief Joseph, and Martin Luther King, Jr., the letters of John Keats and J. Hector St. John de Crèvecoeur, and the *Diary of Anne Frank* become literary objects and part of the canon. Readers have read them in the light of a common experience of literary texts and have derived principles of "literariness" that allow them to accept these works. In part their criteria are formal and structural; in part they arise from consideration of the breadth of the writer's vision.

In a society such as the United States, there may exist a set of texts that a community refers to as "literature," that is, to be viewed functionally as being predominantly poetic and therefore to be read aesthetically. At the same time other communities within the society may read those texts as informing or persuading (or perhaps like a greeting card—who really listens to the sense of "The Night Before Christmas"?). These different communities may also focus primarily on the content, structure, or style and tone depending on their view of the function of the text within the community.

As a result of this communal process, a network of texts grows over time and forms part of the background that weaves a group into a community. From this communal nature of texts comes one of the well-known features of literature—its tendency to feed on itself as well as on folklore, myth, and historical events. Many literary works are clearly situated in a web of culture; many others are situated in a specific time and place (e.g., Jonathan Swift's works, which are clearly situated in eighteenth century England; Gwendolyn Brooks' poetry, in Chicago; Barbara Kingsolver's novels, like *Pigs in Heaven*, in Arizona and Oklahoma).

We may argue that in selecting a given word, a writer is tapping associations and references that are peculiarly hers and her culture's and have reference to her reading as well as her conversation and other linguistic experiences. Literature uses allusion, and many writers presume readers have background knowledge even though the allusions have been transmuted into a new artifact. Non-literary texts presume much the same knowledge. But there is the difference that literary texts form part of a large, interdependent, textual world that forms that thing called literature. So the literary community determines. Even literature that we think of as "trash" forms a part of that world, both for writers and readers. Different communities define some works as "good" and some as "lousy."

From this grouping of texts comes one part of the literature curriculum—but only a part. We're back at a canon again. But it is a canon with a difference, a canon of read works. Louise Rosenblatt (1978) distinguishes between the *text* (what lies inert on the page) and the *poem* (what is read and responded to by an individual).

ALONE/DECEMBER/NIGHT

It's been so long
speaking to people
who think it all
too complex
stupidity in their eyes
&
it's been so long
so far from the truth
so far from a roof
to talk to
or a hand to touch
or anything to really love

it's been so long
talking to myself
alone
in the night
listening to a music
that is me.
                    Victor Hernandez Cruz

The people in any community are simultaneously individuals, changing, and members of a larger community. So when we read a text like "ALONE/december/night," each of us is engaged in a "poem-encounter" or "transaction" that is situated within a system and related to other transactions. The transactions are individual, but not unique. Thinking of them as unique is the error, we believe, in much of the writing about response-based teaching; it is similar to the fallacy of naiveté. Let us suppose that several thousand people read this text in this book. What do they have in common? What does each have individually?

To be conservative, 50 million U.S. citizens share the experience of having read *Romeo and Juliet*, and another 50 million have seen a film version. To what extent is that a common or general experience? They have clearly learned some different things about it and have had different experiences of it and somewhat diverse responses to it. In Rosenblatt's terms, there have been 100 million transactions, resulting in perhaps 40 million poems, the rest being efferent readings (1978). How are these poems related to each other? How are they related to the text? How are they related to some sort of common *Romeo and Juliet*?

Perhaps the best way to think of this phenomenon is to take the analogy from linguistics of type and token. The "poem-text" is the source of all "poem-tokens," the form taken by the poem each time it is read. The relationship between the two is analogous to the relation between the poem-text and some idealized poem. The text of *Romeo and Juliet* is found in schools in the Yale or the Penguin or the Kitteridge or some other "type" which is relatively invariant as each copy emerges from the bindery. It may be modified by having taped or marked pages, highlighters, or sidenotes, but it remains essentially the same, just as the phrase *Romeo and Juliet* remains relatively the same whether it is printed, written, capitalized, or the like. Each of these is a token, and each student reading *Romeo and Juliet* in a class is making a *Romeo and Juliet*-token. What is the relation of the *Romeo and Juliet*-tokens to the *Romeo and Juliet*-type? We suggest that as a result of our educational system, which has developed certain habits in readers over several generations, the tokens can be clustered into some general sets: the romantic token, the *West Side Story* token, the sociopolitical token, the tragic token, and the generation gap token might be a few. The habituated poem-token within our society is another way of thinking about the misconception of the naive reader. Because of the developed habit of reading and doing school literature reading, we should talk less about individual readings than about communal readings, less about the reader's response and more about the habitual discourse about texts.

A group of texts, then, has been set aside by communities as forming a part of the communal experience. These communities have selected them to be read aesthetically. Each encounter with those texts helps to bring an individual reader deeper into a particular community of readers. This is the process by which "schools" of writers, like the Romantics or the magical realists, are formed. It is also the process by which people become "feminist" readers or part of the Native-American community. By virtue of this process, the texts and readers have developed a set of associations with each other. Writers subsequently acculturated into this tradition have produced texts that are highly allusive to this communal set of literature.

We might add that what has happened in the literary world has also happened in certain transnational disciplines such as psychology and economics. Certain texts have emerged as a core on which other texts have built. The core in both cases is added to and challenged, and at times it drops certain writers and texts as it adds others. It is a fluid corpus, not a fixed canon; the organic metaphor is quite appropriate.

Literature as Content.   This brings us back to the content of literature curricula, which consist primarily of a group of literary texts, perhaps specified by genre, date, theme, author, and other classifications. The particular texts are set in part by experts, in part by those who sell books, and in part by teachers and curriculum planners. There are other broad areas of literature content, too: historical and background information concerning authors, texts, and the times in which they were written or set; information concerning critical terminology, critical strategies, and literary theory; information of a broad cultural nature, such as from folklore and mythology, which forms a necessary starting point for the reading of many literary texts.

To These We Add the Fifth, the Crucial Element in the Curriculum: The Responses of the Students Themselves

As we suggested in the first chapter and have just repeated in the example of the poem encounter, the important aspect of literature in our view is that it is read. It is not the text out there apart from the reader that is important but the text as it is read and made into a poem or a play or a novel and shared with the group.

A Theory That Might Be a Good Starting Point for Teaching—Because It Is Ours (and We Want You to Like It)

The recent critical debates raise issues that might have affected the curriculum in literature—but they did not as far as we can tell. The debates center on such questions as the nature of the literary text, and the relation of the text to the reader, the writer, and society. Some debaters promote the writer, some the reader, some the linguistic structure, and some the text's relation to the world as the center of theory and critical attention. Some even want the debate, rather than the literature that the debate is about, to be read.

And that is the reason for this book. The main point of most recent literary theory can be stated thus: Texts are written by authors, deal with something called "the world," and are read by readers.

It used to be that we looked at literature primarily as reflecting the world. That was in an age when the primary form of literature was that which was performed orally or as drama.

Then we thought of literary texts as the outpourings of their authors. That was in the age of print, when writers committed themselves to paper to be read individually in the parlor.

Then we thought of them as isolated specimens to be examined. That was in the age of mass printing, when texts floated freely in several different editions. Each reader was alone with a book to make that book hers or his in a simple transaction. The individual might join an interpretive community, the isolated classroom.

Now we think of literary texts as things written and read by people who enter into a new relationship to each other, a more dynamic one. This we do in an age when we can turn the machine on or off, switch channels, or use the computer and other electronic tools to change texts or images as we see fit and even send them and our comments on them out of the world to a satellite and back to the author. They don't sit still on the page—or the screen. Writers and readers enter into a dialogue through the text.

Today Texts Are Seen as Situated in an Intertextual World and Have an Indeterminacy of Meaning Dependent on the Varying Experiences and Natures of the Writers and Readers

Meaning and text themselves are not objective. In fact there may not be much of an objective world. There is, however, some sort of a common world of subjective experiences, but we don't know that much about it. A part of that subjective world is that of writers who "utter" their thoughts and feelings onto a page or a screen. Another part is that of readers who bring their experiences and feelings to the textual world. They meet in space and work together.

What is individual and what is common across the space? In the world of the paperless electronic book, there has emerged the idea of the hypertext. What text there is exists to be manipulated on the screen, to be gone through in many different paths, to be changed and added to by the person operating the computer, to be seen and explored in its relation to other objects in the screen space and to the large span of human activity, to be responded to individually and communally, and then to disappear into the machine or the disk. This view of the text radically changes the way we think about those neat categories like writer, reader, text.

It used to be that we thought of the purposefully ambiguous nature of the text. It was hard to get scholars and teachers to agree on an interpretation of *Hamlet* or Robert Frost's "Mending Wall." The challenge lay in the text and the author's deliberate plot to confuse us.

It is still hard to get them to agree. The challenge lies in the readers. The author seems remote; in hypertext, the author returns, but differently. The sheltered reader alone with a book is now the reader in a complex community, a universe with a number of galaxies.

The writer-text-reader relationship is a universe to be explored each time a reader sits down with a book. It is also a universe each time a student sits down to write a composition. The writer and reader are not simply convenient fictions but flesh and blood people. Of course there also exists that necessary pair, the "authorial voice" and the "audience," which are not the same as the writer and reader but are what the one infers about or imputes to the other. The two flesh and blood people produce a reading token or poem encounter, which is necessarily a poet encounter as well.

In literature programs, as in the rest of life, our students are not simply reading texts, they are reading writers as well. They are invited to bring the author into the equation just as they are invited to bring the reader into the equation when they write. Students readily include the reader, as shown each time they say, "But what do you want?" They need to learn to bring the author into the equation. They also should acknowledge that as readers they are people with prejudices, ignorances, and beliefs that impinge on their readings and interpretations. They should see this as they are engaged in the interpretative task. They are learning to interpret themselves as readers as well as the authors as writers. They are members of a culture with the habits of that culture, engaged in reading the work of inhabitants of other cultures. They should recognize the otherness of the text and the writer as well as the connection to their world.

A part of that learning is involved in reading the culture. Another part can be seen in the following examples. We can read Virginia Hamilton's novels as those of an American, African American, woman, urbanite, and Midwesterner caught up in the world of southern Ohio and the world of history and pan-African myth. To know these facts of the novelist helps us read *Sweet Whispers, Brother Rush*. We recognize that her world is not our world, and we both encounter that difference and assimilate it into our vision, which broadens our vision and our understanding. But we also read the book as a novel, as a myth, as an imaginative creation that is connected to a long tradition of fantasy that includes Hans Christian Anderson, George MacDonald, Maria Gripe, and Madeleine L'Engle. We enter that world as well and seek to make it our own.

We are not only reading the writer, but reading the writer in a cultural context and understanding ourselves as culturally situated readers. If we follow this approach, we can place school literature in the same context as school writing, which at its best is writing for readers or writing with the reader in mind. The teacher is one of those readers, but so are classmates, other teachers, employers, friends, and the media. The reader should not remain in a solipsistic world of response, nor the writer in a solipsistic world of expression. Each takes the author or the audience into account. And not only the author or the audience, but the culture of the author or audience. And not only the cultures, but the continuity among authors and audiences, as well as their disjunctions. It is a mind-bending, explosive view, yes. But such a view enables and strengthens the reader or the writer by giving each something to hold onto, some way of connecting to others through this complex web in space.

Readers may disagree on the text's function and therefore its "meaning." They may even disagree on what text or segment of text they saw. It used to be that the text was seen as the norm by which a reading and a response could be judged. Now it is no longer the norm, even theoretically. The norms, if there are any, lie in the community of readers—even the two people who talk about a book over coffee. Some argue that the largest community we can find is a class. Others would say that there are larger communities, such as those dominated by examination systems or textbook publishers.

It is no longer sufficient to talk about texts or critical terminology or history. We are nearly driven to talk about writers and readers and texts. As teachers, we are led to plan the curriculum mindful of the ways readers make the texts come alive, which means focusing on what they say and do. Literature comes out of the textbooks and into the minds and hearts and particularly the mouths and pens of our students, who come to meet the author and share in the fact of authorship. It is not direct communication but a meeting place of writer and reader, of culture of the past with culture of the present, of individual with group. That is what the critical shift has done to the curriculum—or what it should do.

Theorists argue that literature education is a combination of reading and some form of articulation of a reasoned response to what is read, at times through dramatic interpretation, at times through discussion, at times through writing. The poem does not exist unless the reader makes some overt commitment to it, finds some way of meeting the writer and the other readers in the world of hypertext surrounding and interconnecting with the text. In the classroom the reader leaves the individual cocoon and becomes part of a number of communities. The reader can be passive and powerless or an active participant.

Research shows that readers within a culture tend to have similar impressions of the poems, stories, and plays they read. Where they differ is in their power of expression concerning what they have read. The "better" or more "experienced" readers are those who can set forth a more reasoned and detailed account of the poem they have created in their heads. The expression and the statements about the poem cause the disagreement among critics, not the experience of reading the text.

OK. You've Talked about the Canon and about Literary Theory. How Does This Get Put Together in the Curriculum? Are You Ready for THE SCHEME?

Let us try to see where all this about the canon and knowledge and hyper-space and literature and language arts and English fit together.

School literature is usually seen as one of the language arts, which have often been defined in terms of reading, writing, speaking, and listening. Because literature involves texts that people read or write and because when students read literature they often write about what they have read, literature is often seen as simply a subset of reading and writing, with an occasional nod to speaking and listening.

But we're uneasy with this definition. We become more uneasy when they look at the world of tests and see that literature is simply a vehicle for reading comprehension tests or for measures of writing skill or proficiency. There's something more. To define the literature curriculum as simply a sub-set of reading and writing neglects a number of things that go on within the activity of literature education.

Literature as a school subject has its own body of knowledge—all that content we said people often bring to their reading of a new text. It is also the cultural world of the writers and readers.

Literature is a school subject where we develop the capacity to read in a supple, flexible fashion. In the past, people separated a kind of reading we call "aesthetic" and contrasted it to the reading that people do with informa-tional texts; but when we read anything we move about among various pur-poses and ends of reading. Thus, a part of literature education is the devel-opment of what one might call preferences, which is to say habits of mind in reading and writing. Reading or writing anything is an act of attention, an act of scrutiny, and an act of play. Literature in school helps encourage such a set of habits. Literature is a school subject that demands not just reading but some activity as a result of that reading. It calls for public performance of the reading in talk, dramatization, writing, art, or some other medium through which each reader can make the reading and the understanding of author, text, and culture apparent to other students and teachers. This is something people can get better at; they can become proficient.

Literature is a school subject that seeks to encourage habits of mind. These habits are what constitute a culture of readers; they are not to be attacked in the name of individualism. That would be a fallacious claim, for it would seek to deny the very importance of our collective nature, our nec-essary community. We should be more aware of these habits than we have been. We should take pride in our success and raise our own consciousness about what we are doing.

Students must practice and learn how to perform this kind of reading and be encouraged to read this way voluntarily. They do this through being encouraged to talk about certain other facets of the text and their experience of it and not to talk about facets. They should be encouraged to see themselves as the makers of meaning, and that meaning is what they negotiate with the teacher and with the "authority" that appears to reside in "Cliff Notes" or the teacher's guide. Above all, they are encouraged to talk and write about the text; they cannot simply parrot "Cliff Notes" as if that were the only interpretation. What is encouraged as well as what is discouraged become a part of their habit of being school readers.

Another set of these habits that we may seek to inculcate is less obvious, but no less important. It concerns the way people make aesthetic judgments about the various texts read and justify these judgments publicly. Because literature education is supposed to develop something called taste or the love of "good literature," the curriculum looks beyond reading and writing to the formation of specific sets of reading and writing preferences and habits. These habits may include the development of a tolerance for variety in literature, a willingness to acknowledge that different kinds and styles of work can be considered literature, and an acceptance that just because we do not like a certain poem does not mean it is not good. The development of such intellectual habits should lead students to an acceptance of cultural diversity in literature, and, by extension, in society. These are often cited as parts of the literature curriculum, but they are not uppermost in the minds of students and teachers because they are not part of the assessed curriculum. In addition, we know less about how to handle the student who resists forming these habits.

By Way of a Conclusion to This Chapter, which Leads Us On to the Rest of the Book

We would argue that the domain of school literature can be divided into three interrelated aspects: knowledge, practice, and habit. The interrelationships are complex, in that one brings knowledge to bear on the practices and preferences, and practices and preferences can influence knowledge. At the same time one can separate them for the purposes of curriculum planning and, as we shall see, testing. We may schematize the three subdomains as shown in Table 3.1.

As we have suggested, cultural background is both in and outside the texts, in the ways people read, respond, and criticize. It is the situation of the text in a broader world, which may include the ways in which the text was produced and printed, read at the time of publication, performed, translated into film or turned into song, or otherwise manipulated. The background is the social, political, historical, domestic context of the text and its readers, down to and including the students in class.

TABLE 3.1   School literature

Knowledge		Practice		Habits	
Textual	*Extratextual*	*Responding*	*Articulating Habits*	*Aesthetic*	*Choice*
Specific text (structures, subject, language)	History and cultural background	Decoding	Retelling	Evaluating	Reading
Intertextual links	Author's life	Summarizing	Criticizing single works	Selecting	Criticizing
	Genres Styles	Analyzing Personalizing	Valuing Generalizing across works	Valuing	
	Critical terms Response Approaches	Interpreting	Re-creating		

Responding includes reading, watching, and listening. It includes decoding or figuring out the plain sense of the text or film, forming some imaginative impression and re-creation of what is read, and undertaking the more detailed aspects of analyzing, personalizing, and interpreting. Often people imagine without analyzing or interpreting.

We have used the term *articulating* to cover a wide variety of ways in which students let others know their response to the writer, the text, and their reading. This is the key to the curriculum in many ways. It's not just reading in a closet; it's bringing an imaginative apprehension of what is read out into the open. It is an act of confrontation with oneself and with others as well as with the text and the author and the broader culture around the text. It is making what is personal dramatic, an event in which sharing, baring, stumbling, formulating, changing, and reflecting are practiced, rehearsed, and performed publicly, not only in the class but across space and time. It is about becoming a part of the community—the community of the classroom and the community beyond the classroom.

All of this is done in a particular way that preserves respect for and enjoyment of the text, and treats the work of literature as the expression of an author who is a real person in a real culture, an author who wanted the text to be read, argued about and chortled and cried over.

The curriculum we present in this book focuses on discourse about literary texts. It seeks to help students to become more reasoning and reasonable, more articulate about what they have read, to share their expressions. It seeks to help them find their place in their community as well as find their individuality. That ain't easy, but it can be fun.

References

Rosenblatt, Louise. *The Reader, The Text, The Poem: The Transactional Theory of the Literary Work*. Carbondale, IL: Southern Illinois University Press, 1978.

Said, Edward. *Culture and Imperialism*. New York: Alfred A. Knopf, 1993.

Said, Edward. *The World, The Text and The Critic*. Cambridge, MA: Harvard University Press, 1983.

Resources

Applebee, Arthur, N. "Studies in the Spectator Role: An Approach to Response to Literature." In *Researching Response to Literature and the Teaching of Literature: Points of Departure*, edited by Charles R. Cooper, pp. 87-102. Norwood, NJ: Ablex, 1985.

Bleich, David. *Subjective Criticism*. Baltimore: Johns Hopkins University Press, 1987.

Eagleton, Terry. *Literary Theory: An Introduction*. Minneapolis: University of Minnesota Press, 1983.

Frye, Northrop. *The Educated Imagination*. Bloomington: Indiana University Press, 1964.

Griffith, Peter, *Literary Theory and English Teaching*. Philadelphia: Open University Press, 1987.

Hirsch, Eric D. *Cultural Literacy: What Every American Should Know*. New York: Vintage Books, 1987.

Holbrook, David. *English for the Rejected*. Cambridge: Cambridge University Press, 1965.

Iser, Wolfgang. *The Act of Reading*. Baltimore: Johns Hopkins University Press, 1978.

Purves, Alan C. "You Can't Teach Hamlet, He's Dead." *English Journal* 57 (1968): 832-836.

Purves, Alan C., and William C. Purves. "Cultures, Test Models and the Activity of Writing." *Research in the Teaching of English* 20 (1986): 174-197.

Richards, Ivor A. *Principles of Literary Criticism*. London: Routledge, 1924.

Richards, Ivor A. *Practical Criticism: A Study of Literary Judgment*. New York: Harcourt Brace Jovanovich, 1929.

Rosenblatt, Louise M. *Literature as Exploration*. New York: Noble and Noble, 1968.

Rosenthal, Robert, and Lenore Jacobson. *Pygmalion in the Classroom*. New York: Holt, Rinehart & Winston, 1968.

Scholes, Robert. *Textual Power: Literary Theory and the Teaching of English*. New Haven: Yale University Press, 1986.

Squire, James R. *The Response Processes of Adolescents while Reading Four Short Stories* (Research Report no. 2). Urbana, IL: National Council of Teachers of English, 1964.

Squire, James R., ed. *Response to Literature*. Urbana, IL: National Council of Teachers of English, 1968.

Thompkins, Jane P., ed. *Reader-Response Criticism: From Formalism to Post-Structuralism*. Baltimore: Johns Hopkins University Press, 1980.

White, E. M. "Post-structuralist Literary Criticism and the Response to Student Writing." *College Composition and Communication* 35 (1984): 186-195.

chapter 4

Enter (Stage Right–or Left) the Response-Based Approach

A response-based approach to literature will help introduce students to a multicultural collection of authors and works, to the community of readers in and beyond their classroom, and to their individual and group nature as readers and participants in a culture. It will allow for supple, flexible, and imaginative reading. It will allow for exploration in talk, drama, media, and writing as ways of articulating their responses. It also cures dull sinus headaches and leaves drains shiny bright.

Four Objectives of a Response-Based Approach to School Literature

1. Each student will feel secure in her response to a poem and not the parrot of someone else's response. A student will trust herself.
2. Each student will know why he responds the way he does to a novel—what in him causes that response and what in the novel causes that response. He will get to know himself.
3. Each student will respect the response of others to the play as being as valid for them as hers is for her. She will recognize her differences from and similarities to other people.
4. Each student will reach through the story to the writer and seek to understand the culture that underlies the story to find both unique elements and points of connection to his own culture and that of other readers. He will recognize his similarity and differences with other places, other peoples, other times.

The basic process connecting the onlooker with any event, real or fictional, involving living things, is that of imagining. The fundamental fact is that we can imagine ourselves in a situation very different from the one we are in, we can create images of the sensations we should have, we can become aware, in part, of the meanings we should see in it, what our intentions, attitudes, and emotions would be, what satisfactions and frustrations we should experience. *(D. W. Harding, 1962, p. 138)*

"Response-based approach" is a fairly accurate definition of the way we suggest literature should be taught.

Of course, you don't teach literature, or English, you teach students. We all know that. People, not things, are the focus of instruction. Recently too much attention has been paid to things, and people have been forgotten.

Of course, people learn all by themselves. People have done it for years. They have learned lots of things without teachers, and outside classrooms. One of the best ways people have devised for learning is by doing things and then figuring out what they have done and why they have done it. If they like what they have done, they try to repeat the operation.

Doing things and looking at yourself while and after you have done them is what this approach is about.

That's why this is a reader-based approach. It is not based on texts alone or students alone. It deals with what happens when student meets text, and through text, meets authors, cultures, other literary works, and himself or herself.

A SHORT STORY

The ant climbs up a trunk
carrying a petal on its back,
and if you look closely
that petal is as big as a house
especially compared to the ant that
carries it so olympically.

You ask me: Why couldn't I carry
a petal twice as big as my body and my head?
Ah, but you can, little girl,
but not petals from a dahlia,
rather boxes full of thoughts
and loads of magic hours, and
a wagon of clear dreams, and

a big castle with its fairies:
all the petals that form the soul of
a little girl who speaks and speaks.

> *David Escobar Galindo, translated*
> *by Jorge D. Piche in* This Same Sky

There's a poem, written by somebody, and that somebody has a life and a history and an environment.

There's a reader who is somebody with his or her world of images, metaphors, symbols, and that somebody has a life and a history and an environment.

One reader reads the poem and something happens:

She understands something of what the words say to her.

She translates the experience read about into her own context.

She may make an estimate of the life and history of the poet.

She has a feeling about the experience.

She has attitudes about the experience and the poem and the poet and the poet's world.

She usually reaches conclusions and makes judgments about all these matters.

Another way of putting it: Another reader takes the words and the images, and the experiences and ideas of that poem and puts them into his or her own way of seeing things. A person reads a poem with the word *castle* and maybe sees a chessboard, maybe a building with dungeons and dragons. Maybe it makes the reader feel funny or sad, and maybe the reader doesn't understand that the image could be one of wonder.

On the basis of that process, each reader might

       draw a picture

 groan

    talk about the poem

        role-play a character

     laugh

write a paragraph

    make a film

      try to forget he read the silly thing.

That's the response of each: Part of it's inside them, part of it's expressed. We all do it. We've been doing it for years. Even critics do it. Saying we respond to pieces of literature is like saying we have been talking prose all our lives. What is new is that we now see the ways in which all of these readings and the texts can be connected and related.

The Particular Response Depends on What Is Being Responded To

THEODORE HELPGOOD

Stranger! I died of hydrophobia.
I was bitten by both the upper and the under dog.
While trying to save the under dog.

E. L. Masters

THE SUDDEN CHILLNESS

The piercing chill I feel:
    my dead wife's comb, in our bedroom,
        under my heel ...

Taniguchi Buson

Those two are quite different.
    The pieces differ:

sounds   words   characters   images
countries   incidents   cultures

The ways of gluing the pieces together differ:

arrangements   syntax   plot   structure   pattern
tone   mood   voice   total   shape

You could even take the same pieces and glue them differently and get a different work.

Stranger, while trying to save the underdog,
I was bitten by both the upper and the under dog.
I died of hydrophobia.
Under my heel, in our bedroom,
my dead wife's comb:
I feel a piercing chill.

The Particular Response We Make Depends on Who Is Reading

People differ in their experience. Many have never been to the seashore. Many have read lots of comic books. Some have been in wars. Some have lost a father or a mother. Many come from another culture or spoke another language. Their past experience affects their response.

People differ in their concepts of things. Say "America" to a group of ten people and ask them to say what their concept of it is. You probably will get ten different concepts. But you can find common threads. People differ in their attitudes toward things. Not everybody hates school or poetry or physical education.

People differ in their interests. Not everybody watches the same soap. Some even turn off the set.

All of these and many other differences affect even the way people perceive things. If you love a boy, you see him in a crowd; you don't "see" the other people. If you read a letter, or a list, you see your name, not all the other names.

If these differences affect the way people see things, they also affect the kinds of reactions they have to things, and the kinds of actions they perform in response to things. Look again at the poems on page 62 of this chapter; jot down all the things that come to mind.

Get a friend to do the same thing. Are the jottings more alike or more different?

Then do it again next week. How have your jottings changed?

> In a reading that results in a work of art, the reader is concerned with the quality of the experience that he is living through under the stimulus and guidance of the text. No one else can read the poem or the novel or the play for him. To ask someone else to experience a work of art for him would be tantamount to seeking nourishment by asking someone else to eat his dinner for him. (Rosenblatt, 1978, p. 13)

If people are different and if stories and poems and plays are different, then we can say that different people respond differently to different pieces of writing (or painting, or whatever). There are only unique readings.

Not quite. Remember what we wrote in the last chapter. There are such things as communities that bring people together and hold them together, too. Studies of response to literature show that at one level readers from the same society have the same emotional apprehension of a text. Where they differ, as we said, is in how they articulate their understanding of their apprehension. Often it depends on what they think it is important to say. Often it depends on the context.

People also generally have common meanings for stories and poems and plays—or at least common boundaries for meanings. There is difference within a common framework—diversity within unity.

That's one philosophical principle of this curriculum: to allow for and foster both individuality and commonalty. It's nice to be yourself and part of a group. You can share without giving up your total independence. Sharing is important; so is the group. For many students sharing and articulating are difficult; for some even reading and responding are difficult. We do not want to minimize those difficulties. They may be difficulties of language, culture, psychological makeup, the capacity to imagine. These need to be worked with and dealt with.

The literature curriculum seeks to change people. It does not want them to become one of the herd or total individuals. Both instincts must be respected. It seeks to change them to accept their commonalty and their individuality.

It also seeks to get them to be careful explorers of themselves and their readings and the text.

Although works are unique and people are unique and responses are unique, there are points where responses touch and overlap. The following are three points of agreement:

> If everybody in a group is responding to the same poem, the common point is the poem.
>
> If a person is responding to a poem, a play, and a novel, the common point is the person.
>
> If a group of people are talking about novels they have read, the common points are the language they are using to talk with and the community they enter.

Preposterous

Mr. Weatherwax buttered his toast carefully. His voice was firm. "My dear," he said, "I want it definitely understood that there shall be no more trashy reading around this apartment."

"Yes, Jason. I did not know—"

"Of course you didn't. But it is your *responsibility* to know what our son reads."

"I shall watch more closely, Jason. I did not see the magazine when he brought it in. I did not know it was here."

"Nor would I have known had I not, after I came in last night, accidentally happened to displace one of the pillows on the sofa. The periodical was hidden under it, and of course I glanced through it."

The points of Mr. Weatherwax's mustache quivered with indignation. "Such utterly ridiculous concepts, such impossibly wild ideas. *Astounding Stories*, indeed!"

He took a sip of his coffee to calm himself.

"Such inane and utterly preposterous tripe," he said. "Travel to other galaxies by means of space warps, whatever they are. Time machines, teleportation, and telekinesis. Balderdash, sheer balderdash."

"My dear Jason," said his wife, this time with just the faintest touch of asperity, "I assure you I shall watch Gerald's reading closely hereafter. I fully agree with you."

"Thank you, my dear," Mr. Weatherwax said, more kindly. "The minds of the young should not be poisoned by such wild imaginings."

He glanced at his watch and rose hastily, kissed his wife and left.

Outside the apartment door he stepped into the antigravity shaft and floated gently down two hundred-odd floors to street level where he was lucky enough to catch an atomcab immediately. "Moonport," he snapped to the robot driver, and then sat back and closed his eyes to catch the telepathecast. He'd hoped to catch a bulletin on the Fourth Martian War but it was only another routine report from Immortality Center, so he quirtled.

Frederic Brown: PREPOSTEROUS.

To take the first common point first: A story like "Preposterous" has a set number of words and a set order of words.

Those words have a limited, although not strictly limited, range of meanings. *Firm* can mean stern, grim, unyielding, opinionated, and so forth. Odds are that it does not mean happy.

"The periodical was hidden under it, and of course I glanced through it" can hardly be reconstructed as "The glance was hidden under the periodical, of course" unless you wanted to change what had been written.

A story like "Preposterous" has a set order of incidents. Mr. Weatherwax quirtles after he scolds his wife, not before.

The story was written nearly forty years ago by an American, Frederic Brown. Frederic Brown is known for writing mysteries and short short stories.

The story also contains only the incidents and people it contains. For the purposes of this story, Gerald might as well have no grandfather and no sister. He might or might not have been locked in his room for three weeks prior to the opening of the story. It has a set number of people speaking: a narrator, a man, his wife, a robot. These are some of the limits set by the text.

Here are some limits *not* set by the text:

Whether Mr. Weatherwax is serious

When the story takes place

Whether Gerald is aware of the outside world

Whether Gerald is Jason's son

Whether the narrator likes Mr. Weatherwax

Whether the narrator approves of Mr. Weatherwax

Whether the parents love the boy

Whether he loves his parents

Whether the parents get on

Why Frederic Brown wrote the story

Whether the boy is imaginative

Whether the author agrees with the narrator

Whether the author agrees with Mr. Weatherwax

What the author's background is

Whether there is a lesson to be learned from the story

Whether the story is well constructed

Whether the story is moving

Whether the story is meaningful to the twentieth-century reader

Whether the story is a classic

Whether the author subscribes to a philosophical position

Whether the whole story takes place in Gerald's mind

Whether the author is a great writer

Whether the author and the story are . . .

To take the second common point: Some of the ways by which an individual's responses to several works may have something in common include the words and word structures one knows; the experiences one has had; the prejudices one has acquired; one's ability to tell about the connotation and implication of certain words; whether one can visualize images, or whether one's imagination is more auditory or kinetic; one's openness to new experiences; the preconceptions one has formed.

To take the third common point: Most people within a community have some things in common.

Most people within a community have roughly the same meaning of some words in their heads.

Most people within a community have comparable experiences of some things.

Most people within a community have similar judgments of human behavior: They know whom to trust, what motivates people to do what they do.

Most people within a community have comparable emotional reactions to such things as colors, sound patterns, the actions of certain people.

Most people within a community make similar judgments about some things, such as what they saw while watching a television show—a person riding a horse, not a series of light and dark dots.

Most people within a community can agree that it is possible for

different people to make different judgments about some things—
whether it was a goodie or a baddie riding that horse—with nobody
being absolutely sure.

So . . .

✓ The text limits our reading.
The limits of human knowledge limit our reading.
Our ability to communicate limits our reading.
Our common understanding limits our reading.

When people in the same cultural community read and respond to and
then talk or write about a piece of literature, the major difference among
them is not in the reading or response, but in the talk or writing. Research
has shown that a person could make more than one hundred different kinds
of individual statements about a text, such as about the language or rhythm
or plot or character or setting or interpretation or genre or theme or moral
or quality of style or historical period or personal reaction or estimate of
worthiness or, or, or . . .

If you combined five of these individual statements, the result would be
one of 500,000,000,000 possible five-sentence paragraphs. Maybe some of
them would make sense. It's the combinations of statements that make up
the thousands of articles on a single Shakespeare play; it's not thousands of
different understandings of the play. And on close examination, the differences mask commonalities set by the four limitations we listed above.

If you were to teach "Preposterous" and ask each student to find out
something about the author and then write an analysis of Mr. Weatherwax or
of the relation of the two parts of the story, you would get thirty different
papers. You would probably find that many of the differences are in the
phrasing and organization of the papers rather than in what is actually said
about the text.

Yet even the phrasing and organization will have common elements,
because the students have learned something of the conventions of writing
about stories and they know what sort of writing you expect and reward.
They have become part of the community you have established.

Given the individuality and connectedness of people's responses to what
they read or see, the educational goal becomes one of helping the students
recognize both the individuality and the connectedness.

Enter: The Reader-Based Approach

It recognizes and explores people's individuality and encourages that indi- ✗
viduality.

It recognizes and explores the connections among people and encour- ✗

ages people to make the connections manifest in sharing their responses with a group.

It recognizes and explores the idea that response is exuberant and spills over all sorts of barriers.

Its procedure is simple.

How do we go about it? Follow this recipe:

Ingredients
Take 1 class of 28 students

Add 1 literary text written by a real person, say Katherine Paterson's *Jacob Have I Loved*

and 1 teacher

Stir vigorously; the result in 48 minutes can be

an exploration by the students of themselves and their reaction to the opening words of the text

a search for as many similar situations as possible

a discussion of the world of Maryland in the 1940s as thorough as they are capable of

a search in Genesis for the Jacob and Esau story

a foray into the life of Paterson as a missionary child

a search for language to help articulate their responses

a hearing of diverse responses and a respect for them

an exploration of areas of agreement and disagreement

a dramatization of one day on the island

an exploration of Paterson's other books

a computer dialogue with another class

and much more

With a response-based approach, the teacher encourages students to express whatever their responses might be and encourages everyone to exchange responses or share in expressing a response freely. In one sense, the teacher is still the boss: the person who selects what is read, initiates the framework of discussion, and ends up as the judge of quality. Within these constraints there can be a great deal of negotiation, and even these power relationships can change, particularly in an environment with computers, hypertext, and portfolios.

Those who need and want to look things up will; those who want to remain silent for a long time may. As students work together, they modify their individuality where it seems appropriate, retain it where it seems appropriate. They come to see where their language can connect them or divide them. As students work together, they find out about authors and writers, about other readers, and about themselves. The teacher's role is to challenge students to justify, explain, and share their responses. The teacher's role is to help the students take responsibility for their reading, their learning, their conduct in school, and, ultimately, their lives.

The aim is to have students come to a greater knowledge of why they are who they are and approach new works of literature by an increasingly diverse set of writers with greater self-confidence.

The aim is to affect students' perceptions of works of art (literary works), to affect their ability to articulate their responses, to affect their tolerance of the diversity of human responses to similar objects, and to bring them together into a community of communities.

Notice That We Call It an Approach, Not a Curriculum

We once thought of what we are advocating as a curriculum, but it is not a curriculum. What we are setting forth is a way of thinking about the curriculum. A curriculum is a planned series of experiences, and in literature, this means a selection of stories, poems, plays, novels, and essays with some sort of order and perhaps some clear thread connecting them. A curriculum includes a planned set of activities (with room for spontaneous ones), and it is set forth in quarters or semesters or units. A literature curriculum can be organized by theme, country or historical period, genre, mood, culture, author; each of these is a good way of arranging the pieces of literature that you want to emphasize. Any of them can be meaningful to the students. But the selection and the arrangement are separate from the approach, and what we are suggesting is an approach. If you adopt the approach, you can use it with a lot of different curricular arrangements.

What Does the Reader-Based Approach Say about All the Information That People Have to Have in Order to Know a Poem or a Story Really Well?

A good bit of the information people really have to have is in the words and structure of words of the text.

Some of the information is in the language we use to talk about our reading and that the students are acquiring as they read literature—language having to do with story, poem, word, repetition, scene, pattern, narrator or speaker, comparison. The distinction between the terms that are useful for talk about a text (metaphor, symbol, plot, irony, rhyme, rhythm, voice, point of view, allegory) and those that belong to the specialist (metonymy, anacrusis, iamb, sonnet, heroic couplet, bildungsroman, litotes, romantic irony) is a fine one. Help the students to find those they want.

The situation is just like that in any field: The same thing can be a pitch or a reverse knuckleball, a leap or a jeté, a layer cake or a kaiser torte. One term is more precise than the other, but either is sufficient for most communication, particularly when the people talking about the thing are trying to understand each other as well as the thing. The critical language that developed came from man's need to classify and categorize his experiences. It came from the same impetus that has led to the elaborate classifications of plant and animal life. In a sense, of course, education is the learning of these classificatory schemes, but too often the learning of the names of plants has replaced looking at them, smelling them, enjoying them. The same thing happened to literature teaching; the language became separated from the experience of reading. But don't deny the students the language; keep it subordinate to the experience.

Another important kind of information that students need lies around them in the library, in databases, and in various other sources and concerns the books, who wrote them, why they wrote them, when they were made, and what people thought and think about them. There is more information about the culture surrounding writers and their subject. All of this information surrounding the text is there for the exploring.

In a response-based approach, the central focus is the experience of the reader with the text and the culture that lies behind and within the text.

History and Authors and Background Help with Some Writers More than Others

Does it affect your judgment of *Roll of Thunder, Hear My Cry* to know that Mildred Taylor was a teacher?

Does it help your understanding of "The Pit and the Pendulum" to know that Edgar Allan Poe drank? How about to know he loved the Middle Ages?

Does it affect your interest in Tom and Becky in the cave to know that Mark Twain was a staunch atheist? How about to know he grew up a mile from that cave? How about to know what school life was like at that time?

Does it affect your understanding, appreciation, interpretation, judgment, or involvement to know that Susan Cooper's *The Boggart* resulted from a trip to Canada, or to know that Cooper is interested in Celtic mythology?

Does it affect your reading to know whether *The Tempest* should properly be called a romance or a tragicomedy? What of knowing about the Elizabethan belief in order? Or the Globe theater?

Of course it does, and of course it does not. There is a time for needing information apart from the works being read, and that is when people are in training to be literary critics, literary historians, literature teachers, or quiz-show question writers. It is not the same time as when people are learning how best to express what has happened when they meet with "The Pit and the Pendulum," "Jabberwocky," *Tom Sawyer*, or *The Tempest*. Information must be used in order to be valuable; otherwise it is trivia.

All that information about the author, the history of the work, the fact that drama started as religious ritual, or the specific references to English politics in *Gulliver's Travels*—all of it affects a person's reading; all may even lead to a kind of reading different from the kind a person would have without any such information. Is one reading the better for having all this information? No. Nor worse. The two readings are different. But if one is going to understand the culture within and behind the work, the information is not trivial.

One of the problems with the teaching of literature is that all this sort of information seems to crowd the reader's response to the text out of the picture. The students get everything but the work. In some countries, literature classes consist of almost nothing except reading literary histories; the students don't read the things the histories are about, just as in some college classes in this country they read the work of theorists and critics, not poems and novels. In part this happens because it's much easier to make up a test of factual knowledge than it is to evaluate a response-based curriculum—or even an analytic curriculum.

Be that as it may, background information should be precisely what it is: background. At times it should be so far back it is out of sight. But don't deny it to those who want it. It can help people read a novel to notice and explore what the author takes for granted. Why doesn't Samuel Beckett mention World War II in *Waiting for Godot*?

But What Does the Response-Based Approach Say about Selections, What the Students Should Read? You Seem To Have Forgotten That

No we haven't. Remember the first chapter.

In one sense, it does not particularly matter what selections you choose. As we see it you have two obligations: to introduce students to works they might never read on their own and works that embody the variety of the cultures of the world. It's OK to have a year of American lit. Just don't forget that the Americas include Canadians, Mexicans, Asian Americans, Native Americans, African Americans, immigrants of all sorts, women, men, the blind, the deaf.

Many anthologies contain good selections, ones students like to read and discuss, and they are not necessarily the enemy of a response-based approach. Just be careful about the apparatus and study questions.

Go ahead and use the anthology series the district bought. You can use some of the class sets that are back in the storeroom. You might even use a picture book and perhaps even a Nancy Drew at some point. Don't forget comics, TV tie-ins, "as-told-to" books, even that adolescent lit book you just can't stand. But don't make a steady diet of any of these.

We have found that students will read and consider almost anything. We have found it impossible to pin down the taste or interest of a whole class— even a class of hardcore nonreaders. Some of them are secret sci-fi buffs. They could try Virginia Hamilton or Andre Norton or Jorge Luis Borges. Some tell you about every baseball player going. They could try John Tunis or Bernard Malamud. Others can tick off all the romance writers. Have they tried Emily Brontë, Isabel Allende or Alice Walker?

Of course, there are some caveats from our experience.

Adolescents will probably not enjoy some fiction about parenthood and the responsibilities of middle age; Ernest Hemingway's *The Sun Also Rises* is not as engaging a novel as *The Old Man and the Sea*. Robert Lipsyte's novels are as engaging as Hemingway's.

It would probably be as good to present Shakespeare's *Troilus and Cressida* as it would *King Lear* in a twelfth-grade class.

Adolescents will probably get more out of Barbara Kingsolver's novels of the road than they will out of John Barth's.

Try Andre Norton as well as Jules Verne.

Billy Budd will probably be more successful than *Moby Dick* with a group of eleventh-graders.

Percy Shelley's political poems will probably evoke a more energetic response than will his poems about art like "To a Skylark." Eve Merriam's political poems may strike some even harder.

e.e. cummings's exuberant language will probably gain more adherents to poetry than T. S. Eliot's measured language.

Better to elicit response with the essays of Annie Dillard than with Charles Lamb.

On man and nature, take Tarzan rather than John Stuart Mill or Alfred, Lord Tennyson. But use Tennyson's mythological material or, better yet, Mary Renault's.

Use modern African-American writers or slave narratives rather than Harriet Beecher Stowe to show the horrors of the pre-Civil War South.

Mad Magazine or *Doonesbury* can be as effective an exponent of satiric technique as *The DeCoverly Papers* of Addison and Steele.

Best yet, try all of these and do not be bound to any preconception.

All right, but isn't it important for a student to have read the classics?

Yes,

But

Often the inclusion of what have been called the classics causes a bad reaction. Teachers tend to want to worship a classic and force students to worship it, too. Students tend to see classics as irrelevant because they are not able to see that there is a great deal that is generalizable from the classic to their lives. Is *Billy Budd* irrelevant because it's about sailing ships? It's also about the problem of relating ends to means, the problem of making unpleasant decisions. Those problems are more likely relevant to the students' world—but it is often hard to see that, when you are so wrapped up in your world.

Teachers can present the classics well, but sometimes they need help. Oftentimes they need to get away from the notion that teaching the classics means revering them and teaching their old lecture notes from English 101.

Remember that Shakespeare wrote plays. He was the Neil Simon and Arthur Miller of his day. These works are to be seen and heard. If you cannot take students to a production of *Macbeth*, have them read the comic version that is the complete folio text. Don't spend a lot of time studying every word.

Remember that Swift wrote pamphlets to get people mad about current issues. Remember that Wordsworth and Coleridge wrote poems for the people. So did Whitman, Sandburg, Frost, Hughes, and Brooks.

Remember that a classic is a good example of its type. "The Most Dangerous Game" is a classic short story. *A Tale of Two Cities* is a classic adventure novel. So is *The Third Man*. A classic psychological novel is *Chronicle of a Death Foretold*. So is *A Wrinkle in Time*. The classic is the work, not the author. Certain of the comic strips of Charles Schulz and Berkeley Breathed are classics.

Many recent works have reached classic status: *A Separate Peace*, *To Kill a Mockingbird*, *The Catcher in the Rye*, *Maus*, *Black Boy*, *Diary of a Young Girl*, *The Earthsea Trilogy*, *Arrow of Gold*, *The Color Purple*, *The Joy Luck Club*—the list goes on. Some classics have lost favor: the works of Kipling, Hardy, and Scott, to name but three. The list is wide-ranging and ever-changing.

The important thing is to try to include the best of its kind, works that repay reading. These may include works written three thousand years ago and yesterday. Whenever they were written and however famous they may be, the works worth teaching are those that get us thinking about what they say and how they say it, those in which the experience of reading the book takes each of us a little bit out of ourselves for the moment and then reminds us of ourselves in a new way when we have finished, rereading the "poem" in one's memory. These are the hallmarks of a classic.

Remember, too, that what is important is not the breadth of coverage, but the depth to which the students explore the works. Don't worry about covering; worry about digging.

But a Lot of These Books—Particularly the Contemporary Ones—Are the Ones That Come Up on Blacklists. What about the Censors?

That's a problem. And it cannot be wished away. For every book there is an enemy. One reason is that we have been taught to read books as if they contain moral messages that we should pay attention to. People think that reading a Sherlock Holmes story will lead to disrespect of the police, that reading *Huckleberry Finn* will make one racist, that reading Hemingway will make one sexist, or that reading Cynthia Voigt will make one anti-adult.

We think there are some books it would be better for our students not to read. So do you. They may be books we find personally repellent. They may be books that deal with subjects we would rather not deal with ourselves. For all sorts of reasons we make selections based on a variety of criteria. One of us would never teach Franz Kafka's *In the Penal Colony* because the experience of reading it was more than could be borne a second time.

So there is a little of the censor in all of us. In our experience, the problem is less censors as such than it is that of forcing students to read something that some of them or some of their parents might find repugnant. We have found that most parents and citizens' groups do not mind if they are told that the students can read alternative texts and that they do not have to accept the supposed message of the book.

There are also censors at publishing houses and people who "speak" for groups of various persuasions that provide "guidelines" to publishers or text adoption committees. These are the censors who do not allow teachers and communities the right of choice. To our mind the local objectors who speak against or for books out of a clear sense of conscience are preferable to those who claim to speak for upright citizens everywhere.

The important point is for the teacher to be sensitive to rights and social harm in selecting works to be read, but not to be intimidated by pressure groups that are themselves insensitive.

If you are approached by someone who is concerned about what their children are reading, there are a number of things you can do. The simplest is to talk with them, listen to them, ask what alternatives they suggest. Confrontation is not necessary. It is less important that all students read a particular book than that all read and respond to something. It is not the text but the response that is paramount in the literature curriculum.

Beyond that, you should enter into the dialogue suggested by the National Council of Teachers of English in their pamphlet, *The Student's Right to*

Read. This suggests that you and your principal ask the objectors to bring their complaint in writing, to answer some questions about whether they have read the whole book and what specially they object to, and then determine what alternatives should be proposed.

There may arise an incident where the "offending" book and you and the students will be hailed before the school board or even taken to court. In that case, organizations like the National Council of Teachers of English and the American Library Association can provide various sorts of support. Do not hesitate to call.

One Last Question: All This Sounds Very Nice, but So Many Students Don't Seem to Know How to Really Read a Text

It depends on what one means by "really read." Teachers often use the phrase *really read* to mean that students do not come up with the teachers' particular reading of a text. Students do not see the same things teachers see, nor do they see things the same way. Surely, out of five hundred billion responses, the teacher's response is not superior to many other responses.

For some, "really read"' is a shorthand people use to denigrate students who come from other cultures, who are not native speakers of English, or who come to school with emotional or intellectual baggage that does not get them engaged in what "we" think they ought to be doing. In this case, the person saying "really read" does not or will not know his or her students, will not look at them in the ways we suggested in Chapter 2 and see them for what they are, not for their failure to be what we would like.

But if one means by "really read" that students do not pay attention to all the verbal details that produce their general responses, there is more than a grain of truth to that. People who respond to Picasso's *Guernica* don't pay attention to the strength and direction of the brushwork. Many people who respond fully to a symphony do not pay attention to what key it's in. The comment may mean people who read poems are not professionals. It may also mean students have been trained to be lazy readers who rely on teachers and multiple-choice tests.

If one means by "really read" that students don't know the procedures for doing what literary people do when they criticize texts, that is probably right. In our experience students in the early years of secondary school don't know how to go about finding the theme or meaning of a story or poem. They are often asked to come up with the theme and then told that the one they selected was wrong. They have not been given the rules or procedures for theme-finding; they don't have a map for exploration. Scolded for not being critical readers, they are not told what critical reading entails.

We teachers expect people to be highly attentive readers, though, because they read so much and because they take twelve years of English. And they can be more attentive than we give them credit for, but they are not used to explaining all the processes by which they come to like or dislike, interpret, evaluate, or make some other summative judgment about what they have read. There remains the question of whether they need to. If you let a group of people talk about a poem for an hour without directing them in any way, you will find that collectively they touch on most of the verbal details that produce the various general impressions. There is no need to lecture them or hold a recitation on all these details. The trick is to get them to be active participants in articulating their responses to the texts and their writers.

Students may know how to really read; give them a chance to prove it.

References

Galindo, David Escobar, "A Short Story," translated by Jorge D. Piche. In *This Same Sky*, ed. Naomi Shihab Nye. New York: Four Winds Press, 1992.

Harding, D. W. "Psychological Processes in The Reading of Fiction." *British Journal of Aesthetics* 2 (1962): 133–147.

National Council of Teachers of English. *The Student's Right to Read*. Urbana, IL: National Council of Teachers of English, 1980.

Rosenblatt, Louise. *The Reader, The Text, The Poem: The Transactional Theory of the Literary Work*. Carbondale, IL: Southern Illinois University Press, 1978.

Resources

Bleich, David. *Readings and Feelings: An Introduction to Subjective Criticism*. Urbana, IL: National Council of Teachers of English, 1975.

Fish, Stanley. *Is There a Text in This Class? The Authority of Interpretive Communities*. Cambridge, MA: Harvard University Press, 1980.

Nelms, Ben, ed. *Literature in the Classroom: Readers, Texts and Contexts*. Urbana, IL: National Council of Teachers of English, 1988.

Onore, Cynthia. "The Student, the Teacher, and the Text: Negotiating Meanings Through Response and Revision." In *Writing and Response: Theory, Practice and Research* (pp. 213–260), edited by Chris Anson. Urbana, IL: National Council of Teachers of English, 1989.

Purves, Alan C. "The Teacher as Reader: An Anatomy." *College English* 46 (1984): 259–265.

Rabinowitz, Peter, J. *Before Reading: Narrative Conventions and the Politics of Interpretation*. Ithaca, NY: Cornell University Press, 1987.

Somers, Albert B., and Janet E. Worthington. *Response Guide for Teaching Children's Books*. Urbana, IL: National Council of Teachers of English, 1983.

Tompkins, Jane, R., ed. *Reader-Response Criticism: From Formalism to Post-Structuralism*. Baltimore: Johns Hopkins University Press, 1980.

chapter 5

If Literature Is Exploration, What's the Territory and Who's the Guide?

We've spent a number of pages on literature, students, and texts. What about teachers? What about you? What is your role?

Teachers are pivotal in the response-based classroom:

You usually select the texts that will be read—perhaps from a list or an anthology.

You choose the sequence and timing of texts, reading discussion, writing, films, tests, drama, talk, and grade.

You choose when to divide the class into groups for reading or discussion or projects and when to bring them back together as a whole. You set the pace.

You provide additional information as needed or send the students to it. You provide resources ... you are a resource.

You guide the talk.

You set up the assessment system.

You give some of the feedback and help the students give the rest.

Louise Rosenblatt wrote a book called *Literature as Exploration* (1968); it is one of the guiding lights of the reader-based approach. Exploration doesn't mean being lost in the woods. It means finding out about new territory for the explorer. The students are the explorers, but they need guides who help them, warn them of dangerous swamps and alligators, have scouted out the territory, and arrange for food and shelter. The guide does not replace the explorer, but is absolutely necessary to a successful exploration.

You Are the Guide

Don't forget these tips for being a good guide:

1. You are probably older than they are (sometimes bigger, too).
2. You probably know more than they do (about the subject, that is).
3. You are also their judge and jury (but they judge you, too).

You can take these tips and be a tyrant or you can use them to become a proper guide—like a gardener or the director of a play. In no case are you sure of the outcome, but you are in charge and responsible for the safety of the journey.

We've found it's a mistake to pretend to be one of the guys with the students. You can be sympathetic and encouraging, but there's an invisible boundary; cross it at your own peril.

Selecting the Texts

We've said a lot about this in the last chapter. The only thing we would add is an admonition that a good guide never stops being curious, never stops reading. Stopping reading is the curse of English teachers and the beginning of mental decay.

Anything you read—a short story in an airline magazine, the front of *The National Inquirer*, a new novel, the latest poem, a book your own children ask you to read, the writing of an African poet—is a potential candidate for the curriculum.

So are the neglected classics, like the works of Sir Walter Scott and Kate Chopin.

So are the journals of slaves and immigrants, the unheard voices of our society.

So are the books found on remainder lists or on junk shop shelves.

So are the angry and sweet voices of your youth.

They may not all be usable, but you have a sense of what the students might want to talk about or what you might want to talk about with them.

You can certainly use the selections in the anthology you've been told to teach or the list of books in the library or the class sets. Just don't worry about the teacher's guide and study questions. Use the selections, but make them yours and your students'.

Don't assume that some books are only for the "bright" students and some for the "dummies." Honors students like to read *The Outsiders*; students in regular classes can get involved with *Julius Caesar*.

Above all you can have the students make their own selections. Don't forget that independent reading is one of the goals of the approach.

Setting Up the Sequence

You have thirty-two weeks divided into four quarters and eight marking periods, four groups of thirty students, and a five-pound anthology. What's the plan?

Regardless of how that anthology is set up, we don't recommend marching through it from cover to cover. Remember that the anthology is meant to be more than you can use. If you don't have an anthology, but a set of books or a list, you will have to select an order. How do you make your own sequence?

One principle for making that sequence, we think, is that a reader-based approach to teaching literature means an emphasis on depth, not breadth. Better to do one play thoroughly to capture the totality of the experience of reading and responding to it than rush to cover the next story in the unit.

Literature courses are traditionally organized by author (usually nationally and chronologically), by genre, or by theme. Each of these is a perfectly good arrangement. Each is artificial. Each makes sense. Each may help the students answer the question, "What are you studying in English this year?" "American poetry." It's nice to be studying something tangible, nicer than studying "thinking skills" or "articulating our responses" or "self-understanding." These are educational by-products, terms for curriculum documents, not for real people.

Real people study people, places or things. Subjects like fractions and grammar and Chicano women's poetry. That's the real stuff.

That's OK. Give the students something to get a handle on. Make up a sequence with a tangibility to it. It can be poems, or black writers, or comedy, or the First People's view of humans and nature. It can at times be a single text like *I Know Why the Caged Bird Sings*.

Remember that any text in a curriculum comes before and after another. You can make all sorts of connections. Some can be based on similarity, some on contrast. You could follow *Macbeth* with Thurber's "The Macbeth Murder Mystery" or with *The Caine Mutiny*. The first takes the play into the world of the reader, with a dash of humor; the second takes the theme of tyranny into a new context.

You could put *Wuthering Heights* and the novels of Georgette Heyer together. You could even toss in some Gothics and some Hispanic romance photo-comics.

You could pair Carl Sandburg with Langston Hughes, or Robert Frost with Maxine Kumin.

You could contrast George Orwell with Aldous Huxley on the future, and then toss in Ursula LeGuin.

You could compare the speeches of Chief Joseph and Martin Luther King. You could follow John Wyndham's *The Day of the Triffids* with Sylvia

SUGGESTIONS

Plath's "Mushrooms." You could run a sequence of love poems from the Elizabethans to e.e. cummings, and Audre Lorde.

You could pair the contrasts of place in *A Tale of Two Cities* with those of time in Madeleine L'Engle's *A Wrinkle in Time* or Alan Garner's *The Owl Service*.

The pairings are infinite: structure, style, culture, tone, theme, myth, mood, characterization, author, setting, fictionality, . . . Why not ask your students what they think should come next?

All they require is a sense of what might be an illuminating comparison or contrast, a sequence that makes some sense, a pairing that will help them see one text in the light of another or several others that they have read before.

Dividing the Group and Bringing It Back Together

In the subsequent chapters we are going to go into various activities in depth. One thing we do want to say at this point: It's not necessary for everyone in the class to read the same book at the same time. We think that a part of the literature program at any level should have room for independent reading. It's a way of encouraging the habit. You can even take the time yourself to read.

At times it's good to have the whole class read and talk about the same text. At times it's good to have everyone reading a different text. At times it's good to have reading groups.

A particular text can be a good common point. Take *A Tale of Two Cities*; it's a good novel for a group to read together. It has romance and adventure. Afterward some of the students might want to pick up another novel by Dickens. Another group might want to follow up with some history and might look at Thomas Paine. Still another might ask if there are other works dealing with escapes. The world of adolescent fiction abounds with such stories: escapes from Nazi Germany, escapes from slavery, escapes from hostile planets, escapes from repressive systems of any sort. Still another might ask about fiction that deals with other revolutions. They might turn to *Across Five Aprils*, *Johnny Tremain*, *Darkness at Noon*, or *Doctor Zhivago*. Or you might send them to the library to find out what other books there are.

That's one way of breaking up the class into groups. After they have worked on their extended reading, they should share it with the rest of the class. Then the task would be to see what connections can be made back to the central book.

Another way of breaking up the class is to have them divide into groups to explore different facets of the selection.

VIGNETTE IV: GETTING INTO A STORY

In an eleventh-grade class on Joseph Conrad's *Heart of Darkness*, the group, after reading it through and having a brief discussion, found themselves baffled. The teacher told them there were a number of ways into the story they could try.

T: What might be some good leads?

ST: Well, there's the journey. Where did they go?

T: Why don't three of you try to make a map diary?

ST: These guys seem to be going to hell.

T: Good. Know any other trip-to-hell stories?

ST: I've heard of Dante.

T: The four of you in the back row look at an outline of his *Inferno* and see what you can find.

ST: I'm sort of struck by the phrase "the heart of darkness." There's a lot of times that comes up.

T: Why don't you and Ines and Kris make a list of all the occurrences of the term?

ST: Marlowe makes a lot of comments.

T: Get a partner and catalog them and see where they lead.

ST: You've got two stories here, don't you?

T: Looks that way, what relationships can you find?

Without even thinking about it they had five working groups. They reported to each other and some of them came up with rich findings. The eleventh graders we saw do this wrote excellent papers after about two weeks of reading, digging, and articulating.

GROUP / INTER PROJECTS AROUND THE BOOK!

Being a Resource

In Chapter 10, we will mention some of the hypertext packages that are becoming available, but with or without the hardware, a class can create its own hypertext around whatever is being read. A part of that lies in the thoughts and backgrounds that each member of the class brings to the reading. But you have to help. Sometimes you may give a lecture or find a videotape on a background topic related to the text. You can provide a parallel from another culture to the text the students are reading and discussing. As we wrote in Chapter 4, don't be afraid to tell the students something about the background if they seem to want to know it. It helps readers to have some information on Emily Dickinson's Amherst or on Jim Crow in Richard Wright's time or to know that the Greek theater, like the Japanese, Hebrew, and early Renaissance theaters, was a place for religious ceremony. If you don't know the answer, you and the students can always go to the encyclopedia and begin your exploration there.

A class assignment on *Bless Me, Ultima,* by Rudolfo Anaya, can lead in many directions, and the hypertext can be huge, expanding to films and articles on the Southwest, the decline of ranching and the life of the cowboy, herbal and holistic medicine, the treatment of the elderly in different cultures, or the transition of learning a new language and losing one's familial language. The book can lead to parallel books and plays on the ways in which cultural forces linger in a mixed society, with examples from the African-American, the Sioux, the Eastern European, the Bengali, the Korean. As the teacher, you can guide and channel this exploration into a large world of texts and commentaries on text, of history, geography, anthropology, and sociology.

Such an exploration of background information helps the works come alive but it should not replace reading the work. If you undertake a search of background information, it might come after the initial reading rather than before, at the point where the addition of information clarifies potential misconception, enriches the reading, and can be brought back to the reading.

Although you are the resource, it doesn't mean you have to know everything before you and the class read the book, but you do have to be alert to where the sources are, what tools exist for finding things out, and what related books there might be. A good resource is a resource to other resources. You can be the student's "whole response catalog."

We recommend having lots of adjuncts: maps and atlases for historical fiction or fantasy, a dictionary with etymology, a history of literature, a database of readings and resources, a dictionary of mythology, photographs of artworks, a set of computer programs of texts and resources, diagrams of theaters and other sites, videos concerning authors or settings, tapes of music contemporary with the work. All of these can be useful for clearing something up or starting a discussion.

Don't try to deny that literature has a context. Don't try to tell the students that all they need to understand a text is their native wit. Neither is true. Don't lie to them—it's not for their own good.

The main thing you will have to do as a resource and guide is to know when to help them as they work toward an articulation of their response.

Just How Does a Teacher Proceed? Very Carefully (Like Those Porcupines)

You assume that students can attend to pieces of writing by listening, viewing, or reading. You know they respond, but they might have trouble expressing their response.

VIGNETTE V: EXPRESSING RESPONSES

A tenth-grade teacher stuffs in background on Margaret Walker and what it was like to write as an African American in the 1940s in the Jim Crow South. The teacher reads aloud as the students follow.

The teacher is silent
 . . . and waits
  . . . and watches
   . . . and listens

For My People
Margaret Walker

For my people everywhere singing their slave songs
   repeatedly: their dirges and their ditties and their blues
   and jubilees,[1] praying their prayers nightly
   to an unknown god, bending their knees humbly to an
   unseen power;

For my people lending their strength to the years, to the
   gone years and the now years and the maybe years,
   washing ironing cooking scrubbing sewing mending
   hoeing plowing digging planting pruning patching
   dragging along never gaining never reaping never
   knowing and never understanding;

For my playmates in the clay and dust and sand of Alabama
   backyards playing baptizing and preaching and doctor
   and jail and soldier and school and mama and cooking
   and playhouse and concert and store and hair and Miss
   Choomby and company;

For the cramped bewildered years we went to school to learn
   to know the reasons why and the answers to and the
   people who and the places where and the days when, in
   memory of the bitter hours when we discovered we
   were black and poor and small and different and nobody
   cared and nobody wondered and nobody understood;

For the boys and girls who grew in spite of these things to
   be man and woman, to laugh and dance and sing and
   play and drink their wine and religion and success, to
   marry their playmates and bear children and then die
   of consumption and anemia and lynching;[2]

For my people thronging 47th Street in Chicago and Lenox
   Avenue in New York and Rampart Street in New
   Orleans, lost disinherited dispossessed[3] and happy
   people filling the cabarets and taverns and other
   people's pockets needing bread and shoes and milk and
   land and money and something—something all our own;

For my people walking blindly spreading joy, losing time
   being lazy, sleeping when hungry, shouting when
   burdened, drinking when hopeless, tied, and shackled
   and tangled among ourselves by the unseen creatures
   who tower over us omnisciently[4] and laugh;

For my people blundering and groping and floundering in
   the dark of churches and schools and clubs and
   societies, associations and councils and committees and
   conventions, distressed and disturbed and deceived and
   devoured by money-hungry glory-craving leeches,[5]
   preyed on by facile[6] force of state and fad and novelty, by
   false prophet and holy believer;

For my people standing staring trying to fashion a better way
   from confusion, from hypocrisy and misunderstanding,
   trying to fashion a world that will hold all the people,
   all the faces, all the adams and eves and their countless
   generations;

Let a new earth rise. Let another world be born. Let a
   bloody peace be written in the sky. Let a second
   generation full of courage issue forth; let a people
   loving freedom come to growth. Let a beauty full of
   healing and a strength of final clenching be the pulsing
   in our spirits and our blood. Let the martial songs be
   written, let the dirges disappear. Let a race of men now
   rise and take control.

In other classes, the students may decide to remain silent; they may decide to act something out; they may decide to draw, to make a film, a song medley; they may decide to hear the poem again or turn to something else in the book; or they may decide to talk about the changes in race relations and the situation of African Americans in the past 50 years. They may decide they need to know more. And not all of them will decide to do the same thing at the same time.

You must allow students this first opportunity to express their responses. It may take a long time or a short time. It may seem dull to the teacher or seem nonintellectual or stupid or philistine. It may be exciting for the students; it's new for them, so accept what they do as genuine; listen, watch, attend to what they are doing, and take notes, mental or written. Help those who want to express something express what they want to express. At the moment when you think the students have expressed their initial responses fully, ask them to clarify, to expand, to explain, to share more fully. Encourage them to ask this of each other—not to put each other down but to understand what each is doing, and why. Encourage them to find out what they need to know.

But What if There Is No Initial Response?

In one class, the teacher put the word *lord* on the board, and the class discussed its connotation. Next they did the same with *flies*. Then the teacher connected them and asked what might be implied in *Lord of the Flies*. The discussion was long and heated. Some suggested the ruler of shit; some suggested a star outfielder; most came out with a sense of paradox. Then the teacher wrote the next words of the text, the section title—*The Call of the Conch*—and the class mulled over where that phrase was taking them— away from the title? Was it the tool of the lord? Then they focused on the first sentence of the book for fifteen minutes. How were they being led? Where were they being led? What was the juxtaposition of two phrases and a sentence doing? The class was now free to read the novel and to talk about how it followed this first impression.

It is quite possible that the students will not know what to say. There are a number of ways to get students to begin thinking about the experience they have had reading and envisioning a new work.

Ask the students to jot down the first question that comes into their heads.

Have them share the questions and see who has answers for which questions.

Have a supply of pictures that might be appropriate to a poem and ask groups to select the picture they think best illustrates the poem. Can they justify their choices?

Present students with a set of scales for the main character of a story and ask them to rate the character and share their ratings. How uniform were they?

	Low in Quality		High in Quality	
Good	1	2	3	4	5
Strong	1	2	3	4	5
Distant	1	2	3	4	5
Calm	1	2	3	4	5
Moral	1	2	3	4	5
Spineless| 1	2	3	4	5
Lovable	1	2	3	4	5
Active	1	2	3	4	5

Good for discussion [handwritten note]

If you are reading a play, ask the class to select the actors for the dramatization and justify their choices.

Have one student read a part of the selection aloud. Then have another student pick it up. How did the two readings change the story?

Try making a drama or a choral reading of the text.

Do anything but don't treat it like a passage in a reading test and ask right away for the theme or the main idea.

Remember the difference between "reading" a message and reading literature.

Don't be fooled because reading tests include stories and poems. You are after the thoughtful articulation of the imaginative re-creation of a story or a poem. Cherish the experience for its own sake.

Don't look for a quick answer to a simple question like those in the teacher's guide.

Don't treat *The Old Man and the Sea* as a descriptive account of how to catch marlin (although some students in your class might want to think of it that way), but as the story of an old man, a boy, a fish, the sea, and their complex relationship.

Remember this is a literature class, one that has its own goals and pursuits. It is not designed to help people read reports fast or to help them answer multiple-choice questions. It is designed to help students think about their experiences, to deepen them, to challenge their assumptions. It is a class about literature and the culture that it forms and formed it. It is about your students and their culture and community.

This approach to literature is to be carried through the subsequent consideration of the text. There may be a number of activities that follow from the initial experience and sharing of that experience. Here is a sampler. Some we will explore in greater depth in the next few chapters.

Suppose that after having read Sandra Cisneros's *The House on Mango Street* some students decide to make a collection of pictures, vignettes, and quotes about aspects of modern life in their community—a collage *House on Whatever Street*. After they have finished, the teacher asks them whether they think they have captured the movement of the book as well as its statement.

Suppose a group of students start complaining about the anthology they are using. The teacher asks them to make up their own. As they begin, the teacher asks them what decisions they have to make—decisions about size, type of selection, whether to have only contemporary selections, what sorts of illustrations and graphic treatment there will be.

Suppose a group of students decide that a poem has a really interesting beat. The teacher asks them to demonstrate this beat and offers the use of a tape recorder to help them record what they mean.

Suppose a student complains that he can't read the story, so he doesn't get what the class is talking about. If it seems appropriate, after class in a conference, the teacher reads the story aloud to the student. If they are in class, the teacher suggests that some of the others dramatize the story; then all have something to respond to.

Suppose a group of students wonder what would happen if they had read a poem and had not known what its title was; would they have responded differently? The teacher asks if they want to try an experiment with another class and sets up a research project that the group can carry out.

Let's Summarize

The teacher selects much of the material because the teacher has a wider repertoire.

The students select some, too.

The teacher suggests alternate forms of response.

If the students are talking, the teacher might suggest that they write.

The teacher structures particular forms of expressing response.

At some point the teacher might ask everyone to improvise the end of a story. Even if they haven't finished it, they can imagine what might happen.

The teacher structures particular modes of response.

At some points the teacher asks the group, "But what do you think it *means*?"

The teacher works to elicit the fullest possible response.

The teacher must be dogged about asking "Why?" "What do you mean?" "Tell us more." "I don't understand." One can't simply accept the first response; one must challenge the students to extend it.

The teacher calls the students' attention to certain parts of the work.

At times the teacher may ask how a comparison, a word, a character affects what a student said. Does it change the student's response?

The teacher encourages the students to be their own teachers, to teach each other.

At times the students must suggest alternate forms of response to each other, must suggest other material.

The teacher encourages the students to teach the teacher and show how they can ask each other to elaborate or check responses.

The teacher encourages the students to try new things.

The teacher points out parts of the work that might lead to different understandings.

Most of all, the teacher seeks to make students aware of how much they already know, how much they already feel, how much they already understand, and how they can deal with their areas of ignorance, unfeeling, and misunderstanding. The teacher encourages the students to be articulate, inquisitive, and imaginative.

Being this kind of a teacher is risky—very risky. You don't know what is going to happen. You partially control the play and certainly note the out-come. But come out from behind the shelter of certainty and teachers' guides. It's fun.

Reference

Rosenblatt, Louise. *Literature as Exploration*. New York: Noble and Noble, 1968.

Resources

Beach, Richard. *A Teacher's Introduction to Reader-Response Theories*. Urbana, IL: National Council of Teachers of English, 1993.

Benton, Michael, and Geoff Fox. *Teaching Literature: Nine to Fourteen*. London: Oxford University Press, 1985.

Bruner, Jerome S. *Actual Minds, Possible Worlds*. Cambridge, MA: Harvard University Press, 1987.

Eeds, Maryann, and Deborah Wells. "Grand Conversations: An Exploration of Meaning Construction in Literature Study Groups." *Research in the Teaching of English* 23 (1989): 4–29.

Karolides, Nicholas, J. *Reader Response in the Classroom: Evoking and Interpreting Meaning in Literature*. New York: Longman, 1992.

Koch, Kenneth. *Rose Where Did You Get That Red? Teaching Great Poetry to Children*. New York: Random House, 1974.

Mandel, Barrett J. H., Jr., ed. *Three Language Arts Curriculum Models: Pre-Kindergarten through College*. Urbana, IL: National Council of Teachers of English, 1980.

Moffet, James, and Betty J. Wagner. *A Student-Centered Language Arts Curriculum, Grades K–13*, 3rd ed. Boston: Houghton Mifflin, 1983.

Murison-Travers, D. Molly. "The Poetry Teacher: Behaviour and Attitudes." *Research in the Teaching of English* 18 (1984): 367–385.

chapter **6**

Putting Your Mouth Where Your Money Is: The Role of Talk in a Community of Readers

But I did not, in life, love Miss Duling. I was afraid of her high-arched bony nose, her eyebrows lifted in half-circles above her hooded, brilliant eyes, and of the Kentucky R's in her speech, and the long steps she took in her hightop shoes. I did nothing but fear her bearing-down authority, and did not connect this (as of course we were meant to) with our own need or desire to learn, perhaps because I already had this wish, and did not need to be driven.

Eudora Welty, One Writer's Beginnings

In many English classroom, teachers teach and students "student." As teachers, we stand up in front of the room and impart wisdom with great authority. Students talk when given permission; otherwise they listen (or pretend to listen) or talk to their friends or write notes or worse.

When we talk about literature we like to think we are having a conversation with our students, yet we carefully guide and monitor that conversation so as to end up at a certain point. We are concerned that what's important or significant about the story will be addressed. Important and significant to whom?

This is how some high school students describe the literature discussions in their classrooms:

"I don't pay attention half the time. It's easier just to read the story. When the teacher explains it, she twists it all around."

"In class discussions, we sort of have our own opinions but they get sort of pushed aside. When the teacher focuses on something, we usually pay attention to her."

"I guess what you do is answer the questions and hopefully maybe you might express some of your feelings along with it."

We engage students in an elaborate dance, choreographing a series of questions and answers that lead toward the "class theme." Often that dance begins with the plot; delves into character, symbolism, style perhaps; and ends with *the meaning.* Students are often amazed and somewhat relieved that the meaning, until then hidden, is uncovered by the teacher's discourse.

This discourse cycle goes something like this: The teacher asks a question, the student answers, and the teacher either interrupts the answer (if it's on the "wrong" track), evaluates that answer, elaborates on the answer (to make it more correct), calls on another student, or answers it herself or himself. Questions asked this way have been called "closed" questions. That is, classroom questions are already answered before they are asked. This type of teaching results in a recitation, with the teacher as the focal point.

In 1956, William Waller described the voice in classrooms as the "didactic voice . . . the voice of authority and ennui. There is in it no emotion, no wonder, no question, no argument" (Edwards and Furlong, 1978, p. 24). Has much changed?

Here's what one student said about his experience with literature and schooling:

> In the first grade, they teach you, they ask you. "How did you like this story?" And then you tell them and you don't have to give them evidence so from second grade on they say, "I want you to give hard evidence and support your ideas," and before you know it you're writing five paragraph essays and they say, "Well, don't use your opinions in your thesis now." And gradually they allow you to use less and less of your emotions until it's not allowed. That's where we are now. I don't get any emotional reaction out of my reading anymore. All teachers want you to do is tell them how this relates to the theme they've given you. What the tests essentially say is "This is the theme, give me evidence." It's like OK that was fun. Instead of saying, "How did you feel about the story? Give examples in your answers."

The descriptions and quotes above describe particular types of interpretive communities—communities in which the interpretive authority rests with the teacher or the text or the teacher's guide. These communities often exist in secondary schools and sometimes in colleges. They are developed in elementary and middle school. These communities support a particular way of reading that is something like what the New Critics described as "close textual reading" and is sometimes called an element or academic approach to teaching literature.

We're taught to break it down, hard and rigid: plot, theme, point of view, and all the elements of a short story.

Another kind of community supports the "main idea" approach to teaching reading; only, in literature class it's the Hidden Meaning.

But how does this affect students' enjoyment of literature? What happens when students no longer have someone to tell them the theme or the hidden meaning?

What if you went to the movies with a friend and afterward you got some dinner and your friend said, "Who were the main characters? What happened in the movie? Who was the narrator?"

Students learn how to read by participating in interpretive communities where people read and talk about what they read. The norms or strategies of interpretation that they learn are the ones that are directly or indirectly signaled to them through the discourse patterns of these communities. Most students are astute learners of the social rules of the classroom: when they can talk, with whom they can talk, what they can say, and how they can say it. Often it takes a week or two to "catch on" to a new teacher. Often the process can be demeaning and can hamper learning. We would like to see classroom communities that are ennobling and that support students' engagement with literature—communities in which individuals may struggle for their own ways of reading and their own interpretations and in which they are heard.

Here is how students say discussions help them interpret literature:

"There is usually a class theme. Everyone gets the same idea. They read the story and then the teacher will tell them what she interpreted and the class will say, 'Oh yeah, that's right.' We don't really form the ideas."

"Usually you find out what the themes are from the teacher. They have to tell you before a test."

"We all have one idea of what the theme is and that's a lot easier for the teacher also. So when she grades something, she can just say she has established the main theme."

Then What a Does Response-Based Classroom Sound Like?

In a response-based classroom, teachers and students really listen to each other. Students have a broader range of expression, and they can even talk to each other. Feelings are shared and authority is shared. Discussions emanate from students' feelings, questions, and responses and build toward a class interpretation or several interpretations that are truly class interpretations, not just the teacher's or the one in the textbook and the one that is

expected on the test. There is as much student talk as teacher talk; sometimes it seems like everyone is talking at once. (Sometimes it's quiet.) Students explain things to each other. Students are allowed to disagree with
each other and with the teacher.

In these classrooms, talk is what Douglas Barnes (1976) describes as
"exploratory" rather than "final draft" talk. In exploratory talk, ideas are only
half-formed and they can be revised based on what other people say and do.
As Edwards and Mercer put it in their book, *Common Knowledge* (1987),
when people communicate and negotiate meanings, "there is a real possibility that by pooling their experiences they achieve a new level of understanding beyond that which [they] had before." (p. 3)

When students and teacher explore ideas and negotiate understandings,
classroom talk more closely reflects how people really read and talk about literature (outside of school). This might be called a response-based interpretive community, but how does it happen?

Suppose you want to teach the poem "Nikki-Rosa," which follows:

NIKKI-ROSA

childhood remembrances are always a drag
if you're Black
you always remember things like living in Woodlawn
with no inside toilet
and if you become famous or something
they never talk about how happy you were to have your mother
all to yourself and
how good the water felt when you got your bath from one of those big
tubs that folk in chicago barbecue in
and somehow when you talk about home
it never gets across how much you
understood their feelings
as the whole family attended meetings about Hollydale
and even though you remember
your biographers never understand
your father's pain as he sells his stock
and another dream goes
and though you're poor it isn't poverty that
concerns you
and though they fought a lot
it isn't your father's drinking that makes any difference
but only that everybody is together and you
and your sister have happy birthdays and very good christmasses
and I really hope no white person ever has cause to write about
me because they never understand Black love is Black wealth and
they'll

probably talk about my hard childhood and never understand that
all the while I was quite happy

Nikki Giovanni

After the students read the poem or you read it to them, you could ask
the questions in the book that would promote a literal rereading of the
poem:

What are some of the narrator's happy memories?

Or you could really kill it by getting right to the point:

What wouldn't the narrator want a white biographer to write about her
childhood?

Or you could somehow try to capture the students' feelings about the poem:

How did this poem make you feel?

Or capture their idiosyncratic responses:

What do you think is the most significant word in the poem?

Or find out how they respond to the writer:

What question would you like to ask the poet?

Or better yet, don't ask any questions at all. Questions somehow always get
misconstrued because students are so used to assuming the teacher already
has *the* answer and that they just need to guess what's in her head. We have
rendered mute so many students who are afraid they will give the "wrong"
answer.

VIGNETTE VI: TALK AS RESPONSE

In one classroom, a teacher asked the students to pretend the poem was
sent to them as a letter, and after they read it, asked them to write back.
  Here's what they wrote:

Dear Nikki:

  I sometimes think about my early childhood years, too. All
childhood memories are different. I understand what your childhood was like and even though you didn't have some of the
things that other people had you had something more special:

your family. Some people have everything a person would dream for but they are not happy. I think you have a lot of courage and you are not selfish at all.

Amy

I got your poem. It was very touching. When you put your childhood life down on paper you make it sound so distinct.

Heather

It is very hard to say something about a poem like this.

Dan

I know that being Black is hard, for I am, but being proud of yourself makes you just like anyone else if you are happy and you know that you are being all you can be.

Sandy

I don't know how you can be so happy when your father drinks and your parents fight a lot.

Joe

If Black love is Black wealth, what is white love?

Susan

You say your childhood remembrances are always a drag, if you're Black. What were some of your memories that were such a drag? Also, what do you mean Black love is Black wealth? Please write back and explain these things to me.

Gloria

I don't think the first line of your poem needed to be put in.

Kenny

When I first read your letter I really didn't know how to react. I was deeply saddened, but then I thought you were happy. Why should I become sad reading about how you were happy? (Did you follow that?) I'm really glad you sent the letter and I'm really glad I had a chance to respond.

Adam

Dear Mrs. Giovanni:

I really can't relate to your poem, but I would like to say that I know my mother, Linda, would. The poem describes her child-hood, too, from the things she has told me. . . . I wish she could get to know you. Although I didn't relate to it, I was really touched by your poem and I think my mother would be, too.

Jason

Any two or three of these letters could be discussed for a whole class period. Why is it hard to say something about a poem like this? Why did Adam feel saddened even though the poet said she was happy? Why couldn't Jason relate to it even though he knew exactly who would relate to it and why?

And what about those first two lines? Why shouldn't they be there? How are they different from the rest of the poem? And what makes Heather say that the poet's life sounds so "distinct"? How *could* she be happy when her father drank and her parents fought?

Can anyone explain to Gloria why black love is black wealth? And to Susan what white wealth is?

These may not be the issues you would want to discuss when teaching this poem but these are the real questions of the students. You may have wanted to discuss the juxtaposition of happy and sad images in one line or the nature of free verse. You are entitled as a member of the interpretive community to bring up your responses to students. But if they are important it is likely they will come up anyway: "How come it doesn't rhyme? I thought poetry had to rhyme."

This is a good place to share your expertise. Students need to know about literary genres and about the analytical tools of literary study—as long as they don't replace response.

Vignette VI continued
Let's listen to parts of the discussion that followed:

ST: It seems like she's feeling sorry for herself at the beginning of the letter.

ST: But if she felt sorry for herself why did she say she was happy at the end?

ST: Yeah. If she wasn't trying to show the bad things why did she write the first two lines? That if you're black, childhood remembrances are always a drag.

ST: She's saying that she's getting sick of other people feeling sorry for her.

ST: She doesn't want you to feel sorry for her. She just wants you to know she had it bad in her life.

ST: I think she contradicts herself by saying how bad it was and that she was happy anyway.

T: Let's explore these contradictions.

ST: How can someone be happy when your father drinks and your parents fight? She said she was happy; she may have been but I wouldn't' have been with a drunk father and living in poverty. I wouldn't like that. It makes me realize . . .

ST: I wouldn't be happy either with a drinking father.

ST: She was with people she loved and cared about. I didn't think she had a bad childhood.

ST: She wanted people to know that even if you have it rough you can still be happy. Some people may not realize that.

ST: I think she just wanted white people to know what her life was like, how she grew up. I don't think she was trying to make people feel sorry for her. She had it sort of rough but she wasn't trying to make people feel sorry for her.

ST: She liked her life. She wanted to say that you can always pull something good out of something bad. She said all the while she was happy.

ST: She's saying if people would concentrate on the good instead of the bad they would see it more.

ST: What would bring this to her mind to write this poem?

T: I don't know. Why do you think she wrote the poem?

ST: Maybe she had something inside she wanted to get out. Maybe she had this on her mind for a long time and she thought people should know. Because when people are famous other people talk about the bad things in their life. But maybe she wanted to say she was happy.

ST: She must have had it bottled up inside her.

ST: She might have just written to say what it was like to grow up black. She didn't necessarily want to make a point.

T: I think you're right. We tend to assume writers write only to convey a message or a point. But that's not necessarily the case, is it?

ST: It's just an expression of feeling. Her anger and frustration. To say that there were good things that happened, too.

. . .

T: What words stood out for you?

ST: Black.

ST: Love.

T: Someone asked in their letter if black love is black wealth; what's white wealth?

ST: Money, money, money.

ST: Health.

ST: You can't live on love.

T: Who has money in our society?

ST: Movie stars, drug pushers.

T: Are these our heroes?

ST: My mother is my hero. She could have left me but she didn't and she takes care of me.

T: Does anyone else have heroes close to home? A local hero?

ST: My grandmother is someone I can talk to; we shop and go to lunch and we talk. She'll give me advice and I love her for it.

T: She's given you things that have no price tag.

. . .

ST: I told her (the author) her letter was very touching.

T: What did you find touching about it?

ST: It made me think how grateful I was because she had a bad life. But I found it depressing.

. . .

ST: Why is Hollydale and Woodlawn capitalized and Chicago isn't?

ST: Maybe she didn't think Chicago was as important.

When students start talking about their responses there will be natural disagreements, differing feelings, and possibly different interpretations. But there is a tendency to converge on an interpretation, too, albeit in different ways. These students seem to agree that the poem expressed frustration about misunderstandings. But they found the expression of other things, too, like love and happiness and being black and famous and the worth of money. And they noticed that it didn't rhyme and that capitalizations carried meaning.

The poem made some of them think about their own life and the people in it. And they listened to each other. Mostly.

Many things about the poem were said. Many things were left unsaid.

If you are concerned about whether students are learning about how to read and analyze literature, look again. The students discussed the following "literary aspects" of the poem:

Tone ("she's feeling sorry for herself")

Irony ("if she wasn't trying to show")

Structure ("she contradicts herself")

Diction ("what words stand out")

Mood ("her anger and frustration")

Atmosphere ("her letter was very touching")

Metaphor ("what's white wealth")

Paradox ("she said all the while she was happy")

Symbolism ("what words stood out for you")

Symbolic punctuation ("why is Hollydale and Woodlawn capitalized?")

They also engaged in the following:

Analysis
Interpretation
Generic criticism
Evaluation of style
Evaluation of impact
Evocation
Analogical reasoning

Not bad! And what did the teacher do?

Listened and recognized what was happening. Encouraged. Asked for more. Took a lot of chances.

Once students are able and willing to express their responses, the language of literary criticism becomes a tool—a language they can use to extend their ability to read, understand, analyze, and talk about literature and people and life.

Broadening Students' Use of Interpretive Strategies

One way to show students that there is not one way of reading, but many ways, is to provide opportunities for students to share the process of interpretation and the strategies that other readers use. Students may also enter into the professional critical conversation by reading various critical articles on a piece of literature.

VIGNETTE VII: EXPANDING INTERPRETIVE STRATEGIES

In one classroom, we asked students to read Hemingway's short story, "A Clean Well-Lighted Place" (1965). After reading the story, students first constructed their own preliminary thematic responses and shared them with the class:

> Think of your home. Every day you come back to it and you cook and watch TV and sleep in it. People are there to talk to you and understand you. This is not the case for the old man in the story. The story centered on the difference between his home and the cafe that was "a clean well-lighted place."

> I think this story is about the difference between young and old. It shows that the younger waiter just wants the old man to go home and even says he wishes his suicide attempt had been successful, which is extremely insensitive. The older waiter sym-

pathizes with the old man and is more sensitive to his wanting to stay in a "clean well-lighted place."

It is through the waiter's introspection that Hemingway expresses his theme that some people believe that everything is nothing and is worth nothing and how nothing really matters. However, he still believes he should try to make everything as nice as it can be. He is a realist and an idealist at the same time.

In the discussion that followed, the teacher asked students to elaborate on their written responses and talk about why they focussed on a particular aspect of the story:

T: Quite a few of you wrote about the theme of the young versus the old in the story in terms of the younger waiter and the older waiter. Let's see, Bob, do you want to start by telling us why you thought that was an important theme?

ST: I remember putting that in as one of two possible themes. It was basically because of the differences in what the two waiters thought of themselves and other people. The young waiter was very concerned about himself and he just kept saying, "I just want to go home and go to bed," and the older waiter feels more concern with the people and the world around him. And he showed that by opening the cafe to people who might need it.

ST: Well, I think the light versus dark theme is more important. It kind of goes along with the young and old theme because, well, the light imagery goes with the older waiter because he liked the lighted place and that it was a bright place. And also the younger waiter like the dark place. Well, that's what I thought.

T: Karen, you mentioned the light and dark theme but you saw it a little differently. Can you tell us about that?

ST: What I thought about the light and dark theme was that the old waiter is dark and the younger waiter is light because the older waiter and the old man had to go to light places and couldn't sleep until it was light, but the young waiter already had light in his life—a wife and comfort—so he didn't need the light.

T: So he didn't seek it out.

ST: Yeah.

T: So either way we might say that the contrasting themes of lightness and darkness are central to our interpretation of the story.

During the discussion of the various themes addressed in the student papers, the teacher pointed out the kinds of strategies the students were using. For instance, some students drew on their responses to the characters (or the contrast between characters), while others responded to the imagery, the central conflict, what they knew about the author, or even the significance of the title.

The teacher then introduced critical pieces published in scholarly books and journals. Critics such as Wayne Booth and David Lodge have drawn on Hemingway's other works and his style as well as his life to draw conclusions about the themes of the work; and, of course, they come to very different conclusions about what those themes are.

In their own final versions of their interpretive essays, the students tended to weave together their original ideas with those of the other students, and sometimes they incorporated ideas from the published critical works as well:

> Although even after the class discussion I'm not absolutely sure what the meaning of the story is, I have discovered a few themes: the bar/cafe theme, the theme of lightness and darkness, and the theme of young versus old. It seems like young people, such as the young waiter, somewhat seem to live more and thrive more during the daylight, while older people, even though they need light, were more like night people. Another theme along those lines is the dirty dark bar as opposed to a lighted and clean cafe. The older waiter could see how important the cafe was to people like the old man in the story. So the bar/cafe theme and the light and dark theme can be incorporated into the young and old theme because the views and tastes of the older people in the story are compared to those of younger people. The older people, like the older waiter, basically see life like Hemingway as nothing (*nada*).

The students continued to struggle with their understandings of the story, but they were now able to enter into the critical conversation because a range of interpretive strategies were made available to them. No longer did the teacher tell them THE theme before the test; instead, the students were encouraged to take responsibility for their own interpretations. This way students are invited into the interpretive process so they can develop their own strategies for coping with complex literary texts. Their responses became richer and more intertextual.

As one student later said, "We might as well get used to it because I don't think there's always going to be someone there telling you what the [interpretation] is, so it's good to figure out what you can for yourself."

Sounds Good. How Do I Change My Community?

If you suddenly change from one kind of community to another, students will get angry because you've changed the rules. You will have to change it carefully (like those porcupines). It will take time for them to believe that you really want to hear what they have to say and that their readings are as valid as anyone else's. Your tests will have to change, too. But more on that later.

Here's what some students said when their community changed.

> . . . it became the students explaining it to other students instead of the teacher. . . . I thought it was good because a lot of the students have different outlooks, different points of view. It was a lot better, because I wasn't being graded on the teacher's interpretation, because she didn't give us one. We were all kind of mad at her for not giving us one, but it may be better for us because it gives us a chance to interpret the way we want.

A good place to begin is to audio- or videotape your class discussions. Listen and watch. What role do you play in the discussion? W hat kinds of questions do you ask? (Ones that already have an answer? What do you do if you get a different answer?) What do you do if someone doesn't raise his or her hand right away. What role do the students play? Do they try to figure out your answers or their own? Do you say something in between each student's utterance? Are you constantly evaluating student responses? Do the students ever talk to each other (about literature)? What are you signaling to students about how to read literature? Do you get a sense of how the *students* responded to the text?

Are you trying to remain in control?

How can you let go?

This Is a Lot to Think about and Change

You could begin by thinking of other ways to stimulate discussion besides asking questions. Have them write first, because writing is often a way to begin a good discussion. Response journals (see Chapter 10) are growing more popular as a way to record students' initial and ongoing responses to literature. You can also start by using a rating scale (Chapter 5) or visuals (Chapter 8) or planning a dramatic activity (Chapter 7) and then have a discussion. There will be plenty to talk about then.

When you do ask questions, ask ones that have no particular answer. Try not to say something right away after a student says something—see if anyone else wants to respond first—and then ask the student to say more, to elaborate or clarify or explain. Listen carefully.

Few things are more gratifying for a teacher than having a real and lively discussion about a good piece of literature.

> You could look at reading a poem this way: if you are thinking and there is a window nearby, you may look out—far. Your thinking will connect now and then to the scene, whenever something out there strikes your attention. Or, even more aptly, you might have a friend with you, and you would interchange, offer beginnings, slanted ideas, linked progressions. There would be a series of mental incidents, not predictable, never to be fully anticipated without the experience that comes about through following the sequence onward, point by point. Your experience would be richer—more would happen—than if you had been alone. (Stafford, 1978, pp. 5-6)

What about Other Kinds of Talk Besides Large-Group Discussions?

If you really want students to talk to each other, you can let them talk to each other in small groups (without you). Talk in small groups is likely to be productive exploratory talk, if students are cooperative and treat each other as equals and with respect.

We remember one teacher saying, "I heard and read a lot about using small groups and so in the beginning of the year I tried it and it was a disaster." Several things are important to keep in mind if you want to set up small-group discussions.

Students need to know what they are supposed to talk about in small groups, such as:

> Argue about an established interpretation.
> Think of issues for the class to discuss.
> Interview each other.
> Talk about what would go into a computer program.
> Rewrite the ending of a story.
> Work on a dramatic activity.

They also need to know what kinds of things they will be expected to produce: a consensus, a list, a paper, a poem, a tableau of a scene from a story.

They should be able to renegotiate and reformulate those goals and procedures.

It is also useful to establish social guidelines for participating in small groups, such as: How does a student gain the floor? Under what conditions can a student interrupt another student? How can it be assured that every student will get a turn? Is one person designated a recorder, a leader? What happens when the group gets off task?

When you circulate from group to group you can encourage productive activity and find out if there are any problems or questions or needed clarifications. We have found that eavesdropping on small groups is one of the most interesting parts of the day.

Think about the outcome of the group work. How will small-group contributions be shared with the rest of the class? What do they contribute to the ongoing interpretations of literature? How do they help build community in your classroom?

Once students know how to work together, you might suggest that they choose their own books to read and talk about just to each other. You might want to set up reading and writing "workshops."

Proceed slowly and, yes, carefully.

Moving toward a Reader-Based Community

In order to build a reader-based community, you will have to relearn how to teach, and students will have to relearn how to "student." In fact, students will have to learn how to teach, and teachers will have to learn how to "student." Everyone will have to learn how to talk to one another in ways that promote learning and response.

Teachers can no longer be the experts, or at least the only experts. (This is not to say they can't or shouldn't share their expertise.)

The class talkers will need to become listeners, and the listeners, talkers.

Feelings will count as much as intellect.

Literary terms can be used to scaffold and bolster responses, but not to build them.

Finally, reading and talking about literature inside the classroom will be a little bit more like reading and talking about literature outside the classroom.

References

Barnes, Douglas. *From Communication to Curriculum*. New York: Penguin, 1976.

Edwards, A. and Furlong, V. J. *The Language of Teaching*. London: Heinemann, 1978.

Edwards, Derek, and Neil Mercer. *Common Knowledge: The Development of Understanding in the Classroom*. London: Methuen, 1987, 3.

Stafford, William. *Writing the Australian Crawl: Views on the Writer's Vocation*. Ann Arbor, MI: University of Michigan Press, 1978, pp. 5-6.

Welty, Eudora. *One Writer's Beginnings*. Cambridge, MA: Harvard University Press, 1983, 23–24.

Resources

Atwell, Nancie. *In the Middle: Writing, Reading and Learning with Adolescents*. Upper Montclair, NJ: Boynton/Cook, 1987.

Barnes, Douglas, James Britton, and Harold Rosen. *Language, the Learner, and the School*. New York: Penguin, 1970.

Bleich, David. *Readings and Feelings: An Introduction to Subjective Criticism*. Urbana, IL: National Council of Teachers of English, 1975.

Bleich, David. *The Double Perspective: Language, Literary and Social Relations*. Urbana, IL: National Council of Teachers of English, 1988.

Edwards, Anthony D., and David P. G. Westgate. *Investigating Classroom Talk*. London: The Falmer Press, 1987.

Fish, Stanley. *Is There a Text in This Class? The Authority of Interpretive Communities*. Cambridge, MA: Harvard University Press, 1980.

Hynds, Susan, and Donald Rubin. *Perspectives on Talk and Learning*. Urbana, IL: National Council of Teachers of English, 1990.

Marland, Michael. *Language across the Curriculum*. London: Heinemann Educational Books, 1977.

Rogers, Theresa. "A Point, Counterpoint Response Strategy for Complex Short Stories." *Journal of Reading* 34, no. 4 (1991): 278–82.

Rogers, Theresa. *Students as Literary Critics*. A case study of the interpretive experiences, processes and communities of ninth-grade students. *Journal of Reading Behavior* 23, no. 4 (1991): 391–424.

Willinsky, John. *The Triumph of Literature/The Fate of Literacy: English in the Secondary School Curriculum*. New York: Teachers College Press, 1991.

chapter 7

Drama: Creating, Improvising, Performing

Drama?

   Do you mean we are going down to the auditorium and we are going to put on costumes and greasepaint and put on a play?

   Do you mean we are going to pretend to be a tree?

   Oh, you mean readers' theater.

Drama can mean many different things to different people. The kind of drama we want to talk about first is "process drama." It can take place in the classroom, it is largely unrehearsed, students and the teacher usually role-play real people, and it is not "theater"; that is, it is informal and without actor/audience separation. It draws on students' natural abilities to pretend, role-play, make believe.

   This kind of drama is not scripted or rehearsed. It focuses on the dramatic process and incorporates improvisational and teacher-in-role strategies to create new dramatic contexts in the classroom. The dramatic worlds that arise through improvised drama are developed and sustained largely through talking and careful listening and responding.

OK, but What Does All This Have to Do with Responding to Literature, Anyway?

When students encounter the literary text through drama, the world of the drama intermingles with the world of the reader and the world of the text (see Figure 7.1). Students are able to participate in what Rosenblatt (1978) calls the "lived through" experience of a literary transaction.

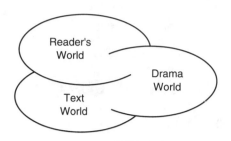

FIGURE 7.1   Interacting Worlds
in Literary Encounters

Let's start with an example. (It is one we learned from Cecily O'Neill, coauthor of a useful guide, *Drama Structures* [1982].)

VIGNETTE VIII: DRAMA AS RESPONSE

We worked with a ninth-grade class that was reading *To Kill a Mockingbird*, by Harper Lee. We wanted the students to really feel what it was like to live in the town of Maycomb—to experience what kind of people lived there.

We started by explaining to the students that we wanted to help them get "inside" the story; that they wouldn't be asked to perform but that they would be asked to pretend a little. Then we divided them into pairs. One was A and the other was B. (If you want groups of three, then one is A and two are Bs.) Then we talked for a few minutes with the students about what is was like in a small Southern town in the 1930s. The Bs were asked to pretend they were a person in Maycomb—not necessarily a named character, such as Miss Maudie or Miss Stephanie or Scout, but anyone who might live in the town: a postal clerk, a barber, a child—whoever might have a perspective on what is happening there.

We asked them to imagine that we were 1930s radio producers who wanted to do a documentary on small-town life in the South. We asked the As to pretend we had hired them as reporters to gather information for the documentary, and explained that we needed some very good reporters. We talked about what skills they would need to capture the nature of a town like Maycomb (how to speak naturally with the people, make them comfortable, dig up a story, etc.).

We explained that oftentimes it is more interesting to take on a point of view in the role you are playing. For instance, as a producer, you might want a "nice" (i.e., censored) portrait of the town—nothing sensationalist—which will likely set you up for an interesting discussion or reflection session later.

We then gave the students time to interview and be interviewed. Some took notes. We walked around and gave support for their interactions as reporter and townsperson as needed.

We met back with the reporters first, asking them to come to the center of the room while the townspeople listen in from the back of the room. We asked them what they had learned from their interviews. They had heard about:

> A mad dog named Tim Johnson who had to be shot.
> The strange Radley family.
> The first snowfall in fifty years.
> A schoolteacher who doesn't want her students to know how to read before they come to school.
> A fire.
> And, of course, the impending trial.

We insisted that the story about a supposed rape and a white lawyer defending a Negro is too sensationalist to put in the documentary. We wanted a "nice" documentary about a small and quiet Southern town. This provoked discussion in role (and out of role when we were done).

Next, we explored the townspeople's perspectives. To do that we changed our roles to that of people in the town—a leading citizen, a storeowner, and a milkman. We then met with the townspeople at a town meeting after church to discuss these strange interviewers gadding about town. We asked the townspeople what kinds of questions they'd been asked. They told us they had been asked about:

> Their families: the children and grandchildren and husbands.
> What they do with their time.
> What it's like to live in the town.
> The fire.
> The dog.
> And the trial.
> Then one of us challenged the townspeople:

> "You didn't tell them about the trial, did you? I don't know what's gotten into that Atticus to defend a Negro, a respected member of society like he was . . ."

And a "townsperson" (student) responded in a slightly Southern accent:

"And still is. I think Atticus has a right to defend who he wants. In all my years I've never seen the difference between a white man and a Negro, anyway."

And the town leader replied:

"And it's just this sort of thing that's splitting up this town . . ."
   "Well, I'll just leave then, if that's how you feel" (and she "left"—in the dramatic sense).

And for that moment, it seemed as though we were really there in Maycomb.

What does this kind of dramatic activity accomplish? <u>It allows students to get inside the story in a tangible way</u>. It might give them new perspectives on the story.
   For instance, one student said, "As a townsperson, I agreed with the town leader, but as me, I didn't."

> Learning in drama is basically a reframing. What knowledge a pupil has is placed in a new perspective. To take on a role is to detach oneself from what is implicitly understood and to blur temporarily the edges of a given world. . . . The ambivalent position between fiction and reality is what creates drama's potency. Attempts by teachers to set up drama as a piece of real life to be lived through is to misunderstand drama. On the other hand attempts by teachers merely to train children to be performers misses drama's potential for significant learning. *(Gavin Bolton, 1985, pp. 155-156)*

What do the students think of it?

> Before a story was just a story, but with drama it became like real life. . . . It's not only that you're reading the story but you're participating in it, like you're in the story. . . . They're writing about you or you're in it. It makes it a lot more fun.
> It helps us to see the situation from the character's point of view.
> It's like I was right in the town.
> I am surprised I liked it. I thought that I'd have to get up in front of the class—the groups were better in the sense that everyone was focusing on the same topic. And I also thought that one had to be very creative.
> I didn't think I'd like dramatic activities, but now I'd rather have dramatic activities than regular class.

According to Cecily O'Neill and Alan Lambert (1982, pp. 11-12), in order to do drama in the classroom students must be able to

* Make believe with regard to actions and objects.
* Adopt a role.

- Maintain the dramatic context (the make-believe) and interact with the rest of the group in a cooperative (not competitive) way.
- Understand and accept the rules of the game. (Sometimes you will have to make the rules more explicit: How did you feel about me as a documentary producer? You're allowed to tell me.)

According to Dorothy Heathcote, this "mantle of the expert system of teaching involves a reversal of the conventional teacher-student role relationship in which the students draw on the knowledge and expertise of the teacher . . . the teacher assumes a fictional role which places the student in the position of being the 'one who knows' " (1985, p. 173).

That is, the dramatic context provides a way for students to discover what *they* know about the story, about their feelings and responses, and about the world.

As one teacher said:

If I stood up in front of the room and tried to tell them to feel the way a certain character felt, it wouldn't have done any good. But when they role-played the part, when they turned into a local townsperson, when they became, say, Stephanie Crawford, then they knew what she felt like.

But I'm Not a Drama Teacher

You don't have to be. All you need is a little imagination, a willingness to take risks in front of your students, and some practice. Some theatrical skills are handy, but you will develop some as you go along. For instance, you will learn to be more convincing in role without overacting.

You will develop some directing skills, too. You will learn to structure the drama from the inside. You will figure out what to do if it's not working—if no dramatic context is being built. Do the students know who they are? Is there something interesting to interact about? Are they listening to each other? It's all right to go out of role to redirect or regroup, and then go back in. O'Neill and Lambert (1982) also offer these guidelines:

- Move the pupils into the drama quickly and economically by inviting an immediate response to the role.
- Present the kind of challenge which may help to focus the pupils' thinking and lead them into a more concerned involvement with the context of the enquiry.
- Provide a model for the pupils' contributions by demonstrating appropriate language, attitudes, action, and commitment.

ʄ Offer encouragement and support through [your] own involvement.

In role, the teacher can be an actual listener, not an evaluator, and thus has a whole new range of communication strategies open to him or her. The teacher can operate through a wide spectrum of roles, as well as using the traditional teacher options of instructor, narrator, side coach. *(David Booth, 1988, p. 10)*

But What Are They Learning?

The discussions or reflection sessions you have during the dramatic activities or afterward provide an opportunity to discuss what happened and to explore what the students have learned about the events, the characters' personalities and feelings and relationships, and about the issues or themes in the story (such as loyalty and prejudice). Students will better understand what happened and why it happened, the characters' motivations, and even why the world was or is the way it is.

The town meeting helped me the most to understand *To Kill a Mockingbird*. It kind of gave me a picture in my mind of the people and the town and a better understanding of why things were what they were in that town.

It helped me understand the people and why they did certain things.

And they will see how the other students interpreted the work:

The town meeting helped me because I got other people's views of the characters.

I found that other people had found things in the story that I didn't and vice versa.

They are also learning how to talk to each other, how to ask each other questions, and how to listen carefully and contribute to the drama in appropriate ways. And they enjoy it.

It was fun because you could use your imagination.

And how often do students use their imagination in school? How often do they use their imaginations to respond to and interpret literature? How often do they have fun?

Dramatic activities also provide a stimulus and a focus for many different genres and functions of writing. We have found that it also gives voice to students' writing, which we don't otherwise hear.

For instance, after the dramatic activity we described, students may want to write a diary entry as Calpurnia, or Scout, or Boo Radley. Maybe it would be written many years later. Here is one example:

Dear Diary—

Today waz a horibl day. Mistur Finch cam hom during the Misionary Society meetin and I new somethin waz wrong cause he never comes hom durin the meetins. He cam in the kitchen and told me Tom had ben killed while trin to escape. Shot 17 times. I dont beleve them prizon guards. Tom wood never tri to escape nowin Atticus was trin his best to get him out. I just felt so bad when I had to tell Mz. Robison the news. I think it waz the worst thing I ever told anyone. When we got to ther house I didnt even hav to say anything.

She droped to the ground lik a sak of potatas. Ill never forget thiz day for the rest of my life.

Yours truly
Cal

The students may want to create a dialogue between two (or more) characters in town.

They may want to write up that documentary.

Or create a town newspaper, as did the students we worked with.

The Maycomb Times Guilty or Innocent?

Negro Tom Robinson has been accused of raping local nineteen-year-old Mayella Ewell. Sheriff Heck Tate describes her condition as severely beaten on the right side of her face with fingerlike bruises around her neck.

Robert Ewell, Mayella's father, claims that while he was carrying firewood back to the house he heard screaming and saw Robinson run off. Mayella said she asked Robinson to come in and help her chop up a chiffarobe for a nickel and when he came inside he tried to take advantage of her.

Link Deas, Robinson's employer, exclaimed, "I've never had a better worker in my life. Tom's been with me for eight years and I can't see him doing anything like that. Robinson had no comment.

The trial is this Saturday and Robinson will be defended by Atticus Finch.

Maycomb Unites to Put Out Blaze

A fire raged through the home of Miss Maudie Atkinson on Thursday, November 28th, at around 3:00 A.M. The fire was determined to be caused by some hanging plants that caught on fire from the fireplace in Miss Maudie's dining room. Miss Maudie said she had left the fire burning all night so her plants wouldn't freeze due to the extreme low temperature.

Maycomb County's sheriff, Mr. Heck Tate, successfully warned the citizens of Maycomb about the fire with the newly purchased town alarm siren. However, the old Maycomb fire truck stalled, so help was sought from Abbotsville and Clark's Ferry, sixty miles away. When the other fire squads arrived and attached their hoses to the hydrant, the water pipes exploded.

Although the fire devoured most of the house, the men of Maycomb salvaged some of the furniture and carried it to a yard across the street. Mr. George Avery, stuck in a window while trying to escape, fell from the second-story window, receiving minor back injuries.

Miss Maudie was thankful and appreciated the help she received. When asked about the damage to her home, Miss Maudie replied, "I hated that old cow barn anyway. Thought of settin' fire to it myself, except they'd lock me up."

It occurred to us that without the dramatic activities these students would not have written their newspapers with such enthusiasm and style.

When Is It Appropriate to Use Process Drama?

Almost always. Drama can be used with all kinds of literature—plays, of course, and novels, short stories, poems, and biographies. Almost any piece of text can become a "pre-text" for developing a dramatic activity (O'Neill, 1991). The dramatic world will illuminate and go beyond the original text. If you're tied to covering the material on your required list or in your literature anthology, you still have many wonderful pre-texts to draw from. The following example was done with the common anthology selection "When the Legends Die," by Hal Borland, the story of a Ute Indian boy who attends an agency school on a reservation.

VIGNETTE IX: CASTING STUDENTS INTO DIFFERENT SPACE AND TIME

The teacher was concerned that the main character would be too removed from the students' experiences. As she said, "We read so many books that cast students in a different place and time—*To Kill A Mock-*

ingbird, *Lord of the Flies*, and *When the Legends Die*, the story of a Ute Indian boy living in a white man's world. Without the quality of empathy, I don't know how students can begin to understand the character." The dramatic frame that was used was one that was familiar to them: a school. In role as the principal of the agency school, the teacher began by welcoming potential teachers to the school.

T: I'm very glad to welcome you here today to the agency school board. I must say I'm very impressed to see so many young people coming into the teaching profession and especially young people like yourselves interested in working under the rather difficult conditions we face here . . . I have to warn you that if you want to work with these young people it will take a good deal of dedication, a great deal of hard work, and sometimes it's very frustrating. These young people coming here, they have no sense of civilization.

S: Why did you take these children in? I mean why did you . . . why do you want them to be more civilized? Why don't you let them be like they want to?

T: Oh, well, like they want to . . . I mean what would that be like? They would be living in shacks in the mountains. They would be unclean. They would be living like wild animals.

S: That would be the way they want to live. That would be the way they were brought up to live.

T: But for our purposes, the civilized ones . . . we are here to educate them. We are here to give them a proper religion.

S: That's your education. They already have their type of education and their type of religion.

T: Yes, but it's not our type and we want them to be more like us.

S: Why?

T: Well, we want them to be citizens of the United States, for instance. We want them to be good citizens.

The students were already beginning to question, challenge, and contradict the teacher in role. The teacher stopped and became herself, encouraging students to reflect on what was happening.

T: Let's stop here for a minute. What do you think of the person I was being?

S: Very prejudiced. Very pushy. Not caring toward other people's feelings. Not very American.

T: Not very American. OK. You [indicating at student and gesturing] went like that once. Did you feel like hitting me?

S: Yeah.

T: You did?

s: Several times.

T: Several times. . . . What was there about me that made you so angry?

s: Like someone coming up to me and telling me that ever since I've been alive I've done wrong and I'm doing wrong . . . I'd laugh in their face.

T: I can see that you felt like that. . . . Was the person I was pretending to be a believable character?

s: Yes.

T: Have you ever met anybody like that?

ss: Yes. Yes.

After this reflection outside the drama, students were invited to choose to be either a prospective teacher or one of the Native-American students at the school. As they talked quietly together in small groups, it became apparent that some of the students were role-playing with greater commitment. In role as the principal again, the teacher spoke again to the prospective teachers.

T: Now do you have any further questions for me, or would you like to tell me how you found the visit? Do speak freely.

s: I understand their ways. I mean, I would be upset if someone came and took my ways away from me. So I understand where they are coming from.

s: And you guys don't seem to treat them very well either.

T: Well, what do you mean? How would you change that?

s: I don't know. You guys treat them like they're some different species. I mean different but—

s: They seem unhappy.

T: Unhappy? Did you all find that they were unhappy?

ss: Yeah. Yes. Yeah

T: Of course, you can't always trust what they say.

s: That's true.

s: You can see it in their faces.

T: You can see it in their faces? What do you mean by that exactly?

s: Well, like when you're talking to them, communicating with them, you can tell whether they are telling the truth or if they are lying.

T: Oh, I see. That's a very useful gift for a teacher, of course you know.

s: They also said you teachers came and took them.

s: Yeah, in the fields . . .

s: Came and took them.

At this point one student, who had taken on the role of a Native-American student, interrupted and began to role-play at a new level of engagement.

s: You took our homes. You expect us to adapt to your ways; why don't you adapt to ours? Our homes, our land. Tell us we have to change—to go to your ways.

t: Are you expecting me to go to your lodges? To your mountains?

s: This is our land. You came here . . . stole it.

t: Well, I'm afraid I don't agree with that . . . I mean . . .

s: How are you going to . . .

t: We made treaties with your people. All the time.

s: And broke them. Broke them. You lied. White man lied.

t: I don't pretend to be a politician; I'm just a teacher. I'm doing the best I can in difficult circumstances.

s. It was our world first. You never owned it. You took it from us.

s: We were here first.

The students had an opportunity to enter the dramatic world and truly empathize with a character who may at first have seemed remote. An overworked selection in a literature anthology briefly came alive, and the students and teacher were given permission to talk to each other in new ways. The use of reflection sessions provided students an opportunity to think more not just about the story but about Native Americans and cultures and history and racism, and they were given new ways to express themselves. Later, when they wrote interim reports on Thomas Black Bear, their level of engagement was apparent in their ability to capture the voices of teachers who were variously sympathetic and hostile toward Black Bear.

Several basic strategies can easily be used in the classroom to create drama activities. The first strategy is *teacher in role*, which is illustrated by the examples of the teacher in role as a radio producer and agency school principal. By using this strategy the teacher can frame and facilitate the drama. The second strategy, *interviewing*, can be carried out with students working in pairs or small groups. One student interviews another from a particular stance or viewpoint, as with the reports and townspeople in Maycomb, or the students and prospective teachers in the agency school. A third strategy is to set up an *inquiry* about the events in the work. A common question that can be asked is, Who's to blame? A character or community can participate in a town meeting or a trial in order to uncover untold events or details and to bring justice. All of these strategies can be used in a larger drama frame or context, such as a media event—a television talk show or documentary, for instance. A documentary on the treatment of Native Americans could include an inquiry into continuing discrimination, an interview with Thomas Black Bull, and tableaux (see Chapter 8) as visual evidence of issues or events.

Using informal dramatic activities can be a powerful way to draw on students' own responses to a literary work, extend those responses, and build community interpretations. It is a particularly useful way to allow students to take on various perspectives and to frame or reframe their responses; it allows them (and us) to momentarily get "inside" a literary work and see things from another perspective. Finally, dramatic activities transfer the authority for interpretations from the teacher back to the students, and they expand the forms and functions of language in the classroom. Process drama is fun but it is also a powerful learning medium.

Gaming

Another dramatic strategy is simulation gaming. There are many role-playing games available commercially, and many teachers have made up their own. Games are often used to help students understand the background of what they are reading. A game is planned in advance with a set of structured roles and activities as well as a period for reflection and debriefing. A teacher might give individual students or groups a set of cue cards telling them who they are and what their situation might be. A game based on a novel like Alice Walker's *The Color Purple* would establish the world of the Depression South and have students given role cards explaining the ways of white males and females and of African-American males and females. Students would be assigned to one of these four groups and then be asked to enact certain scenes of everyday life: encounters in a store, going to school, being paid for labor, preparing for a wedding or a funeral. At some times the races and these sexes would intersect, at others they would talk about each other. After the game is gone through for a brief period, the students would shift groups and enact another scene. The debriefing would include discussion of feelings, appropriate actions, and motives. Following this game, the teacher might take students to various historical sources in documentaries and textbooks. Then the reading of the novel would begin.

Scripted Drama and Oral Interpretation

Of course a great deal of the literature students read is itself dramatic, and a good part of the program should encourage the students to realize the dramatic potential. Performance Drama is also a form of response and interpretation. The performance of *Macbeth* is not the same as the script, just as the reading of a novel is not the same as the text. Students should be encouraged to use performance as a way of articulating their response to the text;

doing so will often force them to come to a decision about how they want others to perceive the text.

That's my last duchess painted on the wall . . .

If you were the Duke in Browning's poem, how would you say that line? Which word would you emphasize?

That's my last duchess painted on the wall . . . Proud?
That's my last duchess painted on the wall . . . Possessive?
That's my last duchess painted on the wall . . . Anticipatory?
That's my last duchess painted on the wall . . . Noble?
That's my last duchess painted on the wall . . . Aesthetic?
That's my last duchess painted on the wall . . . Questioning?
That's my last duchess painted on the wall . . . Unfeeling?

Which is right? Why not let the class decide? Then have them continue the characterization by reading through the rest of the poem. Groups could work up a set of different readings and tape them, then compare the effect.

A great deal of poetry was meant to be heard, to be shared as an oral experience. We think that nearly every poem should be read aloud. In the course of reading poems and dramas over a semester or a quarter, most students will develop an ear for the sound of different kinds of poetry. They will also begin to notice the particular effects that a given poet uses.

THE ECHOING GREEN

The Sun does arise,
And make happy the skies;
The merry bells ring
To welcome the Spring;
The skylark and thrush,
The birds of the bush,
Sing louder around
To the bells' cheerful sound,
While our sports shall be seen
On the Echoing Green.

Old John; with white hair,
Does laugh away care,
Sitting under the oak,
Among the old folk.
They laugh at our play,
And soon they all say:

"Such, such were the joys
When we all, girls and boys,
In our youth time were seen
On the Echoing Green."

Till the little ones, weary,
No more can be merry;
The sun does descend,
And our sports have an end.
Round the laps of their mothers
Many sisters and brothers,
Like birds in their nest,
Are ready for rest,
And sport no more seen
On the darkening Green.

William Blake

The simple, seemingly happy song has small changes from stanza to stanza. Which do they hear? What do the changes suggest?

DREAM VARIATIONS

To fling my arms wide
In some place of the sun,
To whirl and to dance
Till the white day is done.
Then rest at cool evening
Beneath a tall tree
While night comes on gently.
   Dark like me—
That is my dream!

To fling my arms wide
In the face of the sun,
Dance! Whirl! Whirl!
Till the quick day is done.
Rest at pale evening . . .
A tall, slim tree . . .
Night coming tenderly
   Black like me.

Langston Hughes

Are the two stanzas the same? One group could read the first and another the second at the same time. What sort of music would be a good background to the syncopation?

Of course some poems are meant to be read by more than one voice; then the students can try pairing:

THE PHOENIX

I am Phoenix

Phoenix
everlasting!
I am Phoenix

Immortal
eternal.
I live in
Arabia

eagle
My feathers are
scarlet,
purple
golden.

one

there have never been more.
I am my own
daughter
granddaughter
great-granddaughter
I was

will be
my gravedigger.

I gather up twigs of
sweet-smelling spices
and build a nest
on the top of a palm.

Then I wait for noon—

fire
I flap my wings

burst
into flames

I am Phoenix
the fire-bird!
Phoenix

I am Phoenix!
Immortal
eternal
undying.

Arabia
I'm as large as an
eagle

scarlet,
purple.
There is but
one
Phoenix—

I am my own
mother
grandmother
great-grandmother
I was
my own midwife,
will be

for each time I discover
I'm becoming old

sweet-smelling spices

I climb inside.

and when the sun's hot as fire

till the twigs beneath me
burst

which I fan

which I fan	with my wings
with my wings	and fan
and fan	and fan
	till the fire
and I	
are no more.	
Eight days pass.	Eight days pass.
The ashes cool.	
	Then, on the ninth day
in the morning,	
	at dawn,
just as the sun	
	rises in the east
I rise	I rise
from the ashes	
and fly upward—	
	a
new	new
	Phoenix,
my own	
mother	daughter
grandmother	granddaughter
great-grandmother	great-granddaughter
and on	
and on	and on
until the end of time.	until the end of time.

Paul Fleischman

One class that tried this began to develop a choral approach to much of
the poetry. In this poem, they placed the two "voices" in counterpoint or as
melody and harmony. They then moved to find poems that might be read
together like the two voices in the folk song "Scarborough Fair" or the invi-
tation and response poems of the sixteenth century.

THE PASSIONATE SHEPHERD TO HIS LOVE

Come live with me and be my love,
And we will all the pleasures prove
That valleys, groves, hills, and fields,
Woods, or steepy mountain yields.

And we will sit upon the rocks,
Seeing the shepherds feed their flocks,
By shallow rivers to whose falls
Melodious birds sing madrigals.

And I will make thee beds of roses
And a thousand fragrant posies,
A cap of flowers, and a kirtle
Embroidered all with leaves of myrtle;

A gown made of the finest wool
Which from our pretty lambs we pull;
Fair lined slippers for the cold,
With buckles of the purest gold;

A belt of straw and ivy buds,
With coral clasps and amber studs:
And if these pleasures may thee move,
Come live with me, and be my love.

The shepherds' swains shall dance and sing
For thy delight each May morning:
If these delights thy mind may move,
Then live with me and be my love.

Christopher Marlowe

ANSWER TO MARLOWE

If all the world and love were young,
And truth in every shepherd's tongue,
These pretty pleasures might me move
To live with thee and be thy love.

But time drives flocks from field to fold,
When rivers rage and rocks grow cold,
And Philomel becometh dumb;
The rest complain of cares to come.

The flowers do fade, and wanton fields
To wayward winter reckoning yields;
A honey tongue, a heart of gall,
Is fancy's spring, but sorrow's fall.

Thy gowns, thy shoes, thy beds of roses,
Thy cap, thy kirtle, and thy posies
Soon break, soon wither, soon forgotten,
In folly ripe, in reason rotten.

Thy belt of straw and ivy buds,
Thy coral clasps and amber studs,
All these in me no means can move
To come to thee and be thy love.

But could youth last and love still breed,

Had joys no date nor age no need,
Then these delights my mind might move
To live with thee and be thy love.
                                    Sir Walter Raleigh

They tried reading this pair, first alternating the whole poem and then stanza by stanza and then line by line. They then played the recordings of each to another class. There wasn't much more to say about the poems. The readings were the best articulation of a response they could come up with.

Poem after poem repays an oral reading. As the students gain experience, they show that they have learned a good deal about verification and about the tension between the way poems are set up on the page and the way they are read.

They lose the tendency to stop at the end of every line.

They begin to develop an ear for rhythms and meter and to read the poems as if they are poems, not bus tickets.

They begin to hear and present different voices.

They realize that by changing the voice they can control the interpretation.

They find that memorization isn't so hard, and it's fun.

They realize what Robert Frost meant about "the sound of sense."

Now, it is possible to have sense without the sound of sense (as in much prose that is supposed to pass muster but makes very dull reading) and the sound of sense without sense (as in *Alice in Wonderland*, which makes anything but dull reading). The best place to get the abstract sound of sense is from voices behind a door that cuts off the words. Ask yourself how these sentences would sound without the words in which they are embodied:

You mean to tell me you can't read?

I said no such thing.

Well, read then.

You're not my teacher.

                                    Frost, Selected Letters, *1964*

Some classes we have observed have taken these ideas and developed an extensive reading repertoire. The students took the reading out of the classroom and formed a group that read for various community functions. Choral reading can be as exciting and moving as choirs. It's an exciting way to present poetry.

But you don't have to go that far. Simply have the students read aloud and make the reading of the poem an aspect of the response. Sometimes, the reading is all you have to have. Sometimes the students will talk about the reading. A class that read Frost's dramatic poem "Home Burial" with three voices, one for the husband, one for the wife, and one for the narrator, burst into a furious discussion of the relationship between the two characters. They were split over whether she was crazy and unfaithful or he was a murderer. After half an hour they resolved the poem and tried another reading indicating that resolution. Both characters were sympathetic, but the wife came out on top.

And Then There Are Plays

Plays are meant to be heard and seen. They are not to sit on the page and be dissected. This statement is particularly true of Shakespeare. The dialogues that he wrote slipped by the ears fast. The actors did not stop to explain a phrase or repeat a line so that an audience could get it. Much of the imagery and complex language rushed by the audience so that it was the drift, not each individual segment, that was the focus. The words and lines are parts of a speech said by a character in a situation.

> The opening of *Hamlet* presents two scared soldiers half hoping they won't see a ghost.
> Act Three of *Julius Caesar* shows an assassination as hurried and confused as any that might be seen on a nightly news program.
> *Romeo and Juliet* are adolescents meeting on a first date.
> The porter's scene in *Macbeth* presents an ordinary world that contrasts with the horror of the murder in the scene before.

What is true of Shakespeare is true of other plays you will read with your students. They are meant to be seen and heard. The script is to help actors in their performance. That means that in class the plays should be performed. You are not going to turn your students into professional actors and you don't have to be a theatrical type to teach drama this way. But get your students out of their seats—and get off your own backside, too. It won't hurt; and you could have fun.

Reading plays means reading plays as drama. But there are a number of traps to beware of, particularly as a good number of your students are not actors and you aren't aiming for production.

> Take the play scene by scene, with one group of students cast in each scene. Don't switch characters every page in the text.
> Leave the students time to practice and think about their scene. It's hard to read cold.
> Work to get the students listening to each other. They may need some help in learning to avoid concentrating so much on their own lines they forget it's a play. Have them run through the scene at least twice. Encourage the other students to suggest alternatives.

Make sure everyone gets into the act—even the ones in the back row who don't want to get involved in anything. Nobody gets out of having a part and everyone should have a chance at a substantial part. The play then becomes the property of the class.

Run through a whole scene before breaking for comment. Make sure the comments are on the characters, not the students as actors. This isn't acting school; it's a literature class.

Between readings have them decide how the scene should be played: as farce or straight; with lots of emotion or not; fast or slow. These are all decisions they will have to make. These decisions are their response to the text, and the enactment is their articulation of that response. You don't need much "literary discussion." The students have just done it.

Have the students stand when they read. It's hard to get into the part sitting like a student.

Don't take a part yourself. You can be an audience and a critic. You can also be a director. That does not mean being a dictator or forcing your interpretation. But you will have to ask your casts to agree among them on a consistent reading of a character.

The reading should be an enactment, one in which the students have decided something about the characters and how they might move and talk, and particularly how they should relate to each other. On the basis of those decisions they do their reading. What are the inner tensions among the conspirators as they plan to do away with Caesar? What does Willy Loman's family think of him, and how do they show it or hide it? What are the changes in family relationships as we witness the characters in *A Raisin in the Sun*? The students' voices and perhaps some of their movements should work to reflect these relationships. They are an interpretation of the play. They are indeed an articulation of a response to the text.

A class that is reading Thornton Wilder's *Our Town* has to work out the characterization of Emily and George and particularly the Stage Manager. They need to come to decisions about the mood of the play. Is it optimistic or pessimistic? Is the Stage Manager a manipulator or a character on the sidelines? Is the love affair sappy? Is Emily a dumb girl or a mature woman at the end? How do each of the other characters contribute to the mood of the play and its various scenes? These are decisions that can be made during the course of enacting or reading the play. There does not have to be an elaborate production. The students don't have to "learn their lines," but in going through a reader's theater presentation of the play they will have learned their lines, and they will have learned the play, too.

One class we saw worked through a reading of *Death of a Salesman* over the course of two weeks. By the time they came to the end, some were in tears and most had lumps in their throats. There was no discussion. There didn't have to be. That's drama.

References

Bolton, Gavin. "Changes in Thinking about Education," *Theory into Practice* 24, no. 3 (1985): 151–157.

Booth, David. "Talking in Role, Thinking for Life." *Drama Contact* 12 (Autumn 1988): 10.

Frost, Robert. *Selected Letters.* Edited by Lawrance Thompson. New York: Holt, Rinehart & Winston, 1964, 79–80.

Heathcote, Dorothy, and Phyl Herbert. "A Drama of Learning: Mantle of the Expert." *Theory into Practice* 24, no. 3 (1985): 173–180.

O'Neill, Cecily. *Structure and Spontaneity: Improvisation in Theater and Education.* Unpublished Dissertation, Exeter University, 1991.

O'Neill, Cecily, and Alan Lambert. *Drama Structures: A Practical Handbook for Teachers.* Portsmouth, NH: Heinemann, 1982, 11–12.

Rosenblatt, Louise. *The Reader, The Text, The Poem: The Transactional Theory of the Literary Work.* Carbondale, IL: Southern Illinois University Press, 1978.

Resources

Bolton, Gavin. *Toward a Theory of Drama in Education.* London: Longman, 1979.

Booth, David. *Drama Words.* Toronto: Board of Education Language Study Center, 1987.

Bryon, Ken. *Drama in the English Classroom.* London: Methuen, 1986.

Johnson, Liz, and Cecily O'Neill. *Dorothy Heathcote: Collected Writings on Education and Drama.* London: Hutchinson, 1984.

Language Arts 65, no. 1: Special Issue on Drama. 1988.

Morgan, Norah, and Juliana Saxton. *Teaching Drama.* London: Hutchinson, 1987.

O'Neill, Cecily, Alan Lambert, Rosemarie Linnell, and Janet Warr-Wood. *Drama Guidelines.* London: Heinemann, 1977.

Rogers, Theresa, and Cecily O'Neill. "Creating Multiple Worlds: Drama, Language and Literary Response." In *Exploring Texts: The Role of Discussion and Writing*, ed. George Newell and Russell Durst, 69–90. Norwood, MA: Christopher Gordon Publishers, 1993.

Theory Into Practice 24, no. 3 (Summer 1985). Special issue: *Educating through Drama.* Patrick Verriour, guest editor.

Wagner, Betty Jane. *Dorothy Heathcote: Drama as a Learning Medium.* London: Hutchinson, 1979.

chapter **8**

Making the Reading Visible

If the new language of images were used differently, it would, through its use, confer a new kind of power. Within it we could begin to define our experiences more precisely in areas where words are inadequate.
Berger, 1972, p. 33

Why Visuals?

By using visuals we can obtain student responses that we might not otherwise get through talk or writing. Visuals, as response, represent a third "sign" system through which understandings are expressed metaphorically. They provide an opportunity to express aesthetic responses and responses to a word's form and quality as well as to its content. In justifying the use of non-print media as a means of representing our understanding of what we experience, some recent researchers argue that limiting the form through which we respond to literature actually inhibits what we may be able to communicate about our response. For example, although we probably would agree with Kenneth Burke (1950) that "literature is equipment for living," we also believe with Michael Cole and Helen Keysser (1985) that film media, too, is equipment for living.

These two researchers argue that we actually have very little direct experience of the world—that is, "of the knowledge we have of the world very little comes from scenes in which we have literally participated. . . . Rather, much of our knowledge is obtained indirectly. . . . it is not immediately experienced; rather, it is constructed, it is mediated" and as such, this knowledge is an "incomplete rendition of the original event" (Cole and Keysser, 1985, p. 54). Extending their arguments, we would like to suggest that using non-print media represents an effort to extend and enrich interpretations and responses to the literature our students read, for in doing so we broaden the range of perspectives individual students may have of the knowledge they encounter in reading literature.

Semioticians such as C. S. Pierce (1940) have defined literacy as thinking in sign systems, including not only oral and written sign systems but art, music, dance, and drama.

As Eliot Eisner (1982) argues, giving learners a choice in the form in which they are to represent their understandings (e.g., in literature) in effect gives them a choice that reflects their own conceptualizations of the world.

OK, but . . .

How Does This Work in an English Classroom?

In Chapter 2, we said that there would be times when students may not wish to respond in either oral or written form to a piece of literature they have just read. We have had students who have listened quietly during a discussion or sat at their desks with a piece of paper at a loss for words. However, when we gave them the option of articulating their response in another symbolic form or sign system they became unlocked.

As one of us argues elsewhere, the purpose of an initial response to a piece of literature is to begin the process of having students engage with the literary text and (perhaps) share this response with the teacher and other readers. That is, giving space for visual responses as well as oral and written ones acknowledges the subjective aspects of how we respond, and the natural, preferred or spontaneous nature of the response, as well as its content.

VIGNETTE X: ILLUSTRATIONS TO STIMULATE
LITERARY RESPONSE

In one classroom, we read aloud the text of a powerful picture book about the German Occupation during World War II. This book, *Rose Blanche,* by Roberto Innocenti, which follows a little girl who discovers the horrors of the Holocaust and then perishes, is also an allegory of resistance. After reading the text to the students, we gave one group of students a bag of paints and other materials and asked them to create a collage that captured their response to the book (see Figure 8.1).

The students chose to represent the book in abstract and symbolic ways, and we feel their collage captures the underlying drama of the book, particularly the last scene, while also representing Rose Blanche (with a red and white stuffed cloth), military tanks (with aluminum cups), and the fenced-in prisoners (creatively using corks in two ways). The collage also has an integrity of composition and flair. (Activities like these always furnish surprises because we uncover talents we were unaware of among our students.)

We then shared the text illustrations with the students so they could

FIGURE 8.1

read it again (and again) as it was meant to be read, and so they could experience the illustrator's depictions (Figures 8.2 and 8.3).

We also talked about the resemblances between what the illustrator and the students chose to depict, and the power of the book to urge us into a different mode of response.

FIGURE 8.2

SOURCE: Illustration by Roberto Innocenti

FIGURE 8.3
SOURCE: Illustration by Roberto Innocenti

If we want students to respond genuinely to what they read, we must be careful not to cut off that response or to limit it simply because we lean more toward traditional forms of responding in the literature classroom. Words are at times inadequate to represent how we think and feel about literature we have read. Remember the last time you put down a book or left the movie theater and all you could say was "Phew!" or "Wow!"?

What Are Some Other Ways to Respond through Visuals?

Whether the teacher does or does not specify the mode of visual response (and we suggest both options), the variety of possibilities in nonverbal, visual response is surprisingly extensive. We see these ranging across four possible visual dimensions, as shown in Figure 8.4.

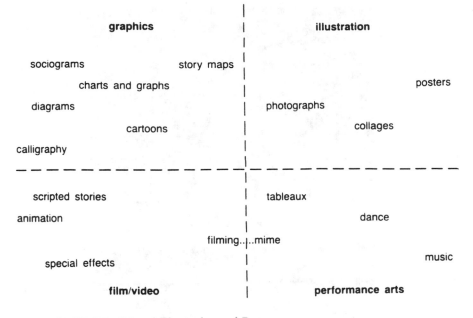

FIGURE 8.4   Visual Dimensions of Response

Take Tableaux, for Instance

A tableau is a "still picture" of a scene or moment from a story that is re-cre-ated by students using gesture, stance, and expression. Students can work in small groups, first deciding what scene they would like to create, then explor-ing different ways to represent that scene physically. When they are ready to present their tableau, it is useful to have someone count to three, at which time the tableau (or picture) is momentarily frozen for the rest of the class to view. It is fun to have other students guess what scene or moment from the story is being depicted, but it is also worth spending time talking about the composition of the tableau, how it represents a scene from a novel, play or short story, or why it was chosen.

VIGNETTE XI: TABLEAUX AS RESPONSE

The following tableaux were created by eleventh-grade students who were reading Lorraine Hansberry's *A Raisin in the Sun*. They had fin-ished Act II, in which Mr. Linder offers to buy back the Youngers's house in order to prevent them from moving into the neighborhood, and Willy makes off with the money Mama gave to Walter.

In response to the first tableau, of Ruth and Walter hugging (Figure 8.5), the rest of the students applauded. We have reproduced some of the discussion here.

FIGURE 8.5

T: What is happening here?
ST: Ruth is feeling sorry for Walter.
T: Why?
ST: Their relationship was falling apart.
ST: And he got gaffled (taken).
T: (sighs)

In the first tableau, the students were able to convey an emotional quality through their gestures and positioning that was immediately recognizable to the rest of the class.

The second tableau (Figure 8.6) creates a scene that was not actually in the play, in which Walter confronts his friend Willy after Willy takes off with his money.

T: Now, watch this: They've made the scene up. One is Walter and one is George.

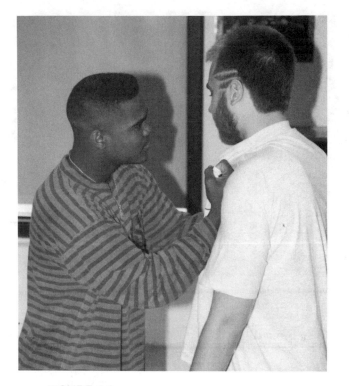

FIGURE 8.6

ST: George?

ST: That ain't George, it's Willy.

T: That's right. Let's look at it. (Freeze)

T: Walter, what would you be saying to him?

ST: Where's my money at?

This tableau is fairly strong and dramatic because it suggests action and movement, although it is frozen. We cannot see Willy's face, but we know simply by his stance how he is responding to Walter's anger. For the students, this was a central scene even though it did not actually appear in the text, because they understood and felt strongly about how this would potentially affect the outcome of the play. This is clear from the discussion that followed the next two tableaux. These (Figures 8.7 and 8.8) depict a scene in which a man from the white neighborhood tries to buy back the house Walter's mother purchased for the family.

In response to the first tableau (Figure 8.7), the rest of the class began modifying the students' frozen composition:

STS: Cory, wait, turn your chair around, like this, 'cause that looks like you're grabbing it. Turn your chair around or turn your head to the

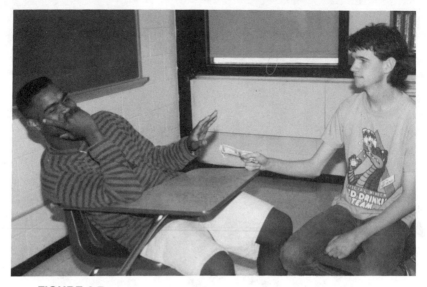

FIGURE 8.7

side or something. Put your hand up again. That's better. Good.
(Applause)

The second depiction (Figure 8.8) includes Walter's son and his sister
Beneatha, which provides a very different framing of the scene and hints
at various perspectives, such as Beneatha's wariness of the man and his
motives.

FIGURE 8.8

Toward the end of the class, the teacher began a discussion in which she asked the students to predict the ending of the play, which they had not yet read, and to think about how things have or have not changed in the 35 years since the play was written.

T: Did you like doing the tableaux?

ST: Yeah!

T: Okay, let me ask you something. The guy comes back tomorrow and he's going to offer Walter the money again. How many of you think he will take it?

STS: I do, I do.

T: Why?

ST: 'Cause he's broke and he needs the money and he's looking for a way out, so . . .

T: Do you all agree?

ST: They'll be the first blacks in that neighborhood. Why should they take that chance?

ST: I think he's gonna be tempted to take the money but he's not gonna do it because, you see, he already let his mother down once, and you know that's just gonna be like letting her down again, because she feels like she wants to stay in that neighborhood, so he's gonna be tempted but I don't think he'll take it.

T: Okay, those are two interesting possibilities. So we'll find out tomorrow. Let me ask another question. It's now 1993. What's happened to Beneatha? She's fifty-something.

ST: She's become a doctor.

T: You think she fulfilled her dream?

ST: I think she set her mind to it and she did it.

T: Was it easy?

STS: No!

T: What did you say, Shaneika? How many of you think she married Asagai and went back to Africa? Or did she marry George, who had all the money?

ST: I think she married Asagai.

ST: In the story didn't she dress up and then go change her clothes? So I don't think she married Asagai.

T: Good point. Why does she marry George instead?

ST: Walter already messed up the money and she knows it's going to be hard because, for one, she's black, and the time period it's in. And George has the money, know what I'm saying?

T: Yes. Let me ask you one more question. What is the same from the play to now, 1993, and what is different?

ST: People having dreams and not having the money for it and, um, families.

ST: A lot of people have dreams, but there are a lot of obstacles.

T: Are the obstacles the same?

ST: Now we got drugs and violence and stuff.

ST: Yeah, but we can move where we want.

T: So you think all our neighborhoods are integrated?

ST: No, but you can move more freely now than you did before. But most people stay with their own people. Black people, too.

STS: (All talking at once. Bell rings.)

T: OK, we'll finish this tomorrow. Nice job.

The students were able to focus on key scenes in or suggested by the play in immediate and graphic ways, enabling a discussion and reflection on the lives of the characters and the play's current and historical meanings. In 1959, Kenneth Tynan reviewed the first production of *A Raisin in the Sun* for *The New Yorker* magazine. He said:

> I will not pretend to be impervious to the facts; this is the first Broadway production of a work by a colored authoress, and it is also the first Broadway production to have been staged by a colored director. . . . I do not see why these facts should be ignored, for a play is not an entity in itself, it is a part of history, and I have no doubt that my knowledge of the historical context predisposed me to like "A Raisin in the Sun" long before the house lights dimmed. Within ten minutes, however, liking had matured into absorption. The relaxed freewheeling interplay of a magnificent team of Negro actors drew me unresisting into a world of their making, their suffering, their thinking, and their rejoicing. (Reprinted in *The New Yorker*, 31 May 1993, p. 118)

Then, as now, the play speaks to readers as a story as well as a comment on our history and our culture(s).

While doing tableaux, talk about what makes a tableau strong, dramatic, and recognizable. The placement of actors in space, the juxtaposition of actors, the suggestion of movement before or after the frozen scene, the shift in perspective, and the framing are all factors that we may use in evaluating the effectiveness of a tableau. Talk about why certain scenes were chosen: for example, their centrality to the story, their visual quality, or their emotional quality. Tableaux can also be a beginning point for role-play and for delivery back into text for further explanation.

We have found that students particularly enjoy creating tableaux because they can actually get out of their seats, using some of that bursting energy we referred to in Chapter 2, and because of the immediacy of the experience.

Story Maps and Sociograms

Story Maps

Story maps are simply illustrations of the terrain of the story, or a map of the characters' travels (e.g., Gulliver's). But their value is greater than the word *simply* implies. Creating maps of stories, poems, and plays can enhance students' understanding of the twists and turns of complex plots and calls for a close reading, which is one of our goals, after all.

Some writers, such as J. R. R. Tolkien, in *The Hobbit*, provide their own maps (Figure 8.9). Stories that might similarly be illustrated by students are *Huckleberry Finn* or *Great Expectations* or the historical novels of Rosemary Sutcliffe. Or Jean Auel's *The Clan of the Cave Bear* or . . .

Sociograms

Literary sociograms are visual displays of characters' relationships. According to teachers we have worked with, adolescents are particularly interested in social relationships between characters and the place of individual characters

FIGURE 8.9 Map from *The Hobbit*

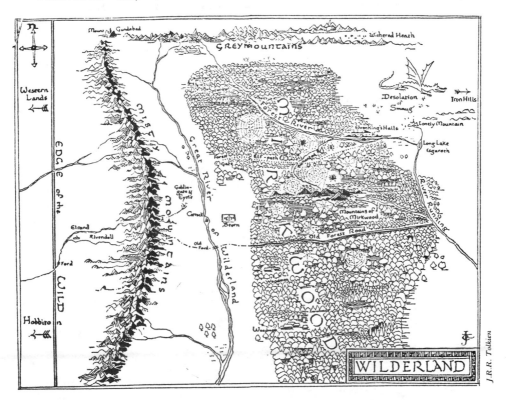

in the larger social framework of a literary work. Sociograms provide a useful tool for expressing character relationships in visual form. For instance, fairly simple sociograms of *West Side Story* and *Romeo and Juliet* might look like the student-drawn ones in Figure 8.10 (bottom, top, respectively).

To do a sociogram, a student will need to think about the central characters and their alignments with one another and with minor characters. Additionally, a sociogram makes visible the minor characters and their role in the action (Figure 8.10, top).

Longer works like *Romeo and Juliet* might even require a series of sociograms that depict the ways in which the relationships between characters shift as a result of events or a series of events. And, as illustrated in Figure 8.10, sociograms can also effectively be used to compare modern versions of literary works with the original classic dramas. One group of students might create a sociogram in which they pair characters from *Romeo and Juliet* and *West Side Story*, particularly the visual parallels in relationships between different characters in each text.

We have used sociograms not only as ends in themselves (final products) but also as stimuli for more extensive exploration in, say, a literary essay on a young adult novel such as *My Brother Sam is Dead*.

But can having students create sociograms tell us what the students know about the book they have read? Sociograms reveal to what extent students have really understood the story, novel, or play because relationships among characters also indicate the relative significance of the characters to each other as well as to the plot, subplot(s), and, ultimately, theme(s). To probe a little deeper, we can also ask students to provide a written rationale of the sociograms they create, justifying their categorization of characters through reference to textual passages.

VIGNETTE XII: SOCIOGRAMS AS RESPONSE

Students in Sarah Edelman's classroom were given the task of creating group sociograms to illustrate their understandings of characters' roles after having read Margaret Craven's *I Heard The Owl Call My Name*.

Each student was asked to be responsible for two or three characters, and each group was to collectively decide how to arrange the characters on their sociograms.

Sarah added the useful suggestion that different colors were to be used to represent the different characters and their relation to the main plot and to subplots. Her preparation made this class highly successful: All students were supplied with crayons or markers, butcher paper was ready for each group, tape was available, her model sociogram (representing characters in another novel they had read) was accessible, and a list of characters' names had been placed on the chalkboard. A composite image of the students' sociograms is represented in Figure 8.11. The following are Sarah's comments of her perceptions of what happened in the lesson.

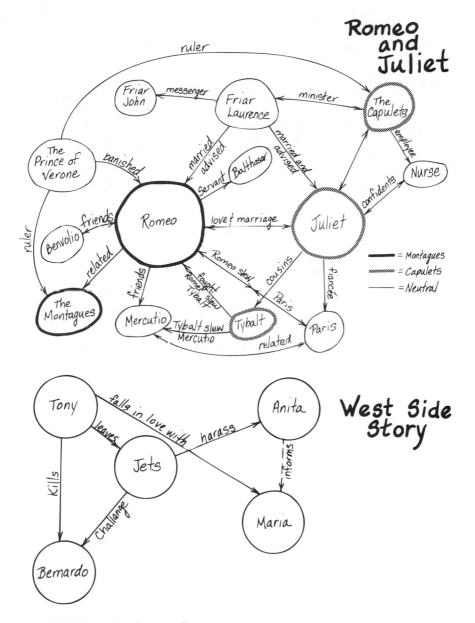

FIGURE 8.10   Student Sociograms

Sarah's comments:

"I feel really good about what happened in this lesson. I am extremely pleased about how the groups worked together, their creativity and their ability to figure out the plot/character relationships on their own. The presentations that followed the

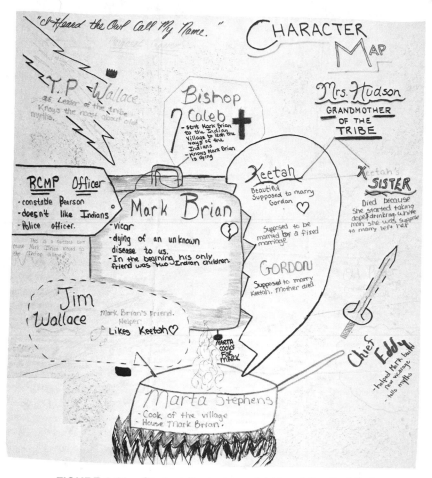

FIGURE 8.11   Student Sociogram of *I Heard the Owl Call My Name*

next day were really fabulous—I felt almost like a proud mother as each group presented their character maps. The students' confusions over plot/character relationship was evident in their presentations. This was a great help to me in targeting problems for later discussion.

It was also interesting to notice group members amending their reporter's explanation of their sociograms. Here, students definitely took responsibility for their own learning and served as learning monitors for each other. I saw peer pressure working at its best in this lesson as students checked each other's perceptions. They also let each other know whether or not they had read closely enough or not at all! If I had to describe the value of this lesson to another teacher I would say it was a fun, creative, engaging activity that definitely helps students understand plot/character relationships in complex fiction. I would give it a fabulous rating." (Edelman, 1993, p. 5)

Filming and Video

Film and video are another means of articulating a response to what is read. Students should be encouraged to create film or video versions representing their responses to literature. Like many of you, we've used film in the teaching of literature for a variety of reasons, including to motivate students to *read the book* and *re-read* the book, to help students to understand a demanding text (e.g., *Hamlet*), to stimulate discussion about issues in a text, to introduce the book by using film as a pre-reading activity, and to provide another angle of the events or characters in the book. Or perhaps it is a hot week, Thursday afternoon, and you know the kids won't be doing any thinking about the book so you might as well use the film to have something productive happen.

Over the past century during which films have become a staple of the artistic fare of the world, many of them have dealt with literary topics. Countless novels and short stories have been made into films, and a large number of plays have also had their movie versions, either directly through a live performance or through a distinctive filmed production.

Films are captured dramas. People in the theater will tell you that theater is a living art in that no two performances are the same. Film takes one performance or an amalgam of several episodes and turns it into a distinct, fixed form.

At the same time, film uses most of the devices of narrative and drama, as well as certain devices that we tend to associate with poetry. Most films have plots and characters and settings, rising actions, and climaxes. Most have episodes or scenes structured to make a whole. Many films will use a particular image as a motif to establish mood or to signal a type of character. The image can be visual or it can be aural, as in the use of a particular bit of theme music.

Films are perhaps more like novels than they are like plays in that the camera serves as the narrator. Film establishes how the viewer will see a scene or a character. The camera can hide things from view as well as reveal them. The camera and the director are clearly central to a film, much as the narrator and the author are to a story or novel.

Key to the camera's manipulation of what you see are the following:

Angle. The relationship of the camera to the object, the angle can be below, above, oblique, or dead-on to the object, which may or may not be in motion. The angle may also be wide or narrow, depending on the lens used, so that one may get a limited or expansive view.

Distance. The object may appear far away or extremely close to the camera (a closeup).

Focus. The camera may bring one object into sharp focus and blur the background or it may put soft or hard focus on all objects.

Position. The camera may remain fixed in one point or it may move with the characters or move around the characters or the whole scene. This last is known as a panorama or "pan" shot.

(What about the trendy Woody Allen-type jiggling of the camera?)

Motion. The film may also be manipulated so that the number of frames seen per second can shift. This manipulation can make the movement of objects or people seem faster or slower than would normally be observed.

If the camera can manipulate the audience's view, so, too, can the director, by editing the film to sequence the various frames.

Shot. What takes place from the moment the camera is turned on until it is turned off.

Scene. A series of related and connected shots usually involving the same locale or characters.

Sequence. A group of related scenes, perhaps in a given time or a given place.

The director can also affect the transition from one scene to another by use of one of the following:

Cut. A straightforward switch from one shot to another without any transition.

Fade. A gradual darkening of one shot to total blackness and then an opening into the light of the next shot.

Dissolve. Without any darkening of the scene, a "melting" of one scene or sequence into another.

These devices clearly affect what the mind of the viewer responds to, just as the various linguistic and rhetorical devices of imagery, diction, structure, and tone in a novel or short story affect the reader's response. A great deal of modern fiction has been influenced by film. Novels like Kundera's *The Incredible Lightness of Being*, Morrison's *Beloved*, Kennedy's *Ironweed*, and Marquez's *One Hundred Years of Solitude* clearly show the influence of film in their organization and sequencing of scenes. In fact, these books lend themselves easily to film treatment for that very reason. It may help students to think of the parallel ways in which literary texts and films deal with literary elements such as point of view, setting, plot, and character portrayal, and for this purpose, we have provided one (though not the only one) way of doing so in Figure 8.12.

It is important to include film in the literature classroom, and film should be studied as an art form in its own right. In studying film and examining students' responses to film, we acknowledge and legitimize the art form and acknowledge the interplay of film and literature in the twentieth century. We show our students Zefferelli's *Romeo and Juliet* not as an illustration of Shakespeare but as an *interpretation* of the play and as a work in its own right that is designed to engage us in its own artistry. If we had time, we would also show other film treatments, such as the old Orson Welles version or the Bugs Bunny parody.

FIGURE 8.12   Elements of Critical Perspectives in Literature and Film

Literary Text (e.g., novel)	Element	Film
Narrative Persona (e.g., first, third persons)	Point of View	Angle of Shot Distance Focus Camera takes narrator role
Narrator important in casting author's perspective		
Period location(s) established early and woven throughout (i.e., integral or backdrop)	Setting	Specific location Focus of shots Panoramic (integral or backdrop)
Protagonist against self Protagonist against other/s Protagonist against system	Plot/Conflicts	[as in literary text] Voice-over Montage Doubling
Typical narrative chronology Flashback	Sequence	Time "warped"/montage Flashback May be more condensed than novel
Embedded sequences		Fewer if any embedded sequences
Character as real Character as symbol Character as central Psychological portrayal central	Character Portrayal	[as in literary text] Dissolves Freeze-frame
Language significant (main medium)	Style	Action/Visual in place of language at times (e.g., cut, fade, dissolve will replace descriptive passages at times)

In film, the director may shift focus from character to plot, especially if the novel focuses on the inner life or world of the character. Film audiences are less likely to enjoy sitting for two hours while a character focuses on him- or herself.

We would not limit ourselves to films of Shakespeare or other "classics"; we might well take up certain films classic in their own right, like *The Red Balloon*, *Citizen Kane*, *Sleeper*, or *High Noon*.

What this means is that showing a film cannot substitute for teaching the book. The film becomes an aesthetic work in its own right, something that provokes a response and is itself worthy of discussion and study. It is compared with the text or "read" version, the point of the comparison is not to establish the superiority of the text to the film. In fact, film and text can now be presented together (and with comments) in hypermedia, using laser disk technology (see Chapter 10).

A Suggestion

If we were to have a unit on the American dream, one of the texts we would certainly include is *The Wizard of Oz*. To us that novel, with its depiction of the Emerald City and the glitter and glamour of the strange world as being nothing compared to the values of home and family, and with its vision of the power of innocence to conquer evil, is the "great American dream." We would want our students to read the original and we would also show them the film. The film takes the novel's view and makes it even more an interpretation typical of the Great Depression. The screenwriters also chose to make it a dream rather than a fantasy. What does this shift do? Why is it important to have the same characters appear in both worlds, only transformed in Oz? These changes create a different experience from the book; they do not make the film inferior to it.

Film belongs in the literature classroom. It should not be reserved for the dull days or the slow classes. It deserves respect and respectable treatment.

Another Suggestion

We could use the film version of Robert Cormier's *A Chocolate War* to explore what happens to our responses, to our understandings of the characters or the plot, to our empathy for the characters, to our predictive powers, and to our perceptions about evil in viewing the film. Have the students read at least the first nine chapters of Cormier's novel. Have them write their responses to their readings. Then have them watch the segment of the film (approximately the first seven minutes) that takes us to the events of Chapter 9 in the novel and have them write their responses to the film segment. These written observations will be useful for subsequent discussion. Questions that will draw their attention to thinking critically about the film and the novel might include asking students to consider how each medium introduces the subject of the film; how long it takes students to read to the end of Chapter 9; how we receive information about what Jerry, the main character, is thinking in the novel and in the film; and how a sense of suspense is introduced in the novel and in the film.

We thought this comparison interesting for several reasons. First, the film opens with credits, voice-overs, music. It is as if there is no narrator. We are given a silent image of an innocent ball game, with only occasional grunts and isolated distant words. Most initial shots are long ones. The novel opens with a blunt statement in the third person: "They murdered him." We are thrust immediately into something that *seems* sinister.

Second, we move early into Jerry's thoughts in the novel, whereas in the film, setting is of primary importance in the opening sequences. We only see Jerry's thoughts from what is apparent through his facial expressions—we don't have a narrator telling us what he is thinking.

Third, these differences are sufficiently interesting to consider questions of interpretation: How does this film director view the characters, situations, and issues in the novel? Is his interpretation the same as ours?

A natural sequel to these questions might be to have students video-tape a sequence that they consider critical in the novel. They would need to script it and act it out in a way that reflects their interpretation. We could follow this up with asking them to argue for their selection and inter-pretation.

Film and video should be used as one means of articulating a response to what is read or watched. The students should be encouraged to make film or video versions of what they have read.

If, as we have argued, film is a respectable medium, film is a respectable and interesting way to allow students to articulate their responses to the text they are reading. The film does not have to be "Oscar" material, but it should represent an understanding or environment of the text. The point of the film, like the point of dramatization, is to effect a coherent interpreta-tion of the text. What we are proposing used to be quite difficult with the more cumbersome Super-8 movie cameras or half-inch video recorders. The activity is easier with a camcorder or palmcorder and cassette. We use the term *film* generically, even though the actual medium is often not film, but tape.

Making the film involves a number of steps:

Selecting the text to be filmed

Choosing an approach

Preparing a script

Preparing a shooting script

Selecting a location

Casting

Rehearsing

Shooting

Editing

Showing

We have found that this whole activity takes about two weeks with a group. The hardest steps are the first ones: determining the text and the approach and then preparing a script and a shooting script, which contains the precise instructions to the camera operator.

The actual run-through and shooting are not too difficult, and there are many cases in which the planned sequence is changed because of the special opportunity of the locale or the day. Editing is somewhat hard without special training, but there is often a student who has the expertise. The viewing is often a revelation for those who have made the film because they realize that the effect they had intended might not be the same as the effect they get, particularly when laughter comes when there should be chills.

VIGNETTE XIII: FILMS AND RESPONSE

On several occasions, we have had two different groups in a class making "rival" films of the same story. One class did two versions of a Damon Runyon story, "Butch Minds the Baby," in which a safe-cracker takes his baby along on a "job." The class was undecided as to whether the story should be done with Butch or one of the other crooks as the central character; they tried both versions. Executing the two versions simultaneously was a somewhat hectic procedure, but it was effective in allowing the class to compare the interpretations and their realizations. The comparison was not on the basis of the quality of the film or the acting, but on what they had done with the characters and what the effect of switching the focus was on the impact of the story. When the class showed the film to another class, the controversy raged all over again, but it was worth it for everyone. The students in both classes realized what the shift could do.

They learned something about point of view and literary techniques as well.

They also learned something about the art of film.

If you don't have the equipment to go through the whole procedure of filming a text, you can go as far as preparing the shooting script with a class. The main point to make with and about the film version is that it is sequential—one image follows another in time. The viewer cannot go back, as the reader can, or even as the person looking at a comic strip can. Will Eisner (see Figure 8.13) refers to comics as "sequential art" and gives a bravura demonstration of how the comic artist can manipulate the reader. This is what film can do as well—perhaps better, because the viewer is the captive of the filmmaker. That is a lesson for your students to learn. Knowing it helps them to realize that the media do indeed manipulate them unless they are aware of how they are being manipulated.

One of the most talented producers of children's films, Morton Schindel,

FIGURE 8.13

has consistently argued the case of film production company Weston Wood for the artistic perspective in film and its educational importance. Schindel once wrote:

> If we keep our eyes open and our imaginations free, we can choose whatever means will work best for us and for the new generation we are entrusted to educate. We can examine impartially all the media in selecting the idea we want to transmit . . . with a realistic view of the role and value of books, we can comfortably begin an exciting romance with the "newcomers" (i.e., film or video) in town—the new media—to derive ever greater satisfaction from professional endeavors. (Schindel, 1967, pp. 44-45)

But Is All This Responding through Images Legitimate? And Why Bother?

Is it really the province of English teachers to concern themselves with such antics? After all, literature is founded on words.

Ultimately, we think English teachers will want to have students express responses in some verbal form and that the English classroom is an appropriate place in which to expect this. However, let's recall one of the main stated objectives of English teachers: to have students love and appreciate literature. If this is our ultimate goal, it won't be well served by limiting how our students may respond to what we want them to love and appreciate. Words alone can become shackles as well as liberators, as at least one dramatist (Samuel Beckett) realized when he turned to mime in preference to verbal drama.

We have been particularly intrigued with the nonverbal or visual response because we've realized that even quite literate college students show a surprisingly high proportion of preference for nonverbal symbolic action in response to literature.

We continue to use the ideas discussed in these chapters with our preservice English language arts teachers. Many of them prefer nonverbal modes of response, including performance (such as dance and mime), drawing, using a camera, and making a film, and of those who prefer verbal responses, relatively few choose the essay form.

We also continue to find that nonverbal responses are a marvelous springboard for lively discussions, which seem to be more difficult to generate without them.

We now know that individual learning styles have a significant impact on how effectively we learn and on our motivation to learn. We believe that allowing students to express visual responses to literature will enhance their responses in writing and talking rather than hinder them, and should not, therefore, be seen as simply giving them "fun" times, which we (and they) don't take seriously.

Bridges to Verbal Responses

As we suggested, people have favorite mediums for expressing what they know, but we also acknowledged that one of the tasks of the English teacher is to help students effectively communicate their responses in writing as well as in talk. Let's concentrate for a moment on the ways in which nonverbal responses can be used as bridges to effective written responses.

Recall again those students who have sat at their desks for twenty or more minutes, having written not a word on their paper. We know they read the book or poem and we may even have heard them say something in class. But the pen is dead.

We happen to know that a student (Martha) is a superb painter and sketch artist. Let's give her the opportunity to present what she responds to in the poem through her natural preferences for representing what she thinks and feels. Martha comes in the next day with a sketch instead of a journal entry. But you really want everyone in the class to write an essay about the poem, and the journal entry as an early step in doing this. The sketch seems even more removed from the ultimate goal you had in mind. So what's the linkup?

What we now know about writing enables us to suggest that *any* activity that promotes thinking about a topic as a precursor to writing and *any* activity that promotes articulation of that thought fosters further thoughts. At some point, students who have written an expressive response to a poem, using their own personal language and perhaps giving little thought to "structure" in what they are writing, will have to translate these words into another style or into another form.

Visual responses can have a similar function of unlocking thoughts and feelings in response to literature, enabling us to stand back from the work itself and develop a sense of what we have not yet seen or an angle we had not previously considered. At the same time, visual response permits us to express with dignity what we feel and think. Our response does not have to die before it ever emerges.

Do we grade visual responses? If so, what criteria do we use? What about students who just don't ever make the grade in verbal responses but can do wonderful things in the visual mediums?

To answer these questions, we'll first have to answer another: What are we actually grading in literature study: the understanding and appreciation of the literature itself (i.e., the response) or the form in which this understanding is presented?

We believe the answer to this question and the answers to the preceding ones have to be aligned with our goals in teaching literature in the first place. If we have to grade, then the focus should be on the process and quality of perception, not on the product itself. For a detailed discussion of assessment and evaluation, we refer you to Chapter 11, but leave you with this one thought:

> A body of research is accumulating to show that when a task can be enjoyable, . . . providing rewards for completing the task has detrimental effects on the learner's motivation to continue with that type of activity when the rewards are no longer offered. When the emphasis is on being rewarded for doing the task the learner's attention becomes geared to mechanical procedures and their enjoyment of it wanes: it becomes an onerous chore. (Johnston, 1987, p. 6)

References

Berger, John. *Ways of Seeing*. London: Penguin, 1972, 33.

Burke, Kenneth. *A Rhetoric of Motives*. Englewood Cliffs, NJ: Prentice-Hall, 1950.

Cole, Michael, and Helen Keysser. "The Concept of Literacy in Print and Film." In *Literacy, Language and Learning: The Nature and Consequences of Reading and Writing*, edited by David R. Olson, Nancy Torrance, and Angela Hildyard. Cambridge: Cambridge University Press, 1985, 50–72.

Edelman, Sarah. "Reflections on Sociograms." Manuscript, Ohio State University, College of Education, 1993, 5.

Eisner, Eliot. *Cognition and Curriculum*. New York: Longman, 1982.

Johnston, Brian. *Assessing English: Helping Students to Reflect on Their Work*. Sydney, Australia: St. Clair Press, 1987, 6.

Pierce, C. S. *Collected Papers*. Cambridge, MA: Harvard University Press, 1940.

Schindel, Morton. "Confessions of a Book Fiend." *School Library Journal* 13 (1967): 44–45.

Tynan, Kenneth. "Review of *A Raisin in the Sun*." *New Yorker* (31 May 1993). First published in *New Yorker* in "Critic's Round Table" (1959): 118–119.

Resources

Eco, Umberto. "Cult Movies and Intertextual Collage." In *Modern Criticism and Theory: A Reader*, edited by David Lodge. New York: Longman, 1988.

Johnson, Terry P., and R. Louis Daphne. *Literacy through Literature*. Portsmouth, NH: Heinemann, 1988.

McCloud, Scott. *Understanding Comics: The Invisible Art*. Northampton, MA: Kitchen Sink Press, 1993.

McKowen, Clark, and William Sparke. *It's Only a Movie*. Englewood Cliffs, NJ: Prentice-Hall, 1971.

Mitchell, W. J. T. *Iconology: Image, Text, Ideology*. Chicago, IL: University of Chicago Press, 1988.

O'Neill, Cecily, and Alan Lambert. *Drama Structures: A Practical Handbook for Teachers*. Portsmouth, NH: Heinemann, 1982.

Paley, Nicholas. "Kids of Survival: Experiments in the Study of Literature." *English Journal* 77 (1988): 54–58.

Sohn, David A. *Film, the Creative Eye*. New York: George A. Pflaum, 1970.

Soter, A. O. "Making the Foot Fit the Shoe: Using Writing and Visual Responses to Evaluate Literary Understanding." In *Exploring Texts: The Role of Discussion and Writing in the Teaching and Learning of Literature*, edited by George Newell and Russell Durst. Norwood, MA: Christopher Gordon Publishers, 1993, 231–258.

chapter 9

But What about Writing and All That?

> *I do not sit at my desk to put into verse something that is already clear in my mind. If it were clear in my mind, I should have no incentive or need to write about it, for I am an explorer. . . . We do not write in order to be understood, we write in order to understand.*
>
> *Lewis, in Murray, 1982, p. 86*

Writing about literature or writing literature? What about writing programs and free writing and expressive writing and writing from experience? How does all that stuff fit into a literature program? It hasn't, but it should. But we hear some say, OK, "they" write poetry and stories, but is it really literature? Our initial response to this is, Does it really matter?

Why include a chapter on writing in response to reading literature? Why shouldn't it be an integrated activity with other kinds of responses such as the visual, the dramatic, and the oral, which we have described in earlier chapters?

In answer to the first question C. Day Lewis provides our own explanation. Writing, unlike the other avenues for response, offers an opportunity to explore what we think and to *record* that exploration simultaneously.

In answer to the second question, we agree that responses to literature should be multimodal and, at times, integrated.

Our intention in providing a chapter on writing in response to literature is not to exclude the possibility of integration. Rather, we wish to focus on the unique properties that writing itself has for pushing the boundaries of response from spontaneous, immediate response to considered, developed, extended response. Having said this, we hasten to add that extended, developed responses are not excluded possibilities in the other response modes we have discussed.

Are we expecting too much to have all secondary students write compelling fiction and nonfiction while they are still gathering experience?

What kinds of writing can we legitimately expect from today's twelve-to seventeen-year-olds?

Is literature an appropriate subject to write about?

What can we expect students to record in their responses to literature?

How long does it take for a "sense of literature" to evolve?

We ask these questions in response to such instructions as the following, which are typical, we think, of what is asked in secondary-school literature anthologies, tacked on to the end of a series of questions about the literature they have just finished reading:

> Find a collection of tall tales in the library. Write a paragraph summarizing one of these tales.
>
> Write a paragraph in which you use several examples to show that animals are protected by their coloration. . . . Open your paragraph with a sentence that states the central idea. You may use this sentence if you like: Natural coloration helps animals conceal themselves from their enemies.

And then there are the types of assignments that simply ask "what" and "why" and sometimes "how" after a reading. Well, we suppose teachers can make of these what they will, but why? What, really, is their purpose? Do the kinds of questions found after the reading selections in many classroom anthologies really take the reader any further than that reader might go without them?

Finally, we pose one last group of questions before trying to suggest some answers to all of them. When we ask students to write in response to literature, should we focus on the writing or, as much as possible, on the content of the response? How does this affect what and how we evaluate what students write in response to literature? What are we really after when we get them to write in response to literature? What can we expect when we ask a whole class to write in response to a common novel or poem or play? What kinds of writing fulfill our differing purposes in the literature classroom?

What about Literature as a Form of Writing?

The nonwriting literature classroom wastes a tremendous opportunity to have the students write about something other than themselves but yet still close to themselves. By experiencing characters and situations and the language crafting that literature provides, writers have always had available to them sources for topics to write about, perspectives on those topics, and inspirations for crafting that lead to new insights, new "statements," and new perspectives still uniquely their own.

We have discussed authors in Chapters 1 and 3. Here, we want to remind ourselves that authors are writers—professionals, yes, but facing the problems and sharing the goals of our students.

We read, for example, about writers who have noted the tremendous influence of one or more writers. For example, Joseph Conrad studied Gustave Flaubert and Guy de Maupassant closely, and they provided him with models in his quest to "find the suitable form without smothering the idea being shaped and released" (Gurko, 1981, p. 31).

Lloyd Alexander claims he has so many authors he relies on for models and inspiration that he forgets the names of half of them. He then goes on to name Shakespeare, Dickens, Twain, and Lewis Carroll and says there might be a dozen.

There exists between literature and writing a very close and natural link—a symbiotic relationship. All writers confess to having been strongly influenced by what others have written and may similarly influence other writers in their immediate surroundings. If their contributions survive, they may also have an impact on writers 100 years later. Students report that reading a new author can give them a new way of organizing their writing.

To explore the possibilities literature offers to its readers through writing, let's consider once more why one might study literature at all. Let's then link these reasons with writing activities that could form the foundation not only for comprehending, responding to, and critically understanding literary texts, but for expressing oneself.

First, literature offers extended vicarious experience of other lives, both imagined and actual. As to whether the latter can be labeled "real," we believe that reality is very much in the eye of the beholder. The streamers of red thread that sweep across a devastated planet long after a large-scale atomic war are as real as what we had for breakfast, once we enter the reality of Anne McAffrey's novel *Dragonsong.*

Second, literature offers the opportunity for insight into human behavior and the hidden thoughts and emotions that few of us have the chance to see in "real life," where much of this is carefully masked for all kinds of reasons. In literature, writers present what they penetrate through their characters and allow us to explore the differences between surface behavior and the hidden self. By the time the child is an adolescent this process is well under way, and much of the adolescent's preoccupation is with the self in relation to others and how others perceive that self. The mask is beginning to be adopted, although the colors and forms that may be added are not fully in place.

Third, literature provides us with the social insights of particularly sensitized people—writers—so that we extend our perspective of individuals to seeing them also as social beings, products of complex social contexts. Men and women are only heroes in the context of certain social situations—for example, repression of one form or another, natural disasters, economic deprivation. Ethics and morality are often presented through situational complexities that leave us perplexed rather than convinced. Is Rochester, in *Jane Eyre*, truly a villain for denying his marriage to Bertha Mason? At times, of course, the writer leaves us in no doubt as to which is the "right course of action" for a hero or heroine dealing with a moral dilemma. For example, you may recall Richie Perry's desire to shoot unarmed villagers, in Walter Dean Myers' *Fallen Angels*, because he is panicky and, after all, "they" are the enemy.

Fourth, literature offers an aesthetic experience and insight into the creative experience. By reflecting on how writers achieve their effects (e.g., moods, senses, rhythms), we can foster awareness of the writer's craft and, in turn, extend that awareness to student writing. Adolescent writers are already intuitively crafters when they write. For example, it isn't uncommon to find them using extremely short sentences to achieve emphasis or a series of short phrases to create cumulative effect. Much of this is, however, intuitive, although it may also be imitative.

Although the essence of what writers say and how they say it is probably essentially unplanned (Robert Hayden observed, "As you continue writing and rewriting, you begin to see possibilities you hadn't seen before"), the process of the activity involves a conscious kind of decision making, much like decisions a potter makes to work some more on refining the original creation so that the clay form is shaped this way rather than that.

John Updike describes the activity as a search for what one is saying. It involves writing and rewriting, and student writers who engage in a process-based activity are already very aware of making conscious choices related to crafting and shaping in their own writing. Literature, therefore, can delight and please through the shaping, not just the content.

Back to Composition

In the past ten years or so, and certainly since the appearance of the first edition of this book, the teaching of writing has undergone a major revolution in secondary schools and colleges. It is by no means widespread, yet more and more English teachers are adopting what has become known as the process approach, or writer's workshop, as the basis for writing instruction in the secondary school. This shift to relating the activity of writing to the text that emerges is particularly beneficial because it provides a great range of opportunities for students to write like "real writers" do and therefore provides a closer link between writing and the study of literature.

The tenets of the process approach to writing instruction have been dealt with extensively elsewhere in articles and such books as Donald Murray's "Write before Writing," Ken McCrorie's *Telling Writing*, Ronald Huff's and Charles Kline Jr.'s *The Contemporary Writing Curriculum*, Ann Berthoff's *The Making of Meaning*, Tom Newkirk's *Only Connect*, and many others.

Much of the research and scholarship of the past two decades confirms what professional writers knew all along: that real writing has real readers; that real writing involves decision making in response to intrinsic motivation and to potential readers; and that real writing is a social activity with both an intrinsic purpose for writing and an audience of readers that helps influence and share the outcome.

All of the following behaviors and attitudes, therefore, lend themselves well to talking, exploring, and writing about literature:

- Writing folders
- Conferences with peers as well as teachers and other adults
- Feedback related to content, purpose, and audience
- The use of journals as writers log or notebooks (compendia for collecting ideas that may or may not be taken up at a later date)
- Revision as a process of working or crafting through the raw material of ideas and experiences

More emphasis is now placed on student writers choosing their own topics, reflecting a belief that they have valid and valuable things to write about. But as teachers are becoming aware of the value of connecting reading and writing, they are also implicitly acknowledging that ideas come from "somewhere," and in this respect writing as part of a literature program offers a potentially extraordinary range of things to write about, either directly or indirectly.

As we noted earlier, professional writers freely acknowledge the influence of other writers, and no one has yet claimed that this influence operates exclusively at the level of form. Freedom of topic choice is an acknowledgment that we write best when we write about what we know most about.

This knowledge, however, need not be exclusively based on firsthand experience. Indeed, if it were, how much could be told? Rather, the knowledge and experience we have is an amalgam of firsthand experience and perception combined with vicarious experience and perception. Literature, again, offers a tremendously rich and diverse set of experiences. Writes Jill Kerr Conway about the verse of T. S. Eliot, "It became as much a part of the inner landscape of my mind as Shakespeare's sonnets . . ." (1989, p. 184).

So What Shall They Write?

If writing about literature is integrated with an activity-based approach to writing, students need not always write in response to the same piece of literature, nor need they always write in response to the same assignment provided by the teacher. Either of these approaches can result in a kind of deadliness that kills both interest in literature and the natural capacity to know one's own response.

Look at the following essays written by two ninth graders when asked to write a letter of advice about how to do well in literature:

Hi Dan,

Thanks for your letter. So you're getting nervous about 9th grade literature classes. Well, don't worry about a thing. Ninth grade is easier than it seems. There are only a few things that you will need to know. First of all, know how to spell and study your spelling vocabulary every week. Every time you have a final 1/2 of it is vocabulary words. Next, always read the book your assigned because the test you have over them will be very specific. Also remember to never use bad grammar in class. The teachers will get on your back for that. That's basically it. I hope that you do as well as I did.

Good luck in 9th grade.

The second letter is less deadly—the writer knows how to work the system somewhat more confidently—but, as with the first letter, it tells us how not to have students respond to literature:

Dear Little Person-
Who-is-one-year-younger-than-me,

English is really a fun class, but you have to have 5 things to be able to succeed in class. Here they are:

(1) Come well dressed, (2) Have a black pen, (3) Have enough money to be able to . . . <<OOPS!>> . . . Wrong list! (Just kidding)

1) Do your vocabulary—every week you get 10 words w/sentences to write. DO THIS because otherwise, you will probably sink.

2) Be nice—the teacher will probably think that you're a head, neonazi, prep, stuck-up, snat, etc. and automatically give you the appropriate grade.

3) Don't do other homework in class (or read, too) I know someone who does that (he sits right next to me), and I don't think he's all that, for lack of a better word, "Here."

4) Do know the names of the authors of the books and stories—these will ALWAYS be test questions.

5) Enjoy yourself—everything seems stupid to you if you don't want to learn something, but the literature is diverse enough for anybody to enjoy as long as you let go of the "I have to please . . ." idea, which is completely stupid, anyway.

Follow this list and enjoy your life in 9th grade.

Good luck.

Writing That Is Directly Related to Literature

Writing in any extended form requires a kind of mental engagement that can be avoided in spoken response. It requires us to organize our thoughts and to think beyond the obvious. Extended writing draws from the mind of the reader more information, more reflection, more wrestling than, for example, either group discussion or brief responses to questions will do. In part, this is a result of not having the conversational situation or the question as a means of providing only the essential information. A good assignment eggs us on to say more than we would on our own initiative, if only because the page has to be filled.

Writing also seems to have a spin-off effect: One sentence generates another sentence, until we have provided a composite view of what we think and feel. In contrast, questions that require short answers (e.g., "Who was the main character in *A Catcher in the Rye*") automatically set up limitations to further growth because they limit exploration.

We could liken extended writing in response to literature to taking a journey with no intention of following any given path (often the impressionistic, personal response) or taking a guided tour of the terrain to be covered (more likely an analytic response). In either case, a journey implies that some distance will be traveled, that the traveler and the terrain will determine the stopping points, that dallying and rendezvous locations may be modified as the journey progresses, and, ultimately, that when the journey is over, the traveler will have a substantial experience to record and ponder.

Another argument in favor of extended written responses relates to the nature of writing itself. When we first explore the extent of our knowledge and perspective on a topic we often discover both what we do and don't want to say about it. Additionally, the early forays into writing about a topic help us to discover what we do and don't know and send us scurrying back to find out more, if need be.

We now understand what real writers have always understood: that the early phases of writing about something enable us to "clear the mental decks"—get rid of intrusive material and unburden our memory capacity. Katherine Paterson reminds us of this: "I'd better get it down any way I can in the first draft. In the next draft I can write it properly" (1981, p. 123). Writing is a juggling act that requires us to balance giving attention to content, structure, style, and perspective with attending to the ubiquitous domains of spelling and usage.

In asking students to write, we ask them to reformulate experiences for themselves and transform them into a form capable of being understood and appreciated by others. Furthermore, writing about literature (particularly in the analytic response mode) requires the ability to generalize, to evaluate, and to synthesize. These critical thinking skills also develop classificatory skills, especially those needed to determine relevance and to relate parts to whole and whole to parts (for example, how plot illustrates theme or how a line in a poem relates to another line in a different stanza).

Literature may also offer a more immediately accessible content to write about than, say, history, biology or economics, because the experiences portrayed in literature are related to all human experience, however remote. So characters who are jealous, disillusioned, sad, delighted, ingenuous, or scheming provide readers with recognizable human traits. In this respect, literature is a natural platform from which to dive in order to explore how others negotiate life's currents.

Exploring Reading Literature through Writing

Writing in response to literature, whether formally or informally, can include a wide range of activity, from brainstorming, writing early drafts, and writing spontaneously to writing work to be published. Not every piece of writing should be graded, not every piece should be "finished," not every piece needs to be read by the teacher or by other students. Writing that the student feels might have potential for development could be filed in a writing folder.

At times, a student may not want to write something in response to a reading, and we suggest that this, too, should be an acceptable alternative. How many times have we finished reading a book in the predawn hours and wanted nothing more than to be allowed to let it soak in?

Are we arguing that letting a book soak in is a response?

Yes, we are.

And for those who fear that we won't know if a student is really responding or merely goofing off, we'd suggest that closer observation of behaviors should put those fears into perspective. We've all been in classrooms, teacher-led and proof-of-response dominated, in which visible signs of paying attention belie the reality of student switch-off: the half-awake pose, the doodling, and the wandering through the rest of the work with a finger on the hopefully right page.

That's not the same as reading intently and then staring into space.

How to entice students to become really interested in the literature we ask them to explore is a vexing question for most teachers. Allowing adult leisure-reading behaviors is one way of doing this.

But does this foster the behaviors of serious students of literature?

Have the students keep a notebook and encourage them to record passages, extracts, whole poems, and the like that intrigue them, delight them, or catch their attention in some way. Encourage them to jot down what literary figures have said or written about their writing, to provide students with their own records of these insights into the creative act. Collections of letters, biographies, autobiographies, literary essays, and interviews with writers are rich sources for these kinds of records.

We're not proposing recipes for writing about literature, but in Figure 9.1 we suggest some ways of grouping the kinds of writing students might do that might help us keep track of what they have attempted and avoided over a period of time.

We have configured the functions of writing in response to literature around groups that represent both the function the writing might fulfill (e.g., writing to learn) and the kinds of writing that might be appropriate for each function (e.g., character profiles).

We are aware of the limitations of presenting these functions in a categorized format. Therefore, Figure 9.2 suggests no particular grouping,

FIGURE 9.1

FUNCTIONS OF WRITING IN RESPONSE TO LITERATURE

Writing to Learn:
    Responses in journals, logs
    Character profiles
    Characters from other characters' perspectives
    Alternative, hypothetical endings
    Summary
    Reviews
    Criticism
    Evaluation

                Writing to Convey Emotions:
                  Letters to friends about book(s) read
                  Journals, diaries
                  Students select form (e.g., a poem, a reflective
                     piece, an episode or scenario) best suited to
                     express written response at the emotional level
                     to a novel, story, or poem

Writing to Imagine:
    Creative spin-offs—not necessarily related to the literary text(s) being dealt with but
        possibly exploring the genre and mode

                Writing to Inform:
                  Open-ended questions for exploring student under-
                     standing of literary texts
                  Analysis of literary aspects of the work
                  Critical appreciation through writing

Writing to Convince:
    Critical arguments
    Discussions about who should and should not be censored
    Book reviews

Functions of Writing in Response to Literature

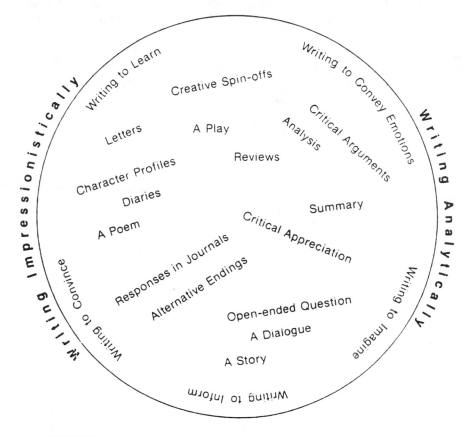

FIGURE 9.2

although the information is essentially the same. In the second figure we want to suggest that the kinds of writing we might have students do (e.g., those character profiles) may fulfill one or more or any of the functions represented inside the rim of the circle (e.g., writing to learn or writing to inform or writing to imagine).

At the same time, this kind of writing (e.g., character profiles again) might be analytical in the sense that students would be required to evaluate the qualities of a character relative to their status in the work, or students might be asked to come to grips with what they feel and think about a character (impressionistic writing) and why (analytic writing).

None of the groupings we have suggested anywhere in this chapter is mutually exclusive and none fits neatly into a separate slot. Ultimately, the teacher and the students determine the types of writing that will be done.

Presenting something as complex as writing in any one- or at best two-dimensional way doesn't really capture just how many simultaneous aspects are involved in the act of writing. For example, we've tried to illustrate some of the main functions we see that writing in response to literature may have. At the same time, we've said that we can ask students to explore responses to literature either impressionistically or analytically. And we have also said that none of the categorizations are mutually exclusive.

All of these activities can be encompassed in a view of writing that permits evolution, process, and refinement and allows for the validity of the spontaneous notation or record. A literature notebook or folder or portfolio (see Chapter 11) could be kept as a record for evaluating students' understanding and their responses to literature.

Elaborations

As we said earlier, response writing may either be impressionistic or analytic. If impressionistic, the focus will be less on the literary work than on the reader's subjective *reaction* to it. If analytic, the focus shifts from the reader's self to the literary work—that is, we write *about* the literary work rather than how we feel or think in reaction to it.

Yet even the analytic response contains elements of the reader's impressionistic response, although in this instance, the reader is actively attempting to understand the literary work itself.

The analytic or text-examining response might be termed an intellectual one in which the reader attempts to distance himself or herself from the literary work. We might add, however, that not allowing adolescents the opportunity to articulate their impressionistic or self examining responses to literary works can hamper subsequent analytic responses; we suggest strongly that room be made for both.

How can writing be used to explore both kinds of response? Typically, teachers have used analytic response writing more frequently than impressionistic response writing. The analytic written response often focuses on having the student declare "the" thematic development of the work or offer an argument for or against an interpretive view of the work.

Typically, the reader is asked to adopt a critical perspective of the literary work and discuss it in terms of such things as theme, characterization, setting, plot, point of view, and style. However, such a response need not be as restrictive and constructive as it appears, and we shall discuss alternative approaches later in this chapter.

At this point we'd like to suggest that the *value* of written response to literature lies primarily in the scope it offers to the student to articulate a range of perspectives about the literary work.

Impressionistic Self-Examining Writing

Impressionistic response writing can be the loosest, freest form of writing. As the word *response* suggests, it is an articulation of how one feels and thinks about something (in this case, something read).

We can write impressionistically to learn, to convey emotions, to imagine, or to inform, just as we can write for these purposes when the focus is on the text itself (i.e., analytic writing).

Therefore, the form of response writing can be whatever the individual chooses and best represents the nature of the response. For example, some students may want to write a poetic response to either prose or poetry because that form allows them to express most faithfully their own thoughts and feelings. Others may choose to write a stream-of-consciousness piece. A number may want to write a more crafted piece—a creative, aesthetically based response. Still others may want to write a journal entry—"talking" to the teacher, to someone else, or to themselves about their thoughts and feelings.

In such cases, we'd expect to see a conversational style, use of the first person, and a more overtly subjective reaction, full of statements like "I like it because . . . I didn't enjoy the way X did Y . . ." and so on.

Another possibility is that students may wish to write a subjective response intertwined with interpretive thoughts, as in the following:

> The main concern or theme of the play *The Fire on the Snow* is somewhat hard to put into words but to me is summed up quite clearly in the author's Foreword to the play: It is, in its simplest terms, a struggle usually of man against man; in *The Fire on the Snow*: essentially of man against snow, the spirit of man against all the conspires to defeat him.

The writer of this excerpt, which is taken from an essay exploring the main issues in Douglas Stewart's *The Fire on the Snow* (a play about the last days of Scott and his companions after discovering they had not beaten Amundsen to the South Pole), concludes:

> To me, the play *Fire on the Snow* is related to the themes I listed above, i.e., qualities of endurance, courage, humanness and determination all of which have a great bearing on the play. I enjoyed the play and think it was a great way of putting together such an historic event.

The student in this example demonstrates that, remote as the experience responded to may be (a South Pole expedition in the early twentieth century), she had nevertheless developed both a close engagement with the text and an intellectual perspective on its power over the reader.

Short-answer and multiple-choice questions don't offer the scope or the space for this kind of textual exploration.

One of the strongest arguments for encouraging students to write impressionistically, or expressively, about literature is that in doing so, they use their own voice and their own language. Writing about something that is not within one's own experience is challenging; trying to do so in a style and from a perspective also not one's own is setting oneself up for frustration and potentially permanent alienation. We can look at impressionistic writing as a springboard for moving from the self to the work—the latter requiring more often than not use of language (i.e., critical, analytical language) that is outside an adolescent's regular experience.

VIGNETTE XIV: IMPRESSIONISTIC WRITING AS RESPONSE

We include here some examples taken from an activity during which eleventh-grade students were asked to write an essay expressing their thoughts on the content of Eudora Welty's short story "A Worn Path" and the meaning or significance of that content. The students were not given any prior information about the story but were provided with a brief biographical sketch of Eudora Welty. They were encouraged to make notes during their reading of the story, including their reactions, confusions, associations or anything else that occurred to them.

Student A:

The story "A Worn Path" is one with no standard plot or course of events. The main character, Phoenix Jackson, is an old woman who has to rely on the kindness of others to get what she needs. The supposed theme will be discussed below, as well as my ways of arriving at my conclusion.

Student B:

The theme of a "Worn Path" is patience. In this story, the granny walks to town to get a present and medicine for her grandson. She must of had much patience to walk the long journey.

Student C (as part of her conclusion):

It is also important to see how Phoenix thinks of the things that she sees on the way to town. She spoke to the animals and a thornbush that caught her dress like they were naughty children. She talks to herself when she crosses a creek on a log. Then, later on, when she rested, she thought she saw a young boy offering her some marble cake. When she goes through a corn field she calls it a maze. Her eyes often fooled her too. She saw a scarecrow and thought it was a ghost.

In this kind of open-ended writing experience, we find that many students do what we all do when writing about anything. We've said elsewhere that the first articulations are usually forays into the forest, trying to discover what it is we really want to say, coming to grips with what we think something means, often halting attempts to define our own understanding.

We may not agree with what the students in the preceding examples think. We may even be discouraged that they are not observant about those aspects of the story that we think are important—for example, that Phoenix is an African-American woman. But recall that these are *initial responses*, which will generate in-depth discussion and further writing and from which students will return to the story for confirmation and disconfirmation of their perceptions.

Analytic Response Writing

When we move to analysis, we move away from the impact a work has on us to examine the work itself and discover what, in the work, causes it to have the effect it does. However, analytic writing does not mean that students have to become entangled in technical jargon. It also does not mean that exploratory writing and revision disappear. After the initial impressionistic responses are recorded in language and forms familiar to the student, teachers and students may select from these pieces those that suggest further possibilities and that may be reworked to move toward a more objective discussion of the literary text.

Analytic response writing requires the writer to move from the private to the public domain. Now we describe for others the work as we perceive it and give our reasons for our perceptions.

Because analytic writing assumes a shift to a more critical stance, using terms such as *theme(s)*, *plot*, *rhyme*, *rhythm*, *figures of speech*, and so on becomes appropriate because we assume an audience familiar with critical writing. Using such terms allows us to highlight certain aspects of the literary text that may be significant to our reading of it.

The use of those terms, however, is not our primary objective in having our students write analytically about the literary text. For example, the following essay illustrates a student's understanding of the role of Iago in Shakespeare's *Othello* but also illustrates the difficulty many students have in using language appropriate for formal critical writing:

Shakespeare has written the play *Othello* as a tragedy, but included a mixture of love, justice and jealousy in writing such a play. Othello, so said by many, is the main character of the play because he is the tragic figure. He leads, and for this he is the tragic hero. However, in the sense of love, justice, and jealousy, Iago plays the main character of the play. Iago forces events to occur the way they do, and is almost totally responsible for the evil set loose in the play."

The student was struggling to understand why *Othello* does not act like a typical main character, who usually directs or influences the action of the play. However, even literary critics don't agree about the roles played by Othello and Iago. We can hardly expect a sixteen-year-old to give a definitive interpretation one way or another!

Although the students doing this writing assignment were given the opportunity for revision and conferencing with their English teacher, they had not been given the opportunity for early writing of the expressive kind previously described. Such writing might have helped this student and the others in the class sort out the thematic and relational complexities in this play at their own level before having to write about them in a formal critical manner.

As we noted earlier, analytic writing may have several primary functions. Among these are writing to learn, writing to inform, and writing to convince.

None of these functions is mutually exclusive. For example, students may be asked to write a critical appreciation of a literary work. This is an act of learning how to generalize (e.g., talk about the thematic development in the work) and how to link whole to parts (e.g., select appropriate examples from the text in support of arguing a particular thematic development). In this example students write to learn as well as to inform.

Additionally, students may be asked to adopt a stance concerning an interpretation of the text (e.g., that the work is or is not reflective of an author's philosophical perspective on life). This requires them to develop an argument and hence, a position that must be defended.

In asking students to engage deeply in the text, we can assume that (a) they have read the text closely; (b) they have remembered most of it and have been able to translate it into their own understanding and experiences; (c) they have already exercised some degree of interpretation about the text; (d) they have analyzed its categorical parts (e.g., plot, theme, episodes, characters who are most and least important); (e) they have synthesized it (related the parts to the whole and perceived the parts in relation to each other); and (f) they have evaluated it (formed some kind of judgment about the text).

In writing a critical appreciation, students learn a great deal about the text and their own response to it. They have also evaluated their own understanding of it relative to that of others. Finally, they have demonstrated that understanding to us (i.e., they are writing to learn, to inform, and to convince).

To clarify the arguments we have made here, we have included an essay written by a tenth grader on George Orwell's *Animal Farm*.

VIGNETTE XV: ANALYTIC WRITING AS RESPONSE

Students were asked to argue the position linked with the following question: *Animal Farm* is a story for children about talking animals. Do you agree? Discuss the reasons for your decision.

Of course it's a loaded question because as teachers of literature, we know the novel is a satire (at least, we believe it is), and therefore, the astute student of literature should argue that it is much more than a story about talking animals. The third and final draft of the essay is reproduced here.

> George Orwell tells us, in *Animal Farm*, of a story about a rebellion by animals over the farm owner, Mr. Jones, who was an oppressor. The story is one of a seemingly victorious rebellion, which is represented by a group of talking animals. However, because the book is not as we would normally expect to find one of this kind—that is, without a leader in history whom we can refer to, and place a name to, we must not, and cannot refer to *Animal Farm* as a children's book or one solely for children.
>
> In writing *Animal Farm*, George Orwell has given us almost two books within the one story; a book on two different levels. One in a superficial way. The other requiring us to interpret the words in greater depth, and relate them to the main theme of the book—Power. This "power" theme is also to show how power causes eventual corruption of an "ideal" society (without class distinction). However, "almost" is an important word, as Orwell's fine line between portraying a message to man, and telling a children's story leans more toward the former, than the latter.
>
> Although Orwell states at the beginning of the book *Animal Farm—A Fairy Story*, we should not read the book thinking that the story is merely for the amusement of a reader who wishes to find out about animals who tend to themselves on a farm. Instead, we should be able to sense something more in the book, even though he welcomes us to the story with the above statement. Some examples of this are: the event of the Rebellion; the partaking human voices, and, a specific example is the ordering of death after "trials" for crimes which were never actually committed (p. 74). These suggest that there is more than a "story about talking animals" because they are taking on many human traits.
>
> However, other factors may attribute to the belief of the book being a children's story. One example of this is the cover of the book—the title *Animal Farm* appears to be childlike, and, with

the cover showing a small pig, one would not imagine that such a simple and plain exterior could contain such an important and interesting experience that Orwell expresses within the bindings of *Animal Farm*. The book, too, as in children's stories, is not long, and on reading it, we find the writing and language are simple, as well as containing a simple plot—all these add up to a children's story.

Yet Orwell's book also shows many traits throughout the story, which point toward the fact that this novel is related greatly to humans, their lifestyles, and his theme and theory of power. In fact, the whole story has animals performing tasks that humans alone can normally accomplish and that animals would be unable to do. This is the case in Napoleon's making of deals for the sale of wood. His cunning ways bring a high price for the wood, and Napoleon is once again thought of as being wise, great and fair to all.

We are shown here, that not only do the animals take on voices, but they also display many human faults. At this time in the story, when the pigs and Napoleon seek and keep on striving for greater power, the condition and health of the overworked "laborers" not only declines, but so does the state of *Animal Farm*. Thus, Orwell is reinforcing his views on power, and how it can break down an equal society into classes such as in *Animal Farm*. His point being to show us that an equal society is a dream and not an achievable reality. Here we can also see Orwell's purpose for writing the book showing through his experiences of war time and fighting for a society without classes, is difficult and even impossible.

We can therefore see that his story carries more than a book holding a fable about talking animals, and remembering that children's fairy stories are concluded with "the underdog" and "the good guy" coming out as victors, after violence and terrorism (as in *Animal Farm* to portray the struggle for the maintenance of power; natural leadership and human nature) we have even further evidence that *Animal Farm* is not a book written entirely for children. This is because the inhabitants of Animal Farm ("the underdogs") are still not happy with their situation. They are once again under an oppressor (Napoleon, the pig) and are once again, divided into groups of authority, and class distinction, as they were before the Rebellion.

Three drafts were written of this essay, and the class enjoyed a prewriting discussion about the issue raised in the essay. A period of five weeks was allowed for the final draft to be submitted, and conferences were held with students after each of the two drafts were submitted for review. Students determined the final draft as being their best effort at the time.

Writing about literature in this way is demanding and requires the student to grapple with abstractions that may be outside the common experience of the adolescent. We can expect that students would find essays of this type very challenging for several reasons.

First, they need to be able to know the function of the specific mode—satire—and they need to be able to select appropriate and telling examples from the work to support any argument they put forth.

Second, they need to be able to argue effectively, a rhetorical mode that many students find very challenging.

Third, although they know about power in its concrete forms (e.g., parent-child struggles, bullies in the locker room, teacher vs. student tugs of war), they need to understand power in the abstract, as a social and political concept.

Given these challenges, the writer of the essay in Vignette XV has demonstrated the value of writing in this way (despite some infelicities of organization and style) for several reasons:

> Such writing moves students from the concrete to the abstract and, consequently, fosters the development of analogical reasoning skills.

> Such writing requires students to focus on text rather than self and, therefore, promotes the development of an objective stance that paves the way for critical appreciation of the _qualities_ of the literature, even though students may not personally like certain aspects of the literary work (e.g., its conclusion or one or more characters).

> Such writing helps students develop generalizing and reasoning skills that, at later stages, enable them to link together other books and issues and, therefore, broaden the scope of literary appreciation.

Of course, these are long-term effects but the process of becoming a critically appreciative reader of literature is a long-term one and certainly not brought about by short-answer questions, which limit the scope of thought and argument.

Any extended writing activity requiring students to stand outside their personal response to the literary text can have similar effects. We should remember, though, that the kinds of skills we're asking for in this kind of writing are, essentially, adult ones, and consequently, we need to modify our expectations of students' products. We're just not going to get a professorial version of a critical essay of the kind represented in this chapter from a fourteen- to sixteen-year-old (and do we really want one?), but we can help them extend their experience of literary text from personal to more public through writing experiences of the analytic kind.

Literature Written by Students

We earlier indicated that one of the functions of writing in response to literature is writing to imagine—that is, writing literature. Included in such writing are creative spin-offs, writing in ways that attempt a modeling of the style adopted by the literary text, and writing in literary genres.

Despite the concerns we may have about students not being able to define such terms as metaphor, oxymoron, hyperbole, rhyme, rhythm, and so on, students, when they write literature themselves, demonstrate remarkable skill in using language illustrative of these devices. Writing literature can, therefore, offer wonderful opportunities for exploring the special manipulation of language that this mode often utilizes.

> ### VIGNETTE XVI: CREATIVE WRITING AS RESPONSE
>
> Janet Lanka had struggled to help her students move on from the expressive, private poetry they typically wrote to thinking about their poetry from an aesthetic perspective. She immersed the students in poetry on a daily basis so that the students "began to realize that poetry could be about anything and could be written in any style or shape."
>
> She then pursued another goal—to introduce students to various techniques favored by poets. Her eighth graders looked at language techniques that dealt with the meaning conveyed by the word.
>
> She wrote, "We studied symbolism and the difference between denotation and connotation. By reading poems that illustrated use of these techniques, my students realized that being aware of the different levels of meaning for a word can affect the poem's meaning. Many of them were fascinated by how a poet could use a word that had more than one meaning and how each of the multiple meanings applied. A third goal, to have the students practice what they had learned, was then pursued.
>
> "No matter what type of poem the writer chose to create, the emphasis was always placed on being a 'language detective,' searching for the best-sounding, best-meaning word each time" (Lanka, 1990, pp. 9–10).
>
> An example of a controlled use of rhyme and meter to maintain a humorous, lighthearted style is demonstrated in the following poem by one of those eighth graders:
>
> MY DOG, MY CAT, MY HAMSTER, AND ME
>
> My dog, my cat, my hamster, and me
> Sleep together so peacefully.
> My cat on my pillow, close to my head;
> My dog on the floor in his little dog bed.
> I roll over which makes my cat hiss,
> And my hamster stops spinning his wheel
> long enough to watch this.

Sometimes I wish I had no pets to lie
by my head or to growl from the floor.
If I had no dog to sit and whine at my door?
Or if I had no cat to hiss or to scratch up my face,
And no hamster to spin and keep me wide awake?

So really I'm glad for my hamster, dog and cat,
Even if they don't really know that.

Shel Silverstein would probably be proud of that young writer! And there is the piece by another eighth grader, perfectly capturing the epitaph style but with the quality of the limerick:

GRAVESTONES BY HENRY BONES

Here lies Danny Lee,
He almost learned,
to water ski.

Here lies John Marks,
Now buddies
With the sharks.

Here lies Brian Sute,
He almost learned
To parachute.

Here lies Peter Nunn,
Was foolin' around
With a gun.

Here lies Henry Bones,
Died engraving,
Funny tombstones.

And the control, the sensitivity to the special power of language we mainly see in literature, is also visible in their prose:

GLADIATOR

Circling the ring, I contemplated my next move. Right now he was ahead, but I knew he wouldn't be for long. He was weak, scared, no fire in his eyes. I decided on an all out attack. With all my might I thrust my shoulder into his gut. Without thinking, I wrapped my arms around his legs. This was it—everything or nothing. My body flexed. In an all out show of power I heaved him to the floor. He had lost his will to live. I wrapped

my arms around his head, wishing only to end the battle mer-
cifully. A hand slapped on the mat. Time rushed before me. I
was not a gladiator fighting for my life. I was back on the school
Wrestling Squad.

Writing literature can provide students with motivation for revision
(often perceived by novices and professionals alike as an onerous chore) if
we provide them with opportunities to use their aesthetic responses to literature they read in their own crafting of literature. Always leaving the writing
of poetry at the level of expressive, impressionistic response, for example,
does not do this.

Students who have written with the idea of language crafting, as these
examples illustrate, say that they develop a better understanding of why
writers revise and a greater enthusiasm for revising their own creative
products. In our discussions, students showed tremendous interest in what
other writers say of their own writing. They strongly related to statements like the following, as could be seen in nods of the head, and the
sudden looks of surprise and flashes of recognition ("that's me") on their
faces:

"Writing to me is a voyage, an odyssey, a discovery because I'm
never certain of precisely what I will find." (Gabriel Fielding)

"As you continue writing and rewriting, you begin to see possibilities you hadn't seen before." (Robert Hayden)

"How do I know what I think until I see what I say?" (E. M. Forster)

"More often I come to an understanding of what I am writing about
as I write it." (Frank Conroy)

Murray, 1982, pp. 85-86

Writing literature offers students the opportunity to gain an appreciation
for the crafting nature of aesthetic writing. And, more than any other form of
writing commonly practiced in school, it offers the opportunity for writers to
develop their own style, to strengthen their own voice.

We add a cautionary note, however. Not all students will be comfortable with writing literary pieces, and perhaps it is best that we should not
assume they ought to be. Some will naturally be more inclined to it than
others, just as some are more naturally inclined to scuba diving or rapping
than others.

We suggest, therefore, that this kind of writing not be used for formal
evaluation of students' general performance as writers. But students may be
invited to include samples of it in their writing portfolios, if they so choose.

Closing Thoughts

We've offered some ways in which writing and literature can be meaningful-
ly related in the English literature classroom. The sensitive English literature
teacher will, without doubt, find other ways. As with other writing done in
the English literature classroom, we would like to suggest several maxims to
help make the experience rewarding, enjoyable, and challenging:

>   Do allow for choice in form as well as topic.
>
>   Do allow for opportunities to *not* write in response to readings.
>
>   Do not expect them to write a response for every reading.
>
>   Do provide for varied writing experiences to encourage variations in
>   how we interpret a literary work.
>
>   Do respond to student writing as one responds to established authors—
>   with anticipation and reverence.
>
>   Do not grade every written piece.
>
>   Do encourage students to "publish" their own literary works.
>
>   Do provide opportunities for nongraded literary creative writing. Do
>   provide opportunities for impressionistic response.
>
>   And *be* like Katherine Paterson's editor of whom she wrote: "She did
>   not brush aside that fragile thread spun from my guts. . . . She
>   understood, . . . what I was trying to do" (1981, p. 63).

References

Berthoff, Ann. *The Making of Meaning: Metaphors, Models and Maxims for Writing
    Teachers*. Upper Montclair, NJ: Boynton/Cook, 1982.

Conway, Jill Kerr. *The Road from Coorain*. New York: Vintage Books, 1989, 184.

Huff, Ronald, and Charles Kline, Jr. *The Contemporary Writing Curriculum: Rehears-
    ing, Composing, Valuing*. New York: Teachers College Press, 1987.

Gurko, Leo. *Joseph Conrad: Giant in Exile*. New York: Collier Macmillan, 1981.

Lanka, Janet. "Instead of Faking It . . . I Told My Students How I Felt." *Literacy Mat-
    ters* 3, no. 2. Columbus, OH: Ohio State University, Martha King Literacy Center,
    1990, 9-10.

McCrorie, Ken. *Telling Writing*. 2nd ed. Rochelle Park, NJ: Hayden, 1976.

Murray, Donald. *Learning by Teaching: Selected Articles on Writing and Teaching*.
    Upper Montclair, NJ: Boynton/Cook, 1982, 85-86.

Newkirk, Thomas, ed. *Only Connect: Uniting Reading and Writing*. Upper Mont-
    clair, NJ: Boynton/Cook, 1982.

Paterson, Katherine. *The Gates of Excellence: On Reading and Writing Books for
    Children*. New York: Elseview/Nelson Books, 1981, 123.

Resources

Alexander, Lloyd. "An Interview." *Language Arts* 61 (1984): 411-413.

Anson, Chris M., ed. *Writing and Response: Theory, Practice, and Research*. Urbana,
    IL: National Council of Teachers of English, 1989.

Atwell Nancie, *In the Middle: Writing, Learning and Reading with Adolescents*. Upper Montclair, NJ: Boynton/Cook, 1987.

Britton, James, Tony Burgess, Nancy Martin, Alex McLeod, and Harold Rosen. *The Development of Writing Abilities (11-18)*. London: Macmillan, 1975.

Bruner, Jerome S. *Beyond the Information Given: Studies in the Psychology of Knowing*. Edited by J. M. Anglin. New York: W. W. Norton, 1973.

Bunge, Nancy. *Finding the Words: Conversations with Writers Who Teach*. Athens: Ohio University Press, 1985.

Donovan, Timothy, and Ben W. McClelland. *Eight Approaches to Teaching Composition*. Urbana, IL: National Council of Teachers of English, 1971.

Emig, Janet. *The Composing Processes of Twelfth Graders* (Research Report 13). Urbana, IL: National Council of Teachers of English, 1971.

Emig, Janet. *The Web of Meaning: Essays on Writing, Teaching, Learning and Thinking*. Upper Montclair, NJ: Boynton/Cook, 1983.

Flower, Linda S., and John R. Hayes, "Images, Plans and Prose: The Representation of Meaning in Writing." *Written Communication* 1 (1984): 120-160.

Freedman, Sarah W. *The Acquisition of Written Language: Response and Revision*. Norwood, NJ: Ablex, 1985.

Gere, Anne Ruggles, ed. *Writing across the Disciplines* Urbana, IL: National Council of Teachers of English, 1985.

Horner, Winifred, ed. *Composition and Literature: Bridging the Gap*. Chicago: University of Chicago Press, 1983.

Langer, Susan. *Mind: An Essay on Human Feeling*. Vol. 1. Baltimore: Johns Hopkins University Press, 1967.

Lloyd, Pamela. *How Writers Write*. Portsmouth, NH: Heinemann, 1988.

Marshall, James D. "The Effects of Writing on Students' Understanding of Literary Texts." *Research in the Teaching of English* 21 (1987): 30-63.

Murray, Donald. *A Writer Teaches Writing*. Boston: Houghton Mifflin, 1968.

Murray, Donald. "Write Before Writing." *College Composition and Communication* 29 (1978): 375-81.

Newell, George, and Russell Durst, eds. *Exploring Texts: The Role of Discussion and Writing in the Teaching and Learning of Literature*. Norwood, MA: Christopher-Gordon Publishers, 1993.

Probst, Robert. *Response and Analysis: Teaching Literature in the Junior and Senior High School*. Portsmouth, NH: Heinemann, 1988.

Purves, Alan, and Victoria Rippere. *The Elements of Writing about a Literary Work*. Urbana, IL: National Council of Teachers of English, 1968.

chapter 10

Reading in Hyperspace

English classes and literature classes in particular should have changed in the past decade, thanks to the introduction of the personal computer and now the CD-ROM and computer networks. It is our sense that these technologies as well as others, except the overhead projector (videocassette recorder), have had a minimal impact on the literature classroom. You will find students using word processors to write their papers, but they won't be using them with literature.

Many students know a lot more about computers and camcorders than their teachers.

Nintendo and Sega exist out of school. Who sees them as a form of literature?

Books are available on diskette and CD-ROM as well as on audiotape. A whole new genre of hypertext novels is now available—or example, novels like *Afternoon*, by Michael Joyce—that allows the reader to interact with the text in a variety of ways. Reading no longer begins on page one and ends on page 220. There is no printed text. Reading takes place on the screen, and the reader creates the book anew with each reading.

Hypermedia presentations of books like *Lord of the Flies* that contain film, questions, exercises, and commentaries are available to teachers. These are not supplements to the book, but new ways of considering its teaching.

The literature classroom has to come to terms with the electronic age. But there is a lot of resistance. And it is odd. After all, the computer is in many ways like the book and perhaps even more like the library. It is a means of storing information and helping people retrieve and manipulate information that has been stored. That is what books are, too, of course, so that the best way to think of the use of computers in literature courses is as extensions and modifications of the page. With a twist—or an olive. As we noted in Chapter 2, the advent of electronic technology in this century has changed our thinking about literature and the way people read and think about their reading. It should make itself known in the classroom.

To think again about what we are after, we can see that computers have two interlocking uses: (1) providing a storage base for the text, sounds, and pictures and for recording articulated responses and (2) providing a means of communication so that this base can be retrieved anywhere on the globe.

The Storage Base

Computers can be used as a means of presenting literature. The machine can present texts and turn the pages on command. It can also provide preprogrammed questions and response starters.

Computers can be used for searching databases about books, authors, historical events, and other resources. Students can use on-line catalogs to find out all sorts of information.

The computer could also be used in articulating a response by creating a computer game based on a text, using desktop publishing to publish a set of papers about a novel, and providing a multiyear record of student responses.

The Communication Tool

Within a classroom a set of computers (or even a single computer) can allow students to share their response journals as they are reading a play or novel. The computer becomes a class notebook.

If school computers are networked, students can create a large, school-wide journal, sharing responses to a text among classes.

As a result of the new information networks, students in one school can converse with students in another about their reading and viewing. A class in South Carolina could ask a class in Alaska to help them understand *Julie of the Wolves*.

Another way to use these networks is to access worldwide databases on all sorts of topics related to what students are reading. They, for example, can search for pictures of different productions of *The Cherry Orchard* or *Raisin in the Sun*.

The computer can create an exciting learning and response environment in the world of hypertext, which brings all these uses together. Let us explore some of these uses further.

Preprogrammed "Teaching" of Response Articulation

As in other fields the idea of programs that teach literature has been attractive. A number of programs have been produced over the past fifteen years, many good ones. But there have been a number of programs that treat the reading of literature as if it were "reading," with all the wrong answers and pseudoresponses—an electronic multiple-choice test. These don't really fit the response-based approach at all.

A few programmers have undertaken experimental versions of response-based programs. Some allow the student to read a poem and select a response to it, or rate the poem or the poet on one of a number of scales. In some cases the students can even write a brief response and the computer can scan it for certain words and then ask the student to elaborate on those words.

Another experimental program type allows the student to choose a question about a text and then trace other students' answers to that question. Still a third type of program starts with question selection and then tells the student what sorts of items must be included in an answer to that question. An example of how it would work follows:

Read the following text:

The Sea

Poor boy. He had very big ears, and when he would turn his back to the window they would become scarlet. Poor boy. He was bent over, yellow. The man who cured came by behind his glasses. "The sea," he said, "the sea, the sea." Everyone began to pack suitcases and speak of the sea. They were in a great hurry.

The boy figured that the sea was like being inside a tremendous seashell full of echoes and chants and voices that would call from afar with a long echo. He thought that the sea was tall and green, but when he arrived at the sea, he stood still. His skin, how strange it was there. "Mother," he said because he felt ashamed, "I want to see how high the sea will come on me." He who thought that the sea was tall and green saw it white like the head of a beer—tickling him, cold on the tips of his toes. "I am going to see how far the sea will come on me." And he walked, he walked, he walked, and the sea—what a strange thing!—grew and became blue, violet. It came up to his knees. Then to his waist, to his chest, to his lips, to his eyes. Then into his ears there came a long echo and the voices that call from afar. And in his eyes all the color. Ah, yes, at last the sea was true. It was one great, immense seashell. The sea truly was tall and green. But those on the shore didn't understand anything about anything. Above they began to cry and scream and were saying "What a pity, Lord, what a great pity."

Anna Maria Matute

Which of the following questions do you think it most important to ask about "The Sea"? Select one response:

- *What do I think the story means?*
- *What sort of a story is this?*
- *Why is this story written the way it is?*
- *Is this a well-written story? Is it any good?*

You have selected *What do I think the story means?* That's a good question. I don't know the answer to it but maybe you can tell me. First tell me which of the following clues to meaning I should pursue. Select one and then hit return.

- *The narrator's comments*
- *Contrasts and oppositions*
- *Sudden shifts and things put next to each other*
- *Repetitions of words, phrases, or images*
- *The title*
- *The character of the boy*
- *Symbols*
- *Allusions to myth or folk tale*

You selected *contrasts and oppositions*. That was an interesting choice. Please enter the contrasts that occur to you.
[*Student enters three: sea and land, boy and those on the shore, and life and death.*]

That's a good list. I've been collecting contrasts, too, from other readers, and I've got several. Which of these did you think of?

- *The sea and the land*
- *The top of the sea and under the sea*
- *The spectrum of colors*
- *The boy and the grownups*
- *The thoughts of the boy and what he saw*
- *The narrator and the characters*

So we picked two that are the same. Please enter the others you thought of that I missed. [*Here the program can add any new ones to its memory.*]

You thought of all of mine and some others as well? What do you think these add up to in the way of meaning? Hit return and type your answer.
[*Student types a paragraph. Here the program stores the paragraph.*]

I have stored your interpretation. Do you want to compare your interpretation to those that other students have written based on this approach? If so, hit RETURN. Do you want to stop here or go on to another approach? Hit RETURN to go back to the menu of approaches. Hit the shift key and RETURN to stop.

The program can cycle the student through all the clues or allow the student to end and summarize the meaning of the story. Each of the questions has a set of alternative avenues for the student to explore in coming up with an answer. This sort of program can be written without having the programmer estimate all of the response possibilities but allows for new ones to be added. That sort of program, involving a reading and storage capacity, is an alternative way of generating responses. It is relatively simple and can be constructed by a class on a system like Hypercard™.

As we have said, few of these sorts of programs exist in commercial form, and there is probably little commercial support for them except as adjuncts to a presentational package like a hypermedia presentation of a novel or a play. Look carefully at these and make sure they are not simply the old kind of true-or-false worksheet. There are programmed tests on some literary selections that seem quite useful as both testing and teaching devices, but again these are not very widespread.

The Computer Could Be Used as a Medium for Articulating a Response

Perhaps the best people to work with computers and texts are your students. We have found that a number of our students who enjoy computers have experimented with creating teaching and learning programs for other students.

Some have taken class profiles of responses to a poem and used statistical packages to examine central tendency and dispersion. One approach was to use the sort of scale we mentioned on p. 85. In this version the scale was attached to *Lord of the Flies*. The teacher had divided the sonnet into four parts, at the end of lines 4, 8, 12, and 14. After each break, the students were to report their ratings of the poem on a number of dimensions, using a scale of 1 (low) to 5 (high): GOOD, STRONG, MORAL, PASSIVE, SIMPLE, DARK, SUBTLE, VIGOROUS, HAPPY. After the students had done their individual ratings, the student programmer entered the results and determined a class rating and a profile of variation on each dimension. The class then discussed the results and through the discussion showed how fully they could articulate their response to and understanding of the poem.

Some of them have come up with games.

Often these games are based on Dungeons and Dragons or similar role-playing games. Others are more like board games. One of the most successful we saw was a game based on *Macbeth*, in which the central characters attempted to gain the castle at Dunsinane. Another class did an elaborate game based on Tolkien's *Lord of the Rings*.

A game based on *A Tale of Two Cities* used maps of London and Paris and had the characters move back and forth. Another student used the same concept for *Wuthering Heights*, with the two houses as the sites. A class used the concept for *A Raisin in the Sun*. A third game had Huck Finn try to get down the river and escape the various people and incidents that came after him. Other journey games have been based on *The Autobiography of Miss Jane Pitman*.

The creation of these games showed an understanding of the story and a nice ability to create a program. Not all of the games were computerized: One senior class created "Pictionary" versions for the characters from the Greek and Elizabethan plays they read, and a junior class created an African-American literature "Trivial Pursuit." But even these could be put on a computer.

The computer as a word processor has enabled students to create their own anthologies. Classes have made collections of legends from all of the cultures represented by the students in the class. Another class created a calendar with quotations from Hispanic poets.

Computer-generated scrapbooks based on literature read in and out of class are popular with many students.

The desktop publishing capability of the computer allows students to explore format and layout as they put their favorite poems on disk and then create anthologies. They have been able to experiment with different typefaces in presenting their text, and some of them have even generated graphics to go with it. They have found that the context, particularly the visual context, is important.

Gray goose and gray gander, waft your wings together, and carry the good king's daughter over the one-strand river.

> *Gray goose and gray gander,*
> *Waft your wings together,*
> *And carry the good king's daughter*
> *Over the one-strand river.*

Gray goose and gray gander,
Waft your wings together,
And carry the good king's daughter
Over the one-strand river.

Gray goose and   gray gander,

                                         wings

              Waft your

   together,

Andcarrythegoodking'sdaughteroverthe

                      one-strand

                                         river.

Each of these versions makes the nursery rhyme different for the reader. So too can the various versions created by the students as they form their anthology. They can also add illustration, set off dialogue differently, and re create a text as a newspaper story.

Some students have taken Stephen Crane's "The Open Boat" and put it next to the newspaper version Crane wrote, then reset the story as if it were in newspaper columns to see the extent to which format affects response. They then gave the new version to another class and taped the discussion.

The Computer Can Be Used for Sharing over Space and Time

A significant use of computer technology is to let students share and compare responses across time and space. Schools can use local-area networking to create a notebook about what they read. The local-area network probably exists in the computer room in most schools. A student at one terminal can read what has been written by a student at another. In some cases the students can communicate directly. Sometimes they have to take turns, but they can comment on each other's responses as they are writing them, and they can compare texts or pictures. They can edit each others work and play games across terminals. These are ways of having the students interact through the technology.

What happens is that small-group work, classroom conversations, and other forms of collaborative learning are now available electronically.

Why do this, when a class can sit in the same room and talk?

There are some advantages, we think, to the electronic classroom. Students who have missed a period can catch up on the class discussion by scanning the electronic bulletin board. A student can respond to another student's comment after thinking about the comment or going to the library. The shy student can take part in the conversation without feeling nervous.

Of course the students will still talk to each other. The conversation is often directed more at the task at hand than at other issues. There is also less competition for the teacher's attention. You are everywhere and nowhere.

Some schools now have the capability to communicate beyond the classroom through user groups on wide-area networks. There are ways for classes in the same school to communicate by taking turns in the computer room, but the classrooms themselves also can be networked and so can schools within and across geographic boundaries.

Wide-area networks enable classes to participate in a common activity. One form of this activity is the simulation game, where students in different schools take parts in a complex simulation. Most of these simulations have been in social studies or history—for example, as taking on the roles of different countries in a conflict in the Middle East—but there have been a few attempts to translate these into literature projects.

One simulation we know of has classes in different schools represent an ancient culture. One school will be Mayan; another Inuit, still another Polynesian. Each class develops and compiles its major folklore, symbols, stories, and a literature anthology. A summary form of these, such as might be found in an archaeological dig, is sent to "anthropologists" in another school who are studying the "lost" world. The only form of communication is through the computer. The anthropologists' report is sent to the originating class to check.

Another form of simulation involves live communication among students in different parts of the country where there are significant numbers from specific cultures. The students share their current folklore, the books they value, the television shows and music they like, their ways of reading a common assignment, and the like, so that the classes can get a real sense of cultural variety. Electronic communication can be supplemented by videotapes. It is also possible to communicate live by satellite through a local cable station. One program of this sort has students in a classroom in the United States "sit in on" a classroom discussion in Australia of a novel both classes have read. The U.S. students were able to explain some aspects of *The Color Purple* that the Australians didn't get.

A commercial form of this approach allows students to correspond online with authors of young adult books and enter into a large-scale dialogue on a book that interests them. The author may be available for a week, and the students can access all of his or her answers to questions from all over the country or the world.

Local and wide-area networking can be exciting forms of sharing responses and building up a complex community of readers who can recognize and explore communal characteristics.

Perhaps the Most Important Use of the Computer Is as a Means of Recording, Organizing, and Sharing Responses to Texts. So Presenting Literature and Recording Responses Become Parts of the Same Package

As we mentioned earlier, there are an increasing number of software packages that present literature in text form, together with a film or film clips of the same selection. This is not a particularly efficient means of presentation except when it is combined with another feature of the computer, its ability to access and add other information quickly and in a complex fashion. This feature is known as hypertext.

Typical computer technology displays one text at a time on a computer screen. With the use of a hypertext system, a student can create or access many related texts and display them on the screen, thus creating hypertext. The flow of reading, then, can be redirected from a basically linear channel to any alternative flow that suits the reader's particular purposes. Suppose you are reading the story, "A Rose for Emily," by William Faulkner, and you come to the part where Colonel Sartoris is mentioned and recall that name from other Faulkner stories. Assuming a rich hypertext program for this story is already in place, you could access information about the use of that character's name in stories such as "Barn Burning." When you found the information you were seeking, you could return to the spot in the story where you left off. Or if the name Homer (Barron) strikes you as an allusion, you could access information about the use of the name *Homer* in literature, or information about what critics have made of the name's symbolism. Perhaps after recovering from the shock of the story's ending, you think it would be interesting to reread the story in chronological order, to grasp the sequence of events that led up to that ending. Or perhaps you are left with the question, Did she really sleep with a corpse? To answer this you might want to access simultaneously a sequential telling of the story and the numerous critical pieces addressing this very question (including one by a nun who draws the obvious conclusion).

In addition to accessing numerous types of related texts, video laser disc technology allows you to access text-related visual material, which can also be displayed on the screen or on a separate screen. It can also be done in Quicktime from magnetic disks. It this case, you might want to view a particular scene from a film version of the story, or several related scenes that are not necessarily in the sequence of the story or in chronological sequence.

The potential of the hypertext and hypermedia technology is limitless. Students themselves can write hypertext programs, and depending on what information sources you link up with (e.g., libraries) there is no limit to information that can be accessed and the programs that can be developed.

One approach that is available is that developed with software called Storyspace™, a hypertext authoring system that allows users to create a complex web of spaces. Jon Landstevt and George Landow (1990) developed one for Tennyson's "In Memoriam" that allows the reader to connect the text of the poem, background information, illustrations, and student comments in a variety of ways. There are also novels presented through the software so that students can follow the text in thousands of different ways. They can add their responses to the text so that the novel and the reading become one. As different students use the program they can add their readings, and the web continues to grow.

VIGNETTE XVII: STORYSPACE™ — THE COMPUTER AND RESPONSE

A simple example is shown with the poem "Dirce." Using Storyspace™, you create five writing spaces, containing the poem, and the other four spaces containing the four paragraphs of information following the poem.

DIRCE
Stand close around, ye Stygian set
With Dirce in one boat convey'd!
Or Charon, seeing, may forget
That he is old and she a shade.

W. S. Landor

Dirce was the name Landor gave a young girl who had recently died. The poem is a tribute to her, and some think an elegy.

Charon was the traditional ferryman of the river Styx. He was responsible for taking the dead across the river from life to Hades. An old man, he was reportedly incorruptible, although each dead person was supposed to be buried with a coin for the ferry. See T. S. Eliot, *The Wasteland*.

Walter Savage Landor lived from 1775 to 1864. He was a friend of many of the major Romantic poets.

An elegy is a poem commemorating the death of a loved one. It is a tribute to the dead and in some cases a prayer for immortality.

In addition to these spaces are a number of blank spaces for the students to write their responses. Each can be labeled with a student's name. What Storyspace™ is able to do is display these on the screen, as in Figure 10.1.

Because each student can access the program, each can open a response space or create a new one. They can write their comments in

FIGURE 10.1 View of Dirce Hypertext

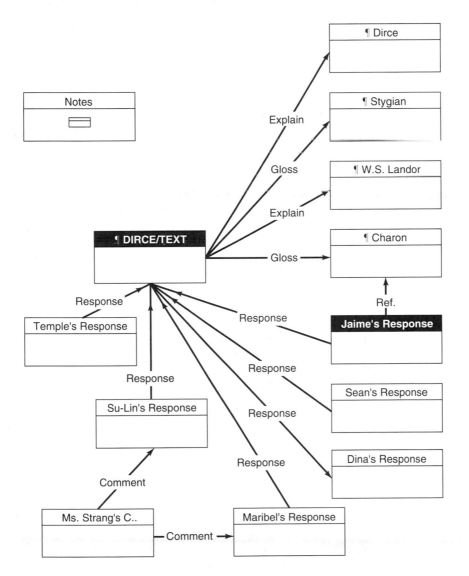

the space (which can hold several pages of text) and can also make links from their response to other responses or to specific words in the text. The students could create a whole glossary on a word like *set*. Each student can also add comments to another student's response, either in the other's space or in a separate one. The resulting hypertext is one that has many connections between text and students.

Some teachers are using Storyspace™ as a way of organizing a novel unit. If the class is to read Amy Tan's *The Kitchen God's Wife*, for example, you can set up a hypertext framework. This might include spaces on background, history, and interpretations. You would list some of the background categories, like "Buddhism," "Chinese folklore," "marriage customs"; historical categories, like "Amy Tan's life," "the publication history of the book," or "early reviews"; and interpretation categories, like "feminist views," "psychological views." In each category you would give a reference source in the library. Each student in the class would pick one of those categories and become the "expert" in that category. The students would fill the space for their category with information, resources, pictures, or whatever they find. They can then make links between the spaces or words or items in the spaces, so there might be a link between "feminist views," "Chinese folklore," and "Amy Tan's life," for example. They can also add spaces with their own comments on the text or on what someone else has written. The teacher can ask questions, too, and make suggestions for elaboration or cross-checking.

With Storyspace™ these links can be given a special name, so that a person can follow the network of relationships around a particular idea. The students can also add their own interpretations to what others have written and can add to or comment on the research of others. The result is a response journal, term paper, final examination, and portfolio all in one.

The benefits of a hypertext program in the response-based literature classroom are clear. It supports the reader's response to a text and allows students to build their own understandings, imaginings, and interpretations of the text's meanings. It also supports the intertextual nature of reading literature that we described in the early part of this book. Readers can access other works of literature by the same or other authors, other "readings" of the text, and information about the author, and juxtapose one aspect of the text with another. If they have the equipment, they can add pictures, film, sound, and music to create a hypermedia event out of the class's response to a text.

This use can play a major role in the lives of students as they read texts and record their understandings of them. However, the hypertext should not take over the classwork, but supplement it. The classroom itself, with all of its talk, drama, and action, is a part of the larger hypertext that brings writer, reader, and text together in myriad ways.

Technology as a Stone Thrown into a Pond

A student enters an initial response to a novel by Sandra Cisneros in a notebook file. Then she adds a series of questions she wants answered. She brings these to class and raises them with her group. Later she and another student enter the answers and their responses to them. These lead to a major question for a paper. The two students and a couple of others go to the library and find a number of sources on the issue. Each enters the quotes and the bibliographic information. With all of this they have a file that can be used for reference and inclusion in their longer papers. The file can grow—just as did the file for this book, which filled two disks.

An individual notebook can grow into a paper on the text. One student's response can be added to by another student, who is linked to the first through a computer network. And then by a third and a fourth. These students do not have to be in the same school, thanks to electronic mail. The first student can then scan the later entries and revise the original note or add to it. This "conversation" can take place over time and space.

The teacher can enter into this network with additional comments or questions.

Another class can also enter into the conversation.

The class does not have to be in the same state.

It does not even have to be in the same year.

From the compiled notebook can come a class composition. It can be reviewed and added to as subsequent readings and responses are entered. Then an editor can produce a final text. It could even be indexed and annotated. It could become a resource for other students writing papers. It could become an annotated bibliography.

Together with the text it can become a different form of the hypertext that next year's students can use to initiate their reading of the same text, thus adding to the cycle.

The result is a "reading" of Sandra Cisneros's text that transcends the individual, space, and time. It can be seen as a historical record, a journal of understandings and perceptions of the text, a collection of commentaries on commentaries. It can enable a variety of students to enter into a community of readers and responders. Without making too much of it, we think this could be a valuable resource for the literature class, particularly in that it can enable students new to a text to have some sense of how other students like them have read it; that these other articulations of response are viable and have merit; that the students are not alone in their doubts and uncertainties.

Of course it could get out of hand . . .

Information overload can result.

But it doesn't hurt to see what the limits are.

Reference

Landstevt, Jon, and George Landow. "The In Memoriam Web" (1992). This excerpt represents only a small portion of the complete hypertext, which can be obtained from Eastgate Systems, Inc.

Resources

Jonassen, David H. "Hypertext Principles for Text and Courseware Design." *Educational Psychologist* 21 (1986): 269-292.

Nelson, Theodor H. *Dream Machines*. South Bend, IN: The Distributors, 1974.

Nelson, Theodor H. *Literary Machines*. 1981. (Available from T. H. Nelson, Box 128, Swarthmore, PA 19081)

Papert, Seymour. *Mindstorms: Children, Computers and Powerful Ideas*. New York: Basic Books, 1980.

Tchudi, Stephen. "Invisible Thinking and the Hypertext." *English Journal* (January 1988): 22-30.

Troutner, Joanne. "Computers and Writers: Software and Other Resources." *English Journal* 77 (1988): 92-94.

chapter 11

Evaluation, Testing, Portfolios: Taking Responsibility

Nearly all that we have been saying in the earlier chapters might as well go unsaid unless something is done about the world of tests that surrounds our students and schools. The United States has been called test mad, and our major testing organizations are happily trying to encourage other countries to join them. Children are tested before they enter kindergarten, and they are subjected to standardized tests that are used to place them, channel them, label them, raise or lower the property values on their parents' homes, reward or punish their teachers and principals, and cause headlines in local papers. Testing is a big industry, and those who reap the greatest profits are test publishers and real estate agents, who can add $20,000 to the value of a property if it is in the "right" school district, which is the one with the highest test scores.

These tests generally do little good in helping teachers do their job better, and they do little to help students learn something more about school subjects except to indicate that certain students may need more help to make it over the hurdles. The result of most of the tests is to label students as "remedial" or "slow" or "gifted," and each label can be used to isolate the students rather than help them work from their strength or shore up their weakness.

A particular problem with these tests is what they do to the teaching of literature. They tend to kill off everything that we suggest should be nurtured. They do so not because the testing companies are malicious or evil but because they simply fill a perceived need and demand—just like gun dealers.

Tests Measure What Our Students Are Learning and Tell Them What to Learn

Three decades of research in literature teaching and testing lead us to a fairly simple summation:

1. Students generally learn what they are taught and don't learn what they aren't taught.
2. What students are taught is not always what teachers think is being taught.

Let us elaborate on these two points. When students are taught a concept or an approach to a text, by and large they demonstrate that they have learned what has been taught and exhibit it in a test situation. Conversely, if they have not been taught a particular type of text or a particular way of looking at texts, and those are on a test, they probably won't get it right. They do not appear to have picked it up naturally.

American students demonstrate that they have learned the lesson of being efficient readers who come up with a single symbolic and moralistic reading of a text, much as if every poem had the characteristic of a fable or the pseudo-texts of the basal reader. This approach to the text is peculiarly American and can be contrasted to the historical and intertextual approach of the Belgian or Italian student, the more stylistic approach of the English or New Zealand student, and the more psychological and evaluative approach of the Swedish student. These groups of students appear to have mastered the critical approach of their teachers. That a few students move from a halting version of the approach to a more fluent version represents, we would argue, not growth but the painful result of a moderately effective educational system that fails to make the rules of the game apparent to the students clearly enough and allows them to learn by trial and error.

Not Learning What Isn't Taught

In addition to showing that students learn what they are taught, studies demonstrate that they do not learn what they are not taught. Analysis of the patterns of performance on particular items and passages revealed that fourteen-year-old U.S. students had greater difficulty both with texts that were more allusive and metaphorical than literal narratives and with items that dealt with style and called for knowledge of literary terms (Purves, 1980). They also had difficulty writing arguments. Such was not the case universally, nor was it true of the older students in the study. An analysis of textbooks and standardized testing programs in the United States shows that the main fare is relatively prosaic and that questions dealing with literary terms or writing arguments are infrequent before the upper years of secondary school, if then.

Lest anyone think we are simply delivering old news, we should say that a recently completed survey of the tests of reading and literature used in secondary schools in this country indicates that little has changed (Brody, DeMilo, and Purves, 1989). Texts are generally straightforward narratives with little figurative language, and the items deal with the efferent message of the text. There is an occasional item on style or structure, but these are insufficient to constitute a meaningful subscore. Most of the essay questions also deal with the description of a determinate meaning. Postmodern critical approaches have yet to find their way into secondary school testing programs in the United States (or into the curriculum, as we mentioned in Chapter 3).

Learning the Wrong Thing

To establish the second of our two generalizations—what students are taught is not always what teachers think is being taught—we could simply point to the first and ask if the specifics that we have outlined match what is desired by the profession or preached by such groups as the California Literature Project or the College Entrance Examination Board.

But we shall go a bit further. Purves, Li, McCann, and Henkin (1991) studied students' perceptions of what constitutes a good literature student. We asked students in the last years of high school to write a letter of advice to students about to attend their school on how to do well in literature classes. (You saw two examples in Chapter 2.) Content analysis of their responses reveals that a large segment of their advice deals with (1) reading strategy: "sit in a hard chair," "take notes on what you are reading," "ask your mother what it means," (2) writing strategy: "watch your spelling," "take a creative approach," and (3) classroom politics: "find out the teacher's interpretation from the class the period before," "sit in the front row and ask questions." Very little advice deals with what we might think of as the substance of reading literature and writing out or discussing one's response to what is read. Literature classes are seen as reading for test taking and clearly not reading for exploration.

There has been a lot of talk in teachers' convocations about growth in English generally and in writing and literature study in particular. If there is growth in U.S. students as they progress through the education system, that growth is not free or natural, but the result of a training and nurturing system that includes a great deal of pruning and the steady administration of manure—particularly in the examination system. We do not think that system is a deliberate plot, but students have become moralizing symbol hunters, and this is not through some sort of natural Piagetian development from the concrete to the abstract and the familiar to the recondite or because literature teachers necessarily desire that outcome.

No, it is simply that such has been the nature of the questions hammered at students beginning in grade one and promulgated by several generations of standardized reading tests. The people who make up the reading tests aren't evil; they just don't know any better. The transition from "What is the main idea?" to "What is the symbolic significance?" is an easy one, and the fact that the main idea or the symbolic significance can be accommodated in a brief response to a multiple-choice question makes the whole matter of literature learning easy to teach, relatively easy to learn (if only you catch onto the system), lacking in joy, and counter to what most serious thinkers believe about the nature of literature and its exploration.

Is there a way out of this situation? We think so. The main way is to redefine the domain of school literature learning for these test makers in school districts, states, and publishing companies and make sure that testing programs cover the domain. It is simple. It is also very, very difficult. It requires convincing parents, school boards, testing companies, and textbook producers. *Change the tests and you change the curriculum and teaching.* It's as simple as that, and yet very complex. There are two approaches: One is to rethink the domain of literature so as to change what is tested; the other is to rethink the mode of assessment so as to change how the assessing is done and by whom. We suggest doing both.

Changing the Tests by Rethinking the Domain

To change the tests, teachers and administrators cannot simply wish them away or attack them as evil. That approach has been tried and it fails. Parents, students, and administrators have a right to know how well students are doing, and they even have a right to know how well they are doing in comparison with some standard. We do not think a comparison with an age group or class is particularly meaningful. We would argue that it is better to see how students are doing with respect to a criterion, such as how well they have covered the subject or how they have changed over time. If we are going to attempt a reasonable alternative to standardized tests, we have to present a clear depiction of the domain and then develop a set of reasonable objectives and a rational means of showing the world the degree to which our students have met those objectives.

To begin that task, let us look again at this domain of literature learning in school as we described it in Chapter 3. The next few pages revisit that chapter from the perspective of assessment.

First, we can say that literature learning is a complex activity that involves not simply individual students but students as a community, who singly and together undertake a set of acts and operations that defines this activity as distinct from others, such as "doing science," or "being historians," or "cooking," or "driving."

Literature as a "Language Art"

The domain of school literature is usually seen as trying to squeeze into one of the language arts, which have often been defined as reading, writing, speaking, and listening. Because literature involves texts that people read or write, and because when students read literature they often write about what they have read, literature tests are simply a subtest of reading and maybe a topic for writing; it's just a different content from social studies.

As we said, we are uneasy with this definition. We become particularly uneasy when we look at the world of tests and see that literature is simply a vehicle for reading comprehension tests or for measures of writing skill or proficiency. To define the literature curriculum as simply a subset of reading and writing neglects a number of the acts that go on within the activity of literature education. We've mentioned a lot of them in this book.

Literature Learning as the Acquisition of Knowledge

Some people would define literature as a school subject that has its own body of knowledge. Recently, this body of knowledge has come to be called "cultural literacy." Narrowly defined, the body of knowledge refers to the names associated with a particular set of texts: authors, characters, plots, and themes. Even more narrowly defined, it limits that body of knowledge to the texts from a particular cultural hegemony. We have suggested that this view is too limited. Literature as a body of knowledge must be expansive and allow for the inclusion of a variety of cultures worldwide particularly within our own melting pot, which keeps refusing to melt. It also must allow for the new, for change. Cultural literacy must include the new and must be ready to shed the outmoded. Schools should include the past and the historical and many of the texts that students would not otherwise read. But they must not be too rigid about it.

The body of knowledge in literature could also be broadened to include critical terms like metaphor, rhyme, plot, and irony, as well as genres, schools and styles of writing, and whole critical approaches. Students should acquire language about literature. They should also become aware of what the properties of novels, drama, and poems are thought to be, even though these definitions should not be too rigid. Poems do not always have to rhyme. Novels and stories can have minimal plots.

Literature Learning as a Special Set of Preferred Acts

Throughout this book we have suggested that literary works are not read and talked about as other kinds of texts are read; they are to be read differently.

Louise Rosenblatt (1978) calls this kind of reading "aesthetic" and opposes it to the more efferent reading that one does with informational texts such as those of social studies and science. Current reading tests only measure efferent reading and by implication signal students that it is the only kind of reading to be valued. As we suggested earlier in this chapter, a part of literature education involves the development of what one might call preferences, that is, habits of mind in reading and writing. These preferences include particular approaches to reading and discussing a text. If we are to inculcate a preference for reading aesthetically, the examination system has to include measures of aesthetic reading.

In addition to ways of reading, literature education is supposed to develop something called "taste" or the love of "good literature," so that literature education goes beyond reading and writing and specific sets of preferences and habits of reading and writing. It includes the development of a tolerance for a variety of literature, a willingness to acknowledge that many different kinds and styles of work can be thought of as literature, and an acceptance that just because we do not like a certain poem does not mean it is not good. It can even lead students to distrust the meretricious or shoddy use of sentiment. Experienced readers of literature can see that they are being tricked by a book or a film even while the trickery is going on.

A Model of the Domain of Literature Learning

The domain of school literature does not need to choose among these three views of literature teaching. In fact the domain is best viewed as divided into three interrelated aspects, as we argued in Chapter 3, and reproduce in Table 11.1.

By way of explaining Table 11.1, we argue first that school literature is different from literature outside of school, simply because schools are self-contained social and cultural institutions with their own rules. Students have to do some things together and respond to certain demands. School literature is like literature outside of school, in that people read and bring their knowledge to bear on what they read and display their preferences about their reading, but in school, students have to do these things more or less on demand. They also have to show their relationship to the group—the community of readers that is the class. In addition, they have to do more writing and talking about their reading, and much of this is quite formal. And they may have to engage in drama or filmmaking or other media work even when they are not quite in the mood to do so.

Interrelationships

This activity appears to involve knowledge, practice, and preference, which are closely interrelated and interdependent. If these aspects are interrelated in the curriculum, they must be interrelated in the assessment. To test on

TABLE 11.1   School literature

Knowledge		Practice		Habits	
Textual	*Extratextual*	*Responding*	*Articulating Habits*	*Aesthetic*	*Choice*
Specific text (structures, subject, language)	History and cultural background	Decoding	Retelling	Evaluating	Reading
Intertextual links	Author's life	Summarizing	Criticizing single works	Selecting	Criticizing
	Genres Styles	Analyzing Personalizing	Valuing Generalizing across works	Valuing	
	Critical terms Response Approaches	Interpreting	Re-creating		

only one of the three aspects is to misconstrue the nature of literature teaching and learning. Practices involve responding and articulating, primarily through reading and writing, but they also might involve listening, viewing, speaking, and moving. These practices are clearly informed and shaped by knowledge, and, in turn, they affect what is known. From two decades of research we know how heavily reading and writing rely on the use of the reader's and writer's knowledge: knowledge of words and their meanings; syntax and grammar; different kinds of organizations and arrangements, such as paragraphs and alphabetized lists; and procedures and strategies for reading. The same applies to writing. At the same time, practice in reading and writing brings the reader and writer new knowledge or reinforces prior knowledge. People both *know* and *know how*. When they know how, their knowledge is moving from practice into habit. The intertwining of these three aspects, knowledge, practice, and habits, is not peculiar to literature; we can see it in driver education, computing, and nearly any other human activity.

In literature, there are certain special kinds of knowledge. Because literary texts often allude to other texts, they demand that readers know something of these texts. *West Side Story* makes its point because the reader knows something of *Romeo and Juliet*. Other works may make general allusions to figures from legend or folklore. These can be thought of as texts, too, of course.

There is another kind of knowledge characteristic of the learning of literature that informs and is affected by the practice of reading: It is knowledge of authors, including other texts they might have written, when they lived, and who influenced their writing.

In addition, there is knowledge of literary terms, genres, and conventions, such as the notation for act and scene divisions in a play, or the form of a sonnet, or the style that is known as realism, or the term *dramatic irony*. It includes knowing the strategies of a whole approach to reading and criticizing, such as Freudian criticism or historical interpretation.

Some test programs include tests solely of this sort of knowledge, but we urge that such testing be minimal and only seen as an adjunct, although an important adjunct, to the practices of reading, writing, responding, and articulating a response to literature in a way that reveals the types of habits formed. Reading literature, as we have suggested throughout this volume, is more than simply decoding or making out the plain sense meaning of the text. That is important and a necessary first step, but it should not be the be-all and end-all of an assessment program—or a curriculum. Reading involves the creation or re-creation of the text in an imaginative peopling of the text in the mind. This re-creation accepts the world of the text as a world that can be personalized and related to the reader's own world. The text can be interpreted as having one or more possible meanings, and it can be analyzed both for its human elements and for its structure, tone, voice, and style.

In school literature, responding is accompanied by articulating, which is to say the production of some sort of formal statement about what has been read. Sometimes this writing is called criticism. People write about their understanding of what they have read and seek to make that understanding accessible to other readers. They seek to persuade other readers that their re-creation, personalizing, analysis, or interpretation is not better than others but certainly acceptable and reasonable.

Another form of writing may be to make some sort of general statement about the body of works that have been read, to draw connections between various texts. One could, for example, show what makes Langston Hughes's poems appear to be by the same author, or how Joseph Conrad's *Heart of Darkness* or Marquez's *One Hundred Years of Solitude* is like Dante's *Inferno*, or how Jane Eyre and Hester Prynne are sisters under the skin. All of these become applications of knowledge.

The use of knowledge in reading and writing has another dimension: the aesthetic. When people read literature (in school or out of it) they should engage in and with the text in such a way as to see it as a work of art to be experienced in and for itself. By the word *should* we are suggesting that practice becomes allied to habit. Readers' judgment of a work may be about its impact on them, its form and structure, its meaningfulness, or a combination of the three.

These sorts of judgments are to be encouraged in literature classrooms, as are discussions that should emerge if, as is to be expected, students disagree about the aesthetic merit of a particular poem or story. Reading's aesthetic dimension should be explored in writing and can be the focus of a part of the assessment program. Certainly a set of tasks could describe the aesthetic principles students hold, and should also call on them to justify their judgments. The aesthetic dimension of a literature program should also manifest itself in what the students select to read.

A literature program should show itself in the habits students develop. At the end of a literature program such as the one we advocate, students should be reading a variety of kinds of works, both classic and contemporary. In addition, they should have the habit of reading. And they should be developing an eclectic approach to the various texts they read, rather than becoming the moralizing symbol hunters we described at the beginning of this chapter.

That's a Nice Theoretical Statement. How Does It Work?

Evaluating your students' performance in a response-based approach—or any literature curriculum for that matter—means that you will have to find out what the students know, how well they read, how well they write about what they have read or are reading, and what the nature of their aesthetic perceptions and judgments is. That's no easy task. It might mean a battery of measures covering literary history, recitations or memorized literature, reading tests, writing tasks, and measures of taste and habits. In the curriculum we propose in this book, however, the central focus is on the practice of responding and articulating, with due attention paid to the uses of knowledge and the aesthetic dimensions of reading literary texts—that is, to judgments and preferences—and particular attention given to establishing reading and responding habits. These habits include such characteristics as openness, flexibility, tentativeness, inquisitiveness, and generosity to others.

The assessment package we propose would feature students writing about what they have read and especially about what they are reading. There would also be records of class discussions, performances, and other sorts of expressions of response, from pictures to computer programs. For each student these papers and records would be assembled into a portfolio that would show to the world outside of the class that the students have learned something and are using their learning.

The Uses of Learning

We think Harry Broudy's (1982) idea of the "uses of learning" has particular relevance to the assessment and evaluation of learning in literature. Broudy sets forth four uses: replicative, applicative, interpretive, and associative. He finds the replicative and applicative uses are most frequently addressed in schools. That is, people are to give back what they learn; and they are to apply what they have learned directly to a new situation. In the case of literature, the replicative use of learning tends not to be directly assessed except in trivia contests and some quizzes. In current literature assessment students are most frequently asked to apply not their knowledge of texts but procedural knowledge of how to interpret texts directly to a new situation. The interpretive use, where the individual later uses what has been learned to gain a conceptual understanding of a phenomenon that may or may not be directly related to what was learned, can be seen in these tasks: A reader is expected to use knowledge about the legend of Pandora to construct a brief article containing an allusion to that legend, or a reader must use knowledge about Jacob and Esau in interpreting Katherine Paterson's novel, *Jacob Have I Loved*. The associative use of learning is seen when something in the new phenomenon elicits an indirect connection with an item previously learned. For example, the reader makes a connection between the story of Hamlet and that of Oedipus Rex: No explicit connection exists, but for the reader steeped in Greek drama, the implicit connections are present. Similarly, there are connections between Nikki Giovanni's "Nikki-Rosa" and Ben Franklin's *Autobiography*, and among many other sets of works as discussed by critical readers.

There are many ways in which students can show they have used their learning—both their prior reading and their preferences and habits in reading. As a result of the response-based curriculum students should be able to demonstrate that they have read and understood a number of texts and that they have deepened their ways of reading and thinking about what they have read. They should also have acquired a sense of openness to other ways of reading and alternative kinds of literature. They should be well-tempered readers.

Changing the Tests by Rethinking the Mode of Assessment

One cannot prove that students have achieved the kinds of learning we have just described with the standardized reading test that is so popular. That does not catch the uses of learning except that of how to read literally.

Not with a test of names, labels, and dates. That catches the replicative use of knowledge, but it does not catch the practice or preference. Not with an essay about what students have already read. That catches the replicative, and it might measure the ability to generalize across texts, but it is likely to be a regurgitation of the class.

NO. To measure across the domain and tap the uses of learning fully, we have to focus on students reading and expressing a response to a new text.

Thus, we can say that achievement in the curriculum is defined as facility and sureness of response to the next selection the student is exposed to.

A student has learned to bat if she makes a hit her next time up, not if she remembers how the pitcher looked the last time or what the coach told her.

A student has mastered the process of responding if he responds surely and easily to a new selection, not if he remembers the teacher's lecture on the last selection.

We prove we can do by doing, not by remembering what we did.

If we prove we can do by doing, the teacher's job is not to devise tests on how well students remember the books they read last quarter but to observe and evaluate performance this quarter.

When we look at present performance, we must observe two things: how well students do what we want them to do, and whether they will do what we want them to do when they're left to their own devices.

After all, if you get students to read T. S. Eliot carefully, finding all the paradoxes and ambiguities and relating them to the mythic background, but they don't ever read a poem or story again, have you succeeded?

If you get people to read a lot of poetry and go to plays but do so without their being able to do much more than grunt, "I like it," have you succeeded?

We want both competence and interest.

If we want both, we have to measure our success both ways.

We have to see whether students will and if students can.

Bringing the Students into the Assessment Act

Recently, there has been a trend away from the single test or grade to what has come to be called the portfolio approach to assessment. In this type of assessment, there is gathered for each student a collection of materials, both trial attempts and finished products. The range of materials has theoretically been broad, but in practice it has comprised mostly written records, either compositions by the student or some sort of log of activities recorded by student or teacher. The portfolio has been heralded as a good way of monitoring student progress. It has also been used to show the nature and quality of a school's program. In some cases, districts and even states have used portfolios.

Portfolio assessment is not just nice but is necessary to the teaching of literature. It is possible and practical, and you can avoid the traps and snares surrounding assessment and get well beyond the trivia of writing folders. Not only that: You can engage the students in their own learning and response in ways you have never even dreamed of. You need to start with some principles; try on these six:

1. A portfolio is meant to present the student to the outside world.
2. A portfolio should seek to reflect the breadth of the student's accomplishments.
3. A portfolio should seek to justify the particular course or curriculum that the student has undertaken.

4. A portfolio should be the responsibility of the student.
5. A portfolio has a rhetorical purpose: to inform and to persuade.
6. Creating a portfolio is different from the portfolio that is created.

Let's elaborate a bit:

1. *A portfolio is meant to present the student to the outside world.* in the professional world, a portfolio is what an artist or a business person takes to the prospective employer or client. It is the first glimpse many people have of that person. A portfolio is an amplified résumé. It seeks to show the person off to the world, to say, "Look, here is what I have done that may serve as an indicator of what I can do." It includes things the person has created or helped to create and it contains comments on and reviews of those things.

So it should be in a school setting. The portfolio is not a mere collection of papers or drafts of papers. It is not an internal document for the student and teacher alone. It should seek to contain those items that best represent the student's accomplishments to a broader world. Some may be things that were assigned, but some may be freely chosen. What you and your students might seek to develop is the sense of the importance of the portfolio. It is the demonstration of people's performance as students of literature, which means their performance as readers, viewers, writers, talkers, dramatizers, artists. It should show what they know, what they can do, and what they do on their own.

Another way to think of the portfolio is as a portrait. Any portrait is taken from an angle. And the angle of the portrait may vary from student to student and class to class. In the classes we have been observing, one kind of portrait is a portrait of mastery, proving to the students and the world that they are indeed competent individuals. Another kind of portrait can be seen in classes where mastery is not an issue (the honors class, for example); there, the portrait may be one to show the student as a thoughtful, sensitive reader with a catholic taste. In some classes, the angle of the portrait is that of growth and change over time. In others it is a portrait of the student as a member of an intellectual or interpretive community.

In all classes, it should be a portrait of the student as a responsible human being.

2. *A portfolio should seek to reflect the breadth of the student's accomplishments.* Literature instruction, however it is conceived (whether as a course focusing on genres, themes, or periods, whether dominated by literary analysis, dramatization, or reader response approaches), includes the three major components that should probably be represented in a portfolio: knowledge, practice, and habits, which we described in the previous section.

The precise mix depends on the approach and the goals of your particular program. Literature instruction, however conceived, does demand that students do something, produce something, be other than couch potatoes, give back something other than plot vomit.

The portfolio should seek to capture all of the aspects of a literature curriculum and students' performance in school literature as they reflect the aims and standards set by the community, the school, and the class. Portfolios represent the curriculum in practice, not a set of abstractions.

3. *A portfolio should seek to justify the particular course or curriculum that the student has undertaken.* This may seem odd, but the point is simple. The portfolio should seek to reflect what the goals and functions of the literature course have been. It should serve to reflect what you have been teaching and what the students have set for themselves. A portfolio should neither be a collection of scores on commercial tests nor items on a behavioral checklist provided by a commercial or state agency. It should contain a statement of the goals and aims of the course and the school. This way anyone looking at the portfolio should be able to reconstruct the literature program that the student has had and should know what its objectives and criteria were. It may well include a listing of the opportunities provided by the school for students to participate in activities related to literature: a student magazine, or a school play, or volunteer reading to the blind.

4. *A portfolio should be the responsibility of the student.* This is the key. A portfolio should be created by the students. It may have guidelines about the kinds of things that might be included (or must be included), such as a number of kinds of writing, a self-evaluation, a list of books read, or a number of original compositions or performances (film, music, writing). But the decision on what specific pieces should be included and how they should be included should remain the students'.

They must also work out how best to put group work into the portfolio. If it is a project that involves the building of a model, they might have to use photographs. If there is a dramatization, there must be an audiotape or videotape. If there is a really good discussion, they must figure out how to put that into the portfolio to show why it is good and what part they took in it.

The students are laying themselves on the line before the whole school perhaps, or before a jury of teachers. It is their choice as to whether they should be seen as uncaring slobs or as people who take pride in their work. Teachers cannot do this for them. By taking responsibility for what they show of themselves to the world they have a new power that they don't have when they are simply handing things in and getting grades. It takes time for them to realize that they are not helpless, that they earn the grade or the rating; you do not give it to them. Teachers who have used this approach have found that students become quite good in judging their own worth. There are a few who don't get the point, who think that just because they did it, they deserve a good grade. Most come to see a difference between doing it and doing it for a portfolio, which is a public document.

One way of encouraging this responsibility is to use the technique of grouping. This is a form of reflection that has been used in other contexts and that works in schools. It relies on having the members of the group use the same format each time they meet. The format is usually one of questions about how the members of the group are progressing toward a set of goals they have defined. Group members share their answers to those questions each time, talk with each other about them, and encourage each other. It is a time of sharing and reflection, generally not one of admonition or assessment, other than self-assessment. What goes on in the group is confidential. It would work in an English class this way: The students divide into groups of three. (The group would remain together for the year.) Every two weeks the three would get together for a half hour and share their answers to the following questions:

What do I know that I didn't know?
What can I do that I couldn't do?
What do I do that I didn't do?

With respect to each question the students should be encouraged to make an individual or collective plan and refer their answers to that plan. The grouping is among the students. The teacher does not participate or even know what the plan of the groups might be; that should come out in the portfolio itself. Grouping is a way of having the students look at themselves and learn how they can take responsibility for their own learning. It is simple, and it works.

5. *A portfolio has a rhetorical purpose: to inform and to persuade.* The portfolio should inform the observer of what students have done in a particular literature course. It should reflect the breadth and depth of the course and the experiences it contains. Because it is public, it should seek to be understandable to the outside world and perhaps to conform to certain principles:

a. The portfolio should tell what has been studied. It should reflect the curriculum of a class and of the school as well as reflect the broader interests of the student. It need not do this chronologically, although that is a possible organization. It might be organized by groups or classes of activity (papers, discussions, dramatizations).

b. The portfolio should convey the value of what has been studied. It should seek to show why it is important to have done what was done, to include what was included, to be judged by the standards that have been established. It should have some sort of introduction and commentary, perhaps by the student, perhaps by the class, perhaps even by some outside juror.

c. The portfolio should convey the merit of the individual student. The portfolio should attempt to show that this student has done as well as she or he has by saying something about change or growth or else about breadth or mastery or knowledge.

One thing that these principles suggest is that a portfolio cannot be slapped together. It should make a good first impression as well as reinforce strong second and third impressions.

Like any composition, a portfolio is known by its content, its arrangement, and its style. A portfolio is to a composition as a book is to a chapter or a hypertext to any of its components. And a portfolio takes time; it is not the work of the night before. It will probably take most of a week per quarter to review portfolios with students. But don't begrudge the time, for the students will have gained in depth of understanding what they might have lost in the one short story that would have been covered.

6. *Creating a portfolio is different from the portfolio that is created.* This is a tricky point—and perhaps the most difficult for students and teachers—and one we alluded to earlier. It is also a key to the reader-based approach, for it defines the role of the teacher. During the course of teaching literature, we act as the coach: the person who encourages the students to bring out their best, who elicits responses, discussion, ideas, and feelings. These may come out in discussions, in drafts of papers, in rehearsals of various sorts. We are generally friendly creatures, helpful beasts in the traditional quest stories. There comes a time, however, when we must drop that role, when the students are showing their stuff for real, when they have to confront the dragon, and we are the dragon-judge. This is hard for many of us and for our students. But it is a shift in role that we must acknowledge in ourselves and explain to our students. What we said about the drafts to encourage pride and revision cannot be said about the final product. We are the judge (unless we can get someone else to take on that role); we are the expert who can describe the performance of students and hold it up against standards that we have set. We have to cast off our mantle of friendliness and look through the lens of the critic or the judge. This is not an inhumane act at all; it is an act of love, and we should try to help our students understand it. We can no longer be the parent/advocate, the attorney for the defense. We cannot rationalize our students' work; it must stand on its own. That is the point at which our students become independent of us, and it is a point toward which we must lead them so that they can be free of us and autonomous. We think it is the hardest part of teaching, but probably the most important. We are seeking to help our students to become independent, responsible human beings who no longer need us. To effect this, we need to balance our tendency to do things for the students with our tendency to serve as the judge. This duality is the crux of the portfolio approach, we think; it is also the crux of what it means to be a teacher. The fact of portfolios encourages us to face ourselves as teachers and as human beings responsible for the education (the leading away from childhood) of our students.

Tools for Making Portfolios

1. A class.
2. Recorders—the teacher, a teacher's aide, a supervisor, some students.
3. A means of recording what is learned—paper, computer printout, programs, games, pictures, a videotape or tape recording of the class, etc., etc.
4. Some criteria to judge by.

These aren't easy tools to use; it takes practice, but no more practice than it takes to write a good multiple-choice test.

Once you and the students have them down, together you can demonstrate what the individuals and the class know, can do, and will do. They have shown that students engage in many kinds of articulating. They are engaged readers.

They have learned to take responsibility for their responses and to share them. They don't need you.

But Maybe They Need to Learn to Trust Themselves

One way to start is go over with your class the following questions (with one warning, that you must be prepared to be brutally frank and be prepared for shocks):

1. What do I look for in student reading and response? In student writing and performance?
2. What do I accept as evidence?
3. What do I see as being better? As being older or more mature?
4. What do I want to communicate about the students and the class? To whom?

The answers to these questions become the standards for you and your class, and they begin to shape the portfolio.

One way to help answer these questions is to use the table on p. 195. Another way is to lay out the answers in a grid like Figure 11.1. In the cells are some responses that teachers have given when we have asked them these questions.

You will need to flesh out the specifics in a grid, discard some, and definitely share them with the students. You might need to clarify with them what the difference is between the way we look at habits (as opposed to knowledge and practice) and the ways we use criteria.

	What's Quality?	**What's More Mature?**

Knowledge	Having read more
	Reading the "right" texts to build
	  up background knowledge
	Getting the lingo
	Knowing the culture
	Knowing the conventions
	  and rules
		Having read older works
		Knowing genres, themes, and
		  movements
		Getting theory and
		  abstractions and/or . . .

Practice	Saying more
	Reading and writing various
	  text types
	Using the right terms and
	  language
	Using detail
	Finding abstractions
	Making connections
	Being clear
	Being coherent
	Being aware of the audiences
		Reading and writing more
		  complex texts
		Being more consistent
		Being more elaborate
		Increasing the variety
		Making alternatives
		Making more abstract
		  connections
		Including more details and/or . . .

Habits	Choosing reading over other
	  activities
	Choosing the preferable texts
	Choosing to write
	Being willing to share
	  and participate
	Using the resources available
	Being self-critical
	Being reflective
		Choosing more complex texts
		Choosing a greater diversity
		  of texts
		Making more subtle
		  judgments of texts
		Broadening the strategies
		  and/or . . .

FIGURE 11.1

When we seek to find out about people's habits, we cast a net and see what we catch; we don't necessarily have tasks or specific criteria in mind. We use terms like "more" and not numbers like 24.

When we seek to find out about knowledge and practice, we ask people to hit a target we set up, or we look at what they do and judge them not on whether they do what we want but on whether they do well what they want to do. We have more definite tasks and criteria in mind.

But when we are creating portfolios with our students, we are asking them to demonstrate what they know, what they do, and what habits they have developed. We are also asking them to help define the tasks and the criteria. Through this activity, we want them to be able to set their own tasks and judge themselves. That's what they will have to do in the world. Why shouldn't we help them along?

Looking at Tasks

In the preceding chapter we discussed writing tasks, and in earlier chapters we discussed other sorts of tasks, those using drama, those involving technology, and those involving talk. All of these need to go into the portfolio.

What tasks should be included? The students can't put in everything from a year or two of talking, acting, drawing, writing, shaping, keyboarding. They have to select, and the selection has to be in terms of what they want to say about themselves. Do they want to show growth? Variety? Daring? Carefulness and precision? Depth? Breadth?

Seeing the Nature of the Problem

As with looking at a writing assignments, so it is with looking at a portfolio, which is, after all, a larger writing assignment, a hypertext that presents the student. They can go through the same sort of analysis:

What's the cognitive demand?

What's the function?

Who's the audience?

Any restrictions on role, tone, content, length, format?

What are the criteria by which it will be judged?

Developing and Exploring Criteria

When we come finally to look at the students' portfolios, we have some expectation of a good performance. Oh, there does not have to be a rigid definition of good, but it should have emerged as we worked through the standards. We use a variety of criteria when we determine a good meal or a good film; we should be as flexible in judging a student's paper, collage, improvisation, or portfolio.

There is no reason to make our criteria as rigorous as those we apply to a highly trained professional, or even a seasoned amateur. The criteria may be built on change or growth or the performance of good students of a particular age. We can, however, help students by sharing with them a sense of the criteria we will use.

We can do this with their drafts and practices. We do not always need to give a grade or a detailed critique, but it helps to share with them something of the range of aspects we are looking at, and our standards. One means of doing this can be to take the following example from writing and adapt it to other activities as well.

When people mark a composition, they don't focus on just one aspect of it, such as spelling or grammar. These are aspects of writing that make it readable, but they do not make it meaningful. The ability to produce effective and meaningful discourse is evaluated in people's commentary on the quality and scope of the composition's content, on the organization of the composition, on the style and tone of the composition, and on the personal impression the writing made on the reader.

When we mark compositions it is useful to keep students' success in writing a legible text separate from their success in creating meaningful discourse. One way of doing this is to prepare a brief form that can be attached to each composition. The form can be used by you or by the students, and it might look like Figure 11.2.

One virtue of this kind of rating is that it helps ensure that one aspect of the composition doesn't sway the appraisal of the whole composition. It may be that a student has very good ideas and has organized them well but has used an inappropriate tone. It may be that another composition is correct in every way but contains very juvenile and unconsidered ideas, given the general level of the student or the class.

By separating out our judgment and examining the various aspects of writing competence, we can give a balanced perspective on a person's writing and prepare them for the varied judgments that the students will receive later on in life.

Teachers can use these categories or ones like them to judge all kinds of tasks, from a brief oral report to a dramatization. Certain aspects will change: The mechanics of writing may translate into audibility in talk or pace in a dramatic presentation.

An effective, consistent style and tone is important in many kinds of performance.

FIGURE 11.2 A Way of Assessing Written Response

	POOR			EXCELLENT	
Discourse Level Qualities					
Quality and development of content					
(response, analysis, etc.)	1	2	3	4	5
Organization and structure	1	2	3	4	5
Style and tone	1	2	3	4	5
Text Level Qualities					
Grammar and wording	1	2	3	4	5
Spelling and punctuation	1	2	3	4	5
Handwriting and neatness	1	2	3	4	5
My personal reaction	1	2	3	4	5
Comments:					

Clear organization and well-thought-out ideas are most important in a discussion, oral reports, and such activities as taking a literary work and turning it into a pantomime or rap.

We can flesh out these criteria with more specific checklists for the individual pieces or the portfolio as a whole: Content can be broken down into such parts as adequacy of information, richness of information, relationships, inferences, synthesis, and evaluation (if such are called for). Organization can be seen in terms of overall framing of the material and grouping of the parts. Style and tone can be seen in terms of consistency, variety, and appropriateness. Each of these characteristics can be explained and discussed with the students. These are not new or unique characteristics; they are the kind of qualities we use to make all sorts of judgments.

All of these checklists and detailed spelling out of criteria are to be used not for the final marking only but to share with the students as they practice or draft their material. Such checklists are as useful for rehearsals as they are for final performances.

Teachers who have discussed marking criteria with their students have found that students appreciate an honest discussion of what is being looked for in their writing. Some teachers have given forms like the one shown in Figure 11.2 to their students for use in peer evaluation. This has been a particularly effective strategy because it forces the student raters to look at many aspects of their colleagues' compositions.

We have found it even more useful to have students look over the work in their portfolio after a quarter, identify a "successful" and a "less successful" piece in their own eyes, and then share the characteristics that make for a better piece of writing. These can take the place of a list.

The whole concept of the portfolio rests less on finding out what students remember in a passive way than on what kinds of thinking, feeling, responding, and imagining they can and do bring to bear on the various experiences of literature and the world they have acquired.

Assessment depends less on your making up a test than on your establishing an arena of interest to you and your students and observing and judging what, in fact, the students do.

Like the curriculum itself, assessment depends on performance and process. It examines the length of the quills without annoying the porcupine.

The Logistics of Handling a Portfolio

One of the problems facing teachers is having to deal with the mountain of material students hand in. It is easy enough to ask students to produce something, but then you have to look at each product and make some estimate of its quality and how it might be improved. It looks worse when you decide to have a portfolio.

We recommend some procedures to follow.

1. It is not necessary to give detailed comments on everything. It is better to save the lengthy comments for those performances that students have a chance to revise or redo.
2. It is best to give feedback as quickly as possible. Having to wait two or three weeks causes students to lose interest in their project.
3. It is always good to have some positive comment on each project and to give students an opportunity to talk about their work. But don't be afraid to ask questions and be critical, as long as it is constructive criticism, not constrictive "crudicism."
4. Whenever it is possible, a good way of giving feedback is in a conference or small-group discussion, when the teacher and student can go over the composition together. We recommend spending a week per semester going over the portfolios with students. It is not a week lost to other things but a week of growing and learning.
5. Usually it is good to have students provide the feedback to each others' writing. They get practice in judging various kinds of work, they often learn how to improve their own work, and they usually give good suggestions for improvement. In fact, they can take over the assessment sessions.

That's Fine, but There Are All These State and National Tests

While we were working on this book, there were a number of people concerned with setting national (or even better, *international*) standards. They were assembling large committees, going over curricula, contemplating their navels, and coming up with statements remarkably similar to ones that had been written before. Students must READ, they must THINK CRITICALLY, they must engage in the WRITING PROCESS, and their assessment must be AUTHENTIC. Of course, any test is authentic for the person taking it . . . it scares the pants off a student, just as a driver's test or a pregnancy test does. All of these new assessment programs probably will improve the quality of statewide testing. They will get us away from the kind of test that asked, "True or False: Huck Finn is a good boy."

Most of those national tests will continue to measure a student's ability to use words, to read unfamiliar texts, and to make inferences and set these down in clear language that is interesting to read. What we have set forth should lead to mastery of that kind of test, bad as it may be, and should do so better than a curriculum that is geared to recall, recognition, and application alone.

Besides, the curriculum we advocate seeks to avoid the trap into which earlier curricula fell. In the past, education in literature spent so much time being scientific, being historical, being something else, that it neglected the fact that literature is written for enjoyment and instruction and that it is intended to be read and responded to, not written about in term papers or made the subject of a recitation.

In one school a teacher asked twenty-three questions on *Macbeth* in fifteen minutes, questions like What does this word mean? What does the next line mean? After class she was asked whether the students liked the play. "I don't know; I haven't time."

If a literature curriculum pays attention only to recitation and term papers, the students may learn to dislike literature, and English, and school, and the mind.

"You've murdered *Hamlet* and *Macbeth*. What more do you want? My blood?" wrote a student on a national examination.

Literature and the arts exist in the curriculum as a means for students to learn to express their emotions, their thoughts, and their imaginations as they enter into the experiences of the works they read and transliterate those experiences into film, talk, silence, writing, drama, pictures, or the like.

Literature and the arts in the curriculum can both free the imagination and help people order their worlds.

This function is served by no other part of the curriculum.

Without freedom of the imagination and personal order there can come a repressive or a revolutionary society.

It might even plug up the hole in the ozone layer.

Such runs the most pragmatic defense of the curriculum we have suggested. It is a curriculum designed to promote individuality, to promote understanding, to promote the imaginative capacity in all parts of our society.

References

Brody, Pamela, Carol DeMilo, and Alan Purves. *The Current State of Assessment in Literature* (Report No. 3.1). Albany: State University of New York, Center for the Learning and Teaching of Literature, 1989.

Broudy, Harry. *Report: On Case Studies on Uses of Knowledge.* Spencer Foundation, 1982.

Purves, Alan C. *Reading and Literature: American Achievement in International Perspective.* Urbana, IL: National Council of Teachers of English, 1980.

Purves, Alan C., Hongru Li, Virginia McCann, and Paul Henkin. *Student Perceptions of Achievement in School Literature* (Report No. 3.5). Albany: State University of New York, Center for the Learning and Teaching of Literature, 1991.

Rosenblatt, Louise. *The Reader, The Text, The Poem: The Transactional Theory of the Literary Work.* Carbondale, IL: Southern Illinois University Press, 1978.

Resources

Bloom, Benjamin S., Thomas Hastings, and George Madaus. *Handbook of Formation and Summative Evaluation of Student Learning.* New York: McGraw-Hill, 1971.

Cooper, Charles R. *Measuring Growth in Appreciation of Literature.* International Reading Association, 1972.

Cooper, Charles R., ed. *On the Nature and Measurement of Competency in English*. Urbana, IL: National Council of Teachers of English, 1981.

Elbow, Peter. *Writing without Teachers*. New York: Oxford University Press, 1973.

Evans, Peter, ed. *Directions and Misdirections in English Evaluation*. Ottawa: Canadian Council of Teachers of English, 1985.

Fagan, William T., Julie M. Jensen, and Charles R. Cooper, eds. *Measures for Research and Evaluation in the English Language Arts*. Vols. 1 and 2. Urbana, IL: National Council of Teachers of English, 1975, 1985.

Fillion, Bryant. "Reading as Inquiry: An Approach to Literature Learning." *English Journal* (January 1981): 39–45.

Holland, Norman. *Five Readers Reading*. New Haven: Yale University Press, 1975.

Johnston, Brian. *Assessing English: Helping Students to Reflect on Their Work*. Milton Keynes: Open University Press, 1983.

Johnston, Peter. "Process Assessment in the Language Arts." In *The Dynamics of Language Learning*, edited by James Squire. Urbana, IL: National Council of Teachers in English, 1987, 355–357.

Loban, Walter. "Language Development and Its Evaluation." In *Reviews of Selected Published Tests in English*, edited by Alfred H. Grommon. Urbana, IL: National Council of Teachers of English, 1976.

Miall, David. "A Repertory Guide Study of a Poem." *Research in the Teaching of English* 19 (1985): 254–268.

O'Dell, Lee, and Charles R. Cooper. "Describing Responses to Works of Fiction." *Research in the Teaching of English* 10 (1976): 203–225.

Purves, Alan C. "Evaluation of Learning in Literature." *Evaluation in Education: An International Review Series* 3 (1979): 93–172.

Purves, Alan, Anna Soter, Sauli Takala, and Anneli Vahapassi. "Towards a Domain-Referenced System for Classifying Composition Assignments." *Research in the Teaching of English 18* (1984): 385–416.

Searle, Dennis, and Margaret Stevenson. "Alternative Assessment Program in Language Arts." *Language Arts* 64, no. 3 (1987): 278–284.

Tierney, Robert J., Mark Carter, and Laura Desai. *Portfolio Assessment in the Reading-Writing Classroom*. Norwood, MA: Christopher Gordon Publishers, 1991.

Index of Literary Texts and Authors